THE TRAGEDY OF
MACBETH
BY WILLIAM SHAKESPEARE

Edited by

GEORGE LYMAN KITTREDGE

GINN AND COMPANY
BOSTON · NEW YORK · CHICAGO
LONDON · ATLANTA · DALLAS · COLUMBUS · SAN FRANCISCO

PR
2823
.A2
K6

The Athenæum Press

GINN AND COMPANY · PRO-
PRIETORS · BOSTON · U.S.A.

PREFACE

THE text is complete and agrees with that in Kittredge's edition of Shakespeare's *Works*. The numbering of the lines accords with that commonly used in citing the plays. This method is preferred to a new counting in order to facilitate reference to such standard works as Bartlett's *Concordance* and Schmidt's *Shakespeare-Lexicon*. In prose passages there results some slight irregularity in computation, but this does not indicate any omission in the text.

G. L. K.

CONTENTS

INTRODUCTION

For the text of MACBETH the only authority is the First Folio.[1]
This prints what is obviously an acting version of the play,
somewhat changed from its original form. Hecate is an in-
trusive character, quite foreign to Shakespeare's conception of
the powers and attributes of the Weird Sisters: the whole
of the fifth scene in Act iii is a manifest interpolation; and
the same is true of iv, 1, 39–43, 125–132, which must stand or
fall with that scene. Two stage directions in the Folio (iii, 5,
33; iv, 1, 43) call for songs that are preserved in Middleton's
tragicomedy *The Witch* (see pp. 237–239, below). This fact,
as well as the character of Hecate in Middleton, suggests that
he may have been the playwright employed to revise Shakespeare's MACBETH in an operatic spirit, out of harmony with the
original design. Two other bits of the Folio text seem to be
spurious ('Whiles . . . gives,' ii, 1, 60, 61; and 'Before . . .
shield,' v, 8, 32, 33), but they do not sound like Middleton.[2]

Several passages besides the Hecate material have been
thought to be interpolated, but without good reason. Coleridge
rejected the Porter's soliloquy (ii, 3), oblivious of its dramatic
irony and of the need for something of the kind to separate the
exit of Macbeth and his wife from their reëntrance. The
speeches of the wounded Sergeant (i, 2) have been attacked on
the ground that their bombastic phraseology is not like Shakespeare's language; but their mixture of bombast and grotesque
bluntness accords perfectly with what was expected of a stage
soldier.

Probably the reviser made some cuts, for the play is very
short; but nothing essential has been lost. The difficulties in
this regard that some critics have found with reference to
the Thane of Cawdor (i, 2, 52–53, 63–64; i, 3, 72–73, 108–116)
and to Macbeth's 'breaking this enterprise' of murder to his

---

[1] For the late Quarto and Davenant's version see pp. 231 ff., below.
[2] With these may be rated iii, 2, 54, 55, and iv, 1, 153, 154 ('No . . .
cool'). One would gladly cancel also v, 2, 29, 30 ('Or . . . weeds'), but
see the note on the passage.

wife and swearing to accomplish it (i, 7, 47–59) are quite imaginary. Nor is there anything mysterious about the Third
Murderer (iii, 3). He is merely the person sent by Macbeth
to give final orders to the other two assassins, in accordance
with his promise (iii, 1, 128–132).

There is no decisive evidence for date. Outside limits are
1603 (the accession of James I)[1] and 1610 or 1611, when
Simon Forman attended a performance of MACBETH at the
Globe (see p. 239 below). 1610 is manifestly several years
too late for the composition of the play, as both style and
metre show. To fix upon a year within the limits many supposed criteria have been cited—all of them interesting, but
none of them decisive. When James I was approaching the
North Gate of Oxford, on his visit to the city in 1605 (August
27), 'tres quasi Sibyllae' emerged from St. John's College, 'as
if from a wood,' and saluted the King, the Queen, and the
Princes Henry and Charles, with a few Latin verses composed
by Dr. Matthew Gwinne. The First Sibyl mentioned the
prophecy spoken by the Weird Sisters to Banquo and desig-
nated King James as Banquo's decendant.[2] He was greeted
also as a ruler of Scotland, England, and Ireland—and likewise
as monarch of Britain (now united), Ireland, and France
(cf. iv, 1, 121). But Shakespeare needed no hint from Gwinne
for the Weird Sisters. They are central figures of the Macbeth
legend as told by Holinshed, with whose standard work he
had been familiar for more than a dozen years. The farmer
(or other speculator in wheat) 'that hang'd himself on th' ex-

---

[1] James I succeeded Elizabeth on March 24, 1603, and was crowned on
July 25.

[2] Fatidicas olim fama est cecinisse Sorores
  Imperium sine fine tuae, Rex Inclyte, stirpis.
  Banquonem agnouit generosa *Loquabria Thanum.*
  Nec tibi *Banquo*, tuis sed sceptra nepotibus illae
  Immortalibus immortalia vaticinatae.

The verses were first printed, so far as we know, in 1607, at the end of the
quarto of *Vertumnus*, the Latin play by Gwinne which was acted before the
King at Christ Church on August 29, 1605.

pectation of plenty' was a stock figure as early as the thirteenth century[1] and is not to be connected especially with the price of wheat in 1606. The Porter's 'equivocator' need not involve an allusion to Garnet, who was tried on March 28, 1606. Possible echoes of MACBETH in almost contemporary plays are interesting but by no means conclusive. The most striking is in *The Knight of the Burning Pestle* (v, 1, 19–29) — itself a play of uncertain date but probably assignable to 1607:

> And never shalt thou sit or be alone
> In any place, but I will visit thee
> With ghastly looks and put into thy mind
> The great offences which thou didst to me.
> When thou art at thy table with thy friends,
> Merry in heart and fill'd with swelling wine,
> I'll come in midst of all thy pride and mirth,
> Invisible to all men but thyself,
> And whisper such a sad tale in thine ear
> Shall make thee let the cup fall from thy hand
> And stand as mute and pale as death itself.[2]

Everything considered, Malone's date for MACBETH, 1606, has stood all tests for more than a century. Style and metre fit this date, but 1605 is also possible; for we cannot be quite sure whether MACBETH came just before *King Lear* or just after it.[3]

[1] Manly has found him in the *Exempla* of Jacques de Vitry, No. 164 (ed. Crane, p. 71): 'Audivi de quodam qui multum de grano congregavit et per multos annos ut carius venderet expectavit. Deus autem semper bonum tempus dabat, unde miser ille, spe sua frustratus, tandem pre tristicia super granum suum se ipsum suspendit.'

[2] Much less likely to be an echo of MACBETH is a passage in *The Puritan or The Widow of Watling Street* (registered and published in 1607; written probably in 1606), iv, 3, 89–91 (*Shakespeare Apocrypha*, ed. Tucker Brooke, p. 246): 'In stead of a Iester, weele ha the ghost ith white sheete sit at vpper end a' th' Table.'

[3] J. Q. Adams, emphasizing the fact that MACBETH deals with subjects of much interest to James I, conjectures that it was one of the three plays acted at court by Shakespeare's company in the late summer of 1606, while Christian IV of Denmark was the King's guest. He believes that it was written in haste for this court performance. Malone had suggested that 'perhaps MACBETH was first exhibited' during this visit.

No evidence exists for any drama on the subject of Macbeth before Shakespeare. Both the 'Tragedie of the Kinge of Scottes' (performed at court in 1567–8)[1] and 'Malcolm Kynge of Scottes' (mentioned by Henslowe as purchased of Charles Massey in 1602)[2] are lost, but nothing suggests that they dealt with Macbeth's career. As for the 'story of Macdoel, or Macdobeth, or Macsomewhat' mentioned by William Kemp in 1600, that was obviously a ballad (if anything)—not a play.[3]

For the plot Shakespeare had recourse to the second edition of Raphael Holinshed's *Chronicle* (1587). Since he was writing a tragedy and not a 'history,' he did not hesitate to take liberties. The rebellion of Macdonwald and the invasion of 'Sweno the Norways' king' are brought together. Banquo, King James's fictitious ancestor, is represented as a loyal subject, whereas in Holinshed he is Macbeth's chief ally in the attack on Duncan. For the murder of Duncan, Shakespeare has used Holinshed's account of the murder of King Duff by Donwald, which includes the drugging of the chamberlains and the prodigies described in ii, 4. The voice that cried 'Sleep no more!' was apparently suggested by what Holinshed tells of the dream of King Kenneth III. The Weird Sisters disappear from Holinshed immediately after their meeting with

---

[1] *Revels Accounts*, ed. Feuillerat, p. 119.

[2] *Diary*, fol. 105 (ed. Greg, I, 165).

[3] In *Kemps humble request to the impudent generation of Ballad-makers* (appended to *Kemps nine daies wonder*, 1600), he writes: 'I haue made a priuie search, what priuate Iigmonger of your iolly number, hath been the Author of these abhominable ballets written of me.' 'The search continuing, I met a proper vpright youth, onely for a little stooping in the shoulders: all hart to the heele, a penny Poet whose first making was the miserable stolne story of Macdoel, or Macdobeth, or Macsomewhat: for I am sure a Mac it was, though I never had the maw to see it: & hee tolde me there was a fat filthy ballet-maker, that should haue once been his Iourneyman to the trade: who liu'd about the towne: and ten to one, but he had thus terribly abused me & my Taberer.' The mention of a 'Ballad of Macdobeth' (or 'Macedbeth') in the Stationers' Register (1596) seems to be a forgery. See Greg, *The Library*, 4th Series, VIII (1928), 418, and *Modern Language Notes*, XLV (1930), 141, 142.

Macbeth upon the blasted heath. The warning to 'beware Macduff' (iv, 1, 71) is given by 'certeine wizzards, in whose words [Macbeth] put great confidence'; the prophecies concerning 'none of woman born' and Birnam Wood (iv, 1, 80, 92–94) are made by 'a certeine witch, whome hee had in great trust.'[1]

Holinshed's authority was the *Scotorum Historiae* of Hector Boece (born *ca.* 1465, died 1536), which goes back to John Fordun's *Scotichronicon* (written in the latter part of the fourteenth century) and to Andrew of Wyntown's *Cronykil* (finished *ca.* 1424). Holinshed used John Bellenden's Scottish translation of Boece (printed *ca.* 1536), but he compared it industriously with the Latin original. The material combines a modicum of sober history with much ancient legend and considerable out-and-out fiction. To sift the actual facts from this conglomerate is a fascinating problem for investigators, but does not much concern the Shakespearean student. One may note, however, that Duncan's reign was A.D. 1034–1040 and Macbeth's A.D. 1040–1057. Macbeth seems to have had some title to the crown, but just what it was cannot be determined. He was certainly not Duncan's cousin-german, as Holinshed (following Boece) and Shakespeare (following Holinshed) represent. He asserted his claim, after the fashion of those times, by attacking Duncan with an armed troop at a place near Elgin. Duncan was killed, but whether or not he fell by Macbeth's own hand is uncertain. In 1054 Macbeth was defeated, probably at Dunsinane, by Siward (not accompanied by Malcolm). He maintained himself in the north until August, 1057, when he fell at Lumphanan in a battle with Malcolm. Banquo and Fleance are unhistorical characters, who make their first appearances in Boece. Macduff is likewise

---

[1] The earliest writer to attach these two prophecies to Macbeth's history is Wyntown (*Cronykil, ca.* 1420; vi, 18, 1929–1930, 2207–2228, ed. Laing, II, 130, 138–139). According to him, the former was uttered by the devil, who was Macbeth's father. The source of the latter he does not specify, but it seems to have been the same demon. Both accord with widespread folktales. For a thorough treatment of the Macbeth legend see Ernst Kröger, *Die Sage von Macbeth bis zu Shakspere*, 1904.

fictitious—at least in any such rôle as he plays in Holinshed and Shakespeare. Macdonwald and Cawdor were also brought into the story by Boece.

The historical Macbeth was a sane and beneficent ruler. Fordun, on the contrary, represents him as a savage tyrant. Boece combines these two characters, and Holinshed follows Boece. Macbeth, he tells us, was 'somewhat cruell of nature,'[1] yet for ten years he ruled wisely and well:

> 'He set his whole intention to mainteine iustice, and to punish all enormities and abuses, which had chanced through the feeble and slouthfull administration of Duncane. . . . But this was but a counterfet zeale of equitie shewed by him, partlie against his naturall inclination, to purchase thereby the fauour of the people. Shortlie after, he began to shew what he was, in stead of equitie practising crueltie. For the pricke of conscience . . . caused him euer to feare, least he should be serued of the same cup, as he had ministred to his predecessor. The woords also of the three weird sisters would not out of his mind, which as they promised him the kingdome, so likewise did they promise it at the same time vnto the posteritie of Banquho. . . . After the contriued slaughter of Banquho, nothing prospered with the foresaid Makbeth: for in maner euerie man began to doubt his owne life, and durst vnneth [i.e., hardly] appeare in the kings presence; and euen as there were manie that stood in feare of him, so likewise stood he in feare of manie, in such sort that he began to make those awaie by one surmized cauillation or other, whome he thought most able to worke him anie displeasure. At length he found such sweetnesse by putting his nobles thus to death, that his earnest thirst after bloud in this behalfe might in no wise be satisfied.'

Shakespeare could not fail to perceive the absurdity of his source in this description of Macbeth's character. How could the King hide his true nature for a decade and then break forth on a sudden in the full strength of inborn savagery? In delineating Macbeth's character, therefore, Shakespeare departed widely from Holinshed. In the first scene of the play we learn nothing about him but his name. The next scene is definitely expository. From beginning to end it is a laudation of Macbeth—'brave Macbeth (well he deserves that name)'; 'valour's minion' (or darling); 'Bellona's bridegroom.' The

---

[1] Cf. Boece: 'nisi ingentem fortitudini crudelitatem natura immiscuisset.'

Sergeant praises him, expressing the sentiments of the army and the common people; then Ross enters and voices the admiration of the peers; and finally King Duncan closes the scene with a kind of suspiration—'noble Macbeth.' The words of Macbeth to his wife, soon after, fitly describe the tenour of the whole—'golden opinions from all sorts of people.'[1] The impression that the expository scene makes upon us is decisive: Macbeth is the first of the Scottish nobles, beloved and admired by everybody, from the rank and file of the army to the King himself—a great soldier, a true patriot, a loyal subject. He is contrasted with 'the merciless Macdonwald' and with 'that most disloyal traitor, the Thane of Cawdor.' Such was Macbeth before the 'supernatural soliciting' that determined his later career.

A second piece of evidence is highly significant, for it concerns two qualities not touched upon in the expository scene. It is Lady Macbeth's soliloquy after she reads her husband's letter. She knows him well. He is 'not without ambition,' but his ambition is of the honourable kind. The thought of kingship attracts him, but he will shrink from achieving the crown by any deed that will stain his conscience: 'What thou wouldst highly, that wouldst thou holily.' And besides, he is gentle and kindly by temperament, and 'the nearest way'—which to her straightforward feminine logic is the only way—will horrify him. Lady Macbeth, then, adds to what we have learned in the expository scene—to valour and loyalty and patriotism—the qualities of a scrupulous conscience and a humane and kindly temper. This last trait, one remembers, has often been noted—to the amazement of superficial observers of human nature—in great military heroes, veritable thunderbolts of war. That the Lady is right in her analysis is confirmed by much circumstantial evidence: by Macbeth's horror when the thought of murder first darts

[1] i, 7, 33. This phrase would be almost enough to prove the genuineness of the second scene, even if that scene were not, as it is, vitally necessary to the understanding of the drama.

into his mind; by his vacillation before the deed[1]; by the hallucinations that precede and follow it; by his naïve wonder
that he 'could not say "Amen!" when they did say "God
bless us!"'; by his remorse. Even the savagery of his later
career, which has deterred some critics from accepting the
unimpeachable evidence of his wife, is in fact a confirmation.
A savage may be little the worse for a murder or two, but
Macbeth has subverted the very foundations of his being.
He has 'cursed his better angel from his side and fallen to
reprobance.'

Macbeth is blessed—and cursed—with an imagination of
extraordinary power, which visualizes to the verge of delirium.
Every idea that enters his mind takes instant visible shape: he
sees what another would merely *think*. And this poetic vision
(which at the outset so presented the hideousness of murder as almost to thwart his purpose) comes later to his aid.
It enables him to think and speak about himself as if he
were a spectator at his own tragedy, and so he finds a
refuge from the direct contemplation of fact. Thus he grows
stronger and more resolute as fate closes in upon him, and is
never greater than in the desperate valour that marks his end.

The rôle and character of Lady Macbeth are barely suggested by Holinshed. He tells us that Macbeth was 'greatlie
incouraged' by 'the woords of the thre weird sisters' to 'vsurpe
the kingdome by force.' 'But,' he adds, 'speciallie his wife
lay sore vpon him to attempt the thing, as she that was verie
ambitious, burning in vnquenchable desire to beare the name
of a queene.' That is all: Holinshed never mentions her again.
Donwald's wife, however, plays a larger part in the murder
of King Duff. 'She counselled [Donwald] (sith the king
oftentimes vsed to lodge in his house without anie gard about
him, other than the garrison of the castell, which was wholie
at his commandement) to make him awaie, and shewed him
the meanes wherby he might soonest accomplish it'; and

---

[1]Note especially the antithesis of ambition and pity in Macbeth's soliloquy in i, 7, 1–28. Cf. the use of 'unfortunate' in iv, 1, 152.

Donwald, 'though he abhorred the act greatlie in heart, yet through instigation of his wife' gave instructions to 'foure of his seruants' to kill the king. The motive in this case was not ambition but revenge.

Lady Macbeth, then, is Shakespeare's own creation. Like all normal women, she is ambitious, but her ambition is rather for her husband than herself. It is for his head that 'fate and metaphysical aid' have destined 'the golden round' (i, 5, 26–31); her task is to remove the obstacles inherent in his nature. With her, to see is to purpose and to purpose is to proceed right onward with an eye single to the end in view: 'the nearest way' is the only way. She sways Macbeth by her strength of will and her feminine charm. She coaxes him and soothes him and taunts him, as the occasion may require; but she does not bully him as Goneril bullies Albany. Their devotion to each other is manifest in every word they speak. Their marriage is the perfect union of complementary natures, each supplying those qualities that the other lacks. Thus the climax of their tragic history is Macbeth's apathy when he hears that his wife is dead: she must have died sometime—and what does it matter when? Life's but a walking shadow.

Lady Macbeth's strength resides in her nervous force and the terrible simplicity of her point of view. She is no creature of heroic frame.[1] She is not a Goneril or a Brynhild or a Clytemnestra. And she has overestimated her nervous energy. It might have sufficed to carry her, unshaken, through the consequences of any act that she could have executed alone. It could not suffice when constantly drawn upon to support and animate her husband, who seems to her to be going mad. Hence the infinite pathos of her final breakdown when the bloody instructions have returned to plague the inventors.

No satisfactory time-scheme for Shakespeare's tragedy can

[1] See iii, 2, 45 ('dearest chuck'); v, 1, 57 ('this little hand'); and note her swoon in ii, 3, 124–131.

be constructed. Somehow, between the accession of Macbeth
in Act ii and his death in Act v, his long reign of seventeen
years (1040-1057) must be accounted for. Much time has
certainly elapsed. Otherwise Malcolm could not have oper-
ated his test of Macduff (iv, 3), for Macduff would have
known his true character; and Malcolm's failure to recognize
Ross (iv, 3, 160-163) would be meaningless; and Macduff's
and Ross's descriptions of Macbeth's tyrannical savagery (iv, 3,
4-8, 164-176) would lose all their force. No computation
satisfies the requirements. There is, to be sure, an interval
between Act ii and Act iii, and another between Scenes ii
and iii of Act iv; but their sum is inadequate. Yet this is a
difficulty that confronts the mathematician alone: it never
troubles the man in the theatre. Indeed, it does not even occur
to him. When Macbeth falls, we feel that it was long ago
that he met the Weird Sisters on the blasted heath. He has
reached the autumn of life and is looking forward to a friend-
less and desolate old age. We reckon the interval, not by clock
and calendar, but in terms of our emotional exhaustion. The
lull in the action during the long dialogue between Macduff
and Malcolm (iv, 3)—with its leisurely movement, so different from the tragic sweep and stress of what comes before—
fills up the requisite interval for us. In short, Shakespeare has
followed his usual method: he has measured time imagina-
tively, not by months and years.

For the Weird Sisters in their relation to Macbeth the earliest
authority is Wyntown, who makes them appear to him in a
dream. Their name comes from the Anglo-Saxon *wyrd*, 'fate.'
One night, Wyntown tells us, Macbeth 'thought in his dream-
ing' that, as he sat beside King Duncan 'at a seat in hunting,'
he saw three women go by:

> He thowcht quhile he was swa syttand,
> He sawe thre wemen by gangand,
> And thai wemen than thowcht he
> Thre werd Systrys mast lyk to be.

thing came to passe as they had spoken.[1] For shortlie after, the thane of Cawder being condemned at Fores of treason against the king committed; his lands, liuings, and offices were giuen of the kings liberalitie to Mackbeth.

In adopting the term 'Weird Sisters' from Holinshed Shakespeare was obviously adopting also Holinshed's definition—'the goddesses of destiny.'[2] The Weird Sisters, then, are the Norns of Scandinavian mythology.[3] The Norns were goddesses who shaped beforehand the life of every man. Sometimes they came in the night and stood by the cradle of the new-born child, uttering their decrees; for their office was not to prophesy only, but to determine. Sometimes they were met

[1] 'Vana ea Maccabaeo Banquhonique visa, atque per ludum Banquho Maccabaeum regem salutabat: Banquhonemque Maccabaeus vicissim multorum regum parentem. Verum ex euentu postea parcas aut nymphas aliquas fatidicas diabolico astu praeditas fuisse interpretatum est vulgo, quum vera ea quae dixerant euenisse cernerent' (Boece, xii, ed. 1526, fol. 258 r°). 'This prophecy and divinatioun wes haldin mony dayis in derision to Banquho and Makbeth. For sum time, Banquho wald call Makbeth, King of Scottis, for derisioun; and he, on the samin maner, wald call Banquho, the fader of mony kingis. Yit, becaus al thingis succedit as thir wemen devinit, the pepill traistit and jugit thame to be weird sisteris' (Bellenden, xii, 3, ed. 1821, II, 259).

[2] The Weird Sisters are styled witches in the stage directions. In the text, however, they are never so called (except for the insulting 'Aroint thee, witch!' of the sailor's wife in i, 3,6), but always 'the Weird Sisters' or 'the Sisters' or 'the Weird Women.' The Folio spells the word *weyard* (iii, 1, 2; iii, 4, 133; iv, 1, 136) or *weyward* (i, 3, 32; i, 5, 6; ii, 1, 20).

[3] On the Norms see J. A. MacCulloch, *The Mythology of All Races*, II, *Eddic* (1930), pp. 238–247, 254, 255. In Scandinavian tradition they are often conceived as powers of evil. Cf. Curry, 'The Demonic Metaphysics of *Macbeth*,' *Studies in Philology* (Chapel Hill), XXX (1933), 395 ff. In the Scottish rhymed *Trojan War* of *ca.* 1400 (l. 2818, ed. Horstmann, *Barbour's Legendensammlung*), 'a werde sistere' translates 'vnam ex illis quam gentes fatam [i.e., fée] appellant' in the *Historia Destructionis Troiae* of Guido delle Colonne (ed. Griffin, p. 269). About the middle of the fifteenth century, Reginald Pecock speaks of the current 'opinioun that .iij. sistris (whiche ben spiritis) comen to the cradilis of infantis, forto sette to the babe what schal bifalle to him' (*Repressor*, ii, 4, ed. Babington, I, 155). These two passages suffice to prove that the term 'Weird Sisters' was not restricted to the classical Parcae, although we know that it was also applied to them.

The first said, 'Lo, yonder the Thane of Cromarty'; the second, 'Yonder I see the Thane of Moray'; the third, 'I see th[e] King.'[1] Banquo is nowhere mentioned in Wyntown's chronicle. Boece took the incident from Wyntown, working it up into the shape in which Shakespeare found it in Holinshed, who uses both Boece's Latin and Bellenden's Scottish translation. The term 'Weird Sisters' Holinshed adopted from Bellenden. Holinshed's account, which is of prime importance for the understanding of Shakespeare's Weird Sisters, is as follows:

Shortlie after happened a strange and vncouth woonder, which afterward was the cause of much trouble in the realme of Scotland, as ye shall after heare. It fortuned as Makbeth and Banquho iournied towards Fores, where the king then laie, they went sporting by the waie togither without other companie, saue onelie themselues, passing thorough the woods and fields, when suddenlie in the middest of a laund, there met them three women in strange and wild apparell, resembling creatures of elder world, whome when they attentiuelie beheld, wondering much at the sight, the first of them spake and said; All haile Makbeth, thane of Glammis (for he had latelie entered into that dignitie and office by the death of his father Sinell). The second of them said; Haile Makbeth thane of Cawder. But the third said; All haile Makbeth that heereafter shalt be king of Scotland.

Then Banquho; What manner of women (saith he) are you, that seeme so little fauourable vnto me, whereas to my fellow heere, besides high offices, ye assigne also the kingdome, appointing foorth nothing for me at all? Yes (saith the first of them) we promise greater benefits vnto thee, than vnto him, for he shall reigne in deed, but with an vnluckie end: neither shall he leaue anie issue behind him to succeed in his place, where contrarilie thou in deed shalt not reigne at all, but of thee those shall be borne which shall gouerne the Scotish kingdome by long order of continuall descent. Herewith the foresaid women vanished immediatlie out of their sight. This was reputed at the first but some vaine fantasticall illusion by Mackbeth and Banquho, insomuch that Banquho would call Mackbeth in iest, king of Scotland; and Mackbeth againe would call him in sport likewise, the father of manie kings. But afterwards the common opinion was, that these women were either the weird sisters, that is (as ye would say) the goddesses of destinie, or else some nymphs or feiries, indued with knowledge of prophesie by their necromanticall science, bicause euerie

---

[1] *Orygynale Cronykil*, vi, 18, 1857–1869 (ed. Laing, II, 127, 128).

in wild places and at unexpected moments. Once they were
seen in a remote den in the woods, weaving the visible web
of doom on the day of a great battle in which many perished.[1]
Now they appear as the guardians of a favourite hero; again,
they are hostile, and bent only on a man's destruction: but
always and everywhere they are great and terrible powers,
from whose mandate there is no appeal. In all probability,
their attachment to the story goes back to the time of Macbeth
himself. Their presence is due to the large infusion of Norse
blood in the Scottish race, and their function is in full accord
with the doctrines of Norse heathendom. That function, then,
was an essential element in the history of Macbeth as it came
into Shakespeare's hands. These were not ordinary witches
or seeresses. They were great powers of destiny, great ministers of fate. They had determined the past; they governed the
present; they not only foresaw the future, but decreed it. All
this was manifest to Shakespeare as he read the chronicle. He
assimilated the conception in its entirety by a single act of sympathetic imagination; and he reproduced it in his tragedy, not
in any literal or dogmatic shape, but coloured and intensified
by his creative genius, and modified by his trained sense of what
it is possible to represent upon the actual stage. The Weird
Sisters, then, are not hags in the service of the devil; they are
not mere personifications of a man's evil desires or his ruth-
less craving for power. They are as actual and objective as the
Furies that lie snoring in bloodthirsty dreams round about the
fugitive Orestes as he clings affrighted to the altar of Apollo.
Thus the tragedy of MACBETH is inevitably fatalistic, but
Shakespeare attempts no solution of the problem of free will
and predestination. It is not his office to make a contribution
to philosophy or theology. He never gives us the impression
that a man is not responsible for his own acts. 'It will have
blood, they say; blood will have blood.'

[1] *Njálssaga*, cap. 157 (*Íslendinga Sögur*, III [1875], 898–902. Here
they are identified with the Valkyries. Their weaving song is translated in
Gray's *Fatal Sisters*.

Obviously, however, Shakespeare could not produce the goddesses of fate *in propriis personis* upon the stage in a Scottish
tragedy. He had to bring them within the range of the specta-
tors' beliefs and experiences. And this he accomplished by
giving them several attributes of a class of women with whom
the audience had perfect familiarity—the witch. They kill
swine, they brew hell-broth, they have familiar spirits, they
dig up the dead to use fragments of mortality in their charms.
Yet they remain indisputably supernatural. They are not
amenable to the halter or the stake. If they choose to wear
the garb of witches for a time, that is their own affair. Their
empire is as wide as the world, and their power extends to
the last syllable of recorded time.

THE TRAGEDY OF
MACBETH

Duncan, King of Scotland.

Malcolm,
Donalbain, } his sons.

Macbeth,
Banquo, } Generals of the Scottish **Army.**

Macduff,
Lennox,
Ross,
Menteith, } Noblemen of Scotland.
Angus,
Caithness,

Fleance, Son to Banquo.
Siward, Earl of Northumberland, General of the English forces.
Young Siward, his son.
Seyton, an Officer attending on *Macbeth*.
Boy, son to *Macduff*.
A Sergeant.
A Porter.
An Old Man.
An English Doctor.
A Scottish Doctor.

Lady Macbeth.
Lady Macduff.
A Gentlewoman, attending on *Lady Macbeth*.

The *Weird Sisters.*
Hecate.
The Ghost of *Banquo.*
Apparitions.

Lords, Gentlemen, Officers, Soldiers, Murderers, Messengers, Attendants.

SCENE.—*Scotland; England.*]

THE TRAGEDY OF
MACBETH

Act I. Scene I. [*Scotland. An open place.*]

Thunder and lightning. Enter three *Witches.*

1. Witch. When shall we three meet again
In thunder, lightning, or in rain?
2. Witch. When the hurlyburly's done,
When the battle's lost and won.
3. Witch. That will be ere the set of sun.   5
1. Witch. Where the place?
2. Witch.   Upon the heath.
3. Witch. There to meet with Macbeth.
1. Witch. I come, Graymalkin!
2. Witch. Paddock calls.
3. Witch.   Anon!
All. Fair is foul, and foul is fair.   10
Hover through the fog and filthy air.   *Exeunt.*

Scene II. [*A camp near Forres.*]

Alarum within. Enter *King* [*Duncan*], *Malcolm, Donalbain,
   Lennox,* with *Attendants,* meeting a bleeding *Sergeant.*

King. What bloody man is that? He can report,
As seemeth by his plight, of the revolt
The newest state.
Mal.   This is the sergeant
Who like a good and hardy soldier fought
'Gainst my captivity. Hail, brave friend!   5
Say to the King the knowledge of the broil
As thou didst leave it.

3

Serg.   Doubtful it stood,
As two spent swimmers that do cling together
And choke their art. The merciless Macdonwald
(Worthy to be a rebel, for to that   10
The multiplying villanies of nature
Do swarm upon him) from the Western Isles
Of kerns and gallowglasses is supplied;
And Fortune, on his damned quarrel smiling,
Show'd like a rebel's whore. But all's too weak;   15
For brave Macbeth (well he deserves that name),
Disdaining Fortune, with his brandish'd steel,
Which smok'd with bloody execution
(Like valour's minion), carv'd out his passage
Till he fac'd the slave;   20
Which ne'er shook hands nor bade farewell to him
Till he unseam'd him from the nave to th' chaps
And fix'd his head upon our battlements.
   King. O valiant cousin! worthy gentleman!
   Serg. As whence the sun gins his reflection   25
Shipwracking storms and direful thunders break,
So from that spring whence comfort seem'd to come
Discomfort swells. Mark, King of Scotland, mark.
No sooner justice had, with valour arm'd,
Compell'd these skipping kerns to trust their heels   30
But the Norweyan lord, surveying vantage,
With furbish'd arms and new supplies of men,
Began a fresh assault.
   King.   Dismay'd not this
Our captains, Macbeth and Banquo?
   Serg.   Yes,
As sparrows eagles, or the hare the lion.   35
If I say sooth, I must report they were
As cannons overcharg'd with double cracks, so they

Doubly redoubled strokes upon the foe.
Except they meant to bathe in reeking wounds,
Or memorize another Golgotha,   40
I cannot tell—
But I am faint; my gashes cry for help.
  King. So well thy words become thee as thy wounds;
They smack of honour both. Go get him surgeons.
                      [*Exit Sergeant, attended.*]
                Enter *Ross.*
Who comes here?
  Mal.   The worthy Thane of Ross.   45
  Len. What a haste looks through his eyes! So should
    he look
That seems to speak things strange.
  Ross.   God save the King!
  King. Whence cam'st thou, worthy thane?
  Ross.   From Fife, great King,
Where the Norweyan banners flout the sky
And fan our people cold. Norway himself,   50
With terrible numbers,
Assisted by that most disloyal traitor
The Thane of Cawdor, began a dismal conflict,
Till that Bellona's bridegroom, lapp'd in proof,
Confronted him with self-comparisons,   55
Point against point, rebellious arm 'gainst arm,
Curbing his lavish spirit; and to conclude,
The victory fell on us.
  King.   Great happiness!
  Ross.   That now
Sweno, the Norways' king, craves composition;
Nor would we deign him burial of his men   60
Till he disbursed, at Saint Colme's Inch,
Ten thousand dollars to our general use.

King. No more that Thane of Cawdor shall deceive
Our bosom interest. Go pronounce his present death
And with his former title greet Macbeth.   65

     Ross. I'll see it done.

     Dun. What he hath lost noble Macbeth hath won. *Exeunt.*

Scene III. [*A blasted heath.*]

Thunder. Enter the three *Witches.*

     1. Witch. Where hast thou been, sister?

     2. Witch. Killing swine.

     3. Witch. Sister, where thou?

     1. Witch. A sailor's wife had chestnuts in her lap
And mounch'd and mounch'd and mounch'd. 'Give me,'
     quoth I.   5
'Aroint thee, witch!' the rump-fed ronyon cries.
Her husband's to Aleppo gone, master o' th' Tiger;
But in a sieve I'll thither sail
And, like a rat without a tail,
I'll do, I'll do, and I'll do.   10

     2. Witch. I'll give thee a wind.

     1. Witch. Th' art kind.

     3. Witch. And I another.

     1. Witch. I myself have all the other,
And the very ports they blow,   15
All the quarters that they know
I' th' shipman's card.
I will drain him dry as hay.
Sleep shall neither night nor day
Hang upon his penthouse lid.   20
He shall live a man forbid.
Weary sev'nights, nine times nine,

Shall he dwindle, peak, and pine.
Though his bark cannot be lost,
Yet it shall be tempest-tost.   25
Look what I have.
   2. Witch. Show me! show me!
   1. Witch. Here I have a pilot's thumb,
Wrack'd as homeward he did come.

                                  Drum within.
   3. Witch. A drum, a drum!   30
Macbeth doth come.
   All. The Weird Sisters, hand in hand,
Posters of the sea and land,
Thus do go about, about,
Thrice to thine, and thrice to mine,   35
And thrice again, to make up nine.
Peace! The charm's wound up.

           Enter *Macbeth* and *Banquo.*

   Macb. So foul and fair a day I have not seen.
   Ban. How far is't call'd to Forres? What are these,
So wither'd, and so wild in their attire,   40
That look not like th' inhabitants o' th' earth,
And yet are on't? Live you? or are you aught
That man may question? You seem to understand me,
By each at once her choppy finger laying
Upon her skinny lips. You should be women,   45
And yet your beards forbid me to interpret
That you are so.
   Macb.   Speak, if you can. What are you?
   1. Witch. All hail, Macbeth! Hail to thee, Thane of
     Glamis!
   2. Witch. All hail, Macbeth! Hail to thee, Thane of
     Cawdor!   49

   3. Witch. All hail, Macbeth, that shalt be King hereafter!
   Ban. Good sir, why do you start and seem to fear
Things that do sound so fair? I' th' name of truth,
Are ye fantastical, or that indeed
Which outwardly ye show? My noble partner
You greet with present grace and great prediction   55
Of noble having and of royal hope,
That he seems rapt withal. To me you speak not.
If you can look into the seeds of time
And say which grain will grow and which will not,
Speak then to me, who neither beg nor fear   60
Your favours nor your hate.
   1. Witch. Hail!
   2. Witch. Hail!
   3. Witch. Hail!
   1. Witch. Lesser than Macbeth, and greater.   65
   2. Witch. Not so happy, yet much happier.
   3. Witch. Thou shalt get kings, though thou be none.
So all hail, Macbeth and Banquo!
   1. Witch. Banquo and Macbeth, all hail!
   Macb. Stay, you imperfect speakers, tell me more!   70
By Sinel's death I know I am Thane of Glamis;
But how of Cawdor? The Thane of Cawdor lives,
A prosperous gentleman; and to be King
Stands not within the prospect of belief,
No more than to be Cawdor. Say from whence   75
You owe this strange intelligence, or why
Upon this blasted heath you stop our way
With such prophetic greeting. Speak, I charge you.

                              Witches vanish.
   Ban. The earth hath bubbles, as the water has,
And these are of them. Whither are they vanish'd?   80

Macb. Into the air, and what seem'd corporal melted
As breath into the wind. Would they had stay'd!
    Ban. Were such things here as we do speak about?
Or have we eaten on the insane root
That takes the reason prisoner?   85
    Macb. Your children shall be kings.
    Ban.   You shall be King.
    Macb. And Thane of Cawdor too. Went it not so?
    Ban. To th' selfsame tune and words. Who's here?

Enter *Ross* and *Angus.*

    Ross. The King hath happily receiv'd, Macbeth,
The news of thy success; and when he reads   90
Thy personal venture in the rebels' fight,
His wonders and his praises do contend
Which should be thine or his. Silenc'd with that,
In viewing o'er the rest o' th' selfsame day,
He finds thee in the stout Norweyan ranks,   95
Nothing afeard of what thyself didst make,
Strange images of death. As thick as tale
Came post with post, and every one did bear
Thy praises in his kingdom's great defence
And pour'd them down before him.
    Ang.   We are sent   100
To give thee from our royal master thanks;
Only to herald thee into his sight,
Not pay thee.
    Ross. And for an earnest of a greater honour,
He bade me, from him, call thee Thane of Cawdor;   105
In which addition, hail, most worthy Thane!
For it is thine.
    Ban.   What, can the devil speak true?

Macb. The Thane of Cawdor lives. Why do you dress me
In borrowed robes?

    Ang.   Who was the Thane lives yet,
But under heavy judgment bears that life   110
Which he deserves to lose. Whether he was combin'd
With those of Norway, or did line the rebel
With hidden help and vantage, or that with both
He labour'd in his country's wrack, I know not;
But treasons capital, confess'd and prov'd,   115
Have overthrown him.

    Macb.   [*aside*] Glamis, and Thane of Cawdor!
The greatest is behind.—[*To Ross and Angus*] Thanks for
    your pains.
[*Aside to Banquo*] Do you not hope your children shall be
    kings,
When those that gave the Thane of Cawdor to me
Promis'd no less to them?

    Ban. [*aside to Macbeth*] That, trusted home,   120
Might yet enkindle you unto the crown,
Besides the Thane of Cawdor. But 'tis strange!
And oftentimes, to win us to our harm,
The instruments of darkness tell us truths,
Win us with honest trifles, to betray 's   125
In deepest consequence.—
Cousins, a word, I pray you.

    Macb.   [*aside*] Two truths are told,
As happy prologues to the swelling act
Of the imperial theme.—I thank you, gentlemen.—
[*Aside*] This supernatural soliciting   130
Cannot be ill; cannot be good. If ill,
Why hath it given me earnest of success,
Commencing in a truth? I am Thane of Cawdor.
If good, why do I yield to that suggestion

Whose horrid image doth unfix my hair   135
And make my seated heart knock at my ribs
Against the use of nature? Present fears
Are less than horrible imaginings.
My thought, whose murther yet is but fantastical,
Shakes so my single state of man that function   140
Is smother'd in surmise and nothing is
But what is not.
    Ban.   Look how our partner's rapt.
    Macb. [*aside*] If chance will have me King, why, chance
      may crown me,
Without my stir.
    Ban.   New honours come upon him,
Like our strange garments, cleave not to their mould   145
But with the aid of use.
    Macb.   [*aside*] Come what come may,
Time and the hour runs through the roughest day.
    Ban. Worthy Macbeth, we stay upon your leisure.
    Macb. Give me your favour. My dull brain was wrought
With things forgotten. Kind gentlemen, your pains   150
Are regist'red where every day I turn
The leaf to read them. Let us toward the King.
[*Aside to Banquo*] Think upon what hath chanc'd; and, at
    more time,
The interim having weigh'd it, let us speak
Our free hearts each to other.
    Ban.   [*aside to Macbeth*] Very gladly. 155
    Macb. [*aside to Banquo*] Till then, enough. — Come,
    friends.   *Exeunt.*

Scene IV. [*Forres. The Palace.*]

Flourish. Enter *King* [*Duncan*], *Lennox, Malcolm, Donal-
        bain*, and *Attendants.*

   King. Is execution done on Cawdor? Are not
Those in commission yet return'd?
   Mal.   My liege,
They are not yet come back. But I have spoke
With one that saw him die; who did report
That very frankly he confess'd his treasons,   5
Implor'd your Highness' pardon, and set forth
A deep repentance. Nothing in his life
Became him like the leaving it. He died
As one that had been studied in his death
To throw away the dearest thing he ow'd   10
As 'twere a careless trifle.
   King.   There's no art
To find the mind's construction in the face.
He was a gentleman on whom I built
An absolute trust.

Enter *Macbeth, Banquo,* and *Angus.*

            O worthiest cousin,
The sin of my ingratitude even now   15
Was heavy on me! Thou art so far before
That swiftest wing of recompense is slow
To overtake thee. Would thou hadst less deserv'd,
That the proportion both of thanks and payment
Might have been mine! Only I have left to say,   20
More is thy due than more than all can pay.
   Macb. The service and the loyalty I owe,

In doing it pays itself. Your Highness' part
Is to receive our duties; and our duties
Are to your throne and state children and servants,   25
Which do but what they should by doing everything
Safe toward your love and honour.
   King.   Welcome hither.
I have begun to plant thee and will labour
To make thee full of growing. Noble Banquo,
That hast no less deserv'd, nor must be known   30
No less to have done so, let me infold thee
And hold thee to my heart.
   Ban.   There if I grow,
The harvest is your own.
   King.   My plenteous joys,
Wanton in fulness, seek to hide themselves
In drops of sorrow. Sons, kinsmen, thanes,   35
And you whose places are the nearest, know
We will establish our estate upon
Our eldest, Malcolm, whom we name hereafter
The Prince of Cumberland; which honour must
Not unaccompanied invest him only,   40
But signs of nobleness, like stars, shall shine
On all deservers. From hence to Inverness,
And bind us further to you.
   Macb. The rest is labour, which is not us'd for you!
I'll be myself the harbinger, and make joyful   45
The hearing of my wife with your approach;
So, humbly take my leave.
   King.   My worthy Cawdor!
   Macb. [*aside*] The Prince of Cumberland! That is a step
On which I must fall down, or else o'erleap,
For in my way it lies. Stars, hide your fires!   50
Let not light see my black and deep desires.

The eye wink at the hand; yet let that be,
Which the eye fears, when it is done, to see.   *Exit.*
   King. True, worthy Banquo: he is full so valiant,
And in his commendations I am fed;   55
It is a banquet to me. Let's after him,
Whose care is gone before to bid us welcome.
It is a peerless kinsman.   *Flourish. Exeunt.*

Scene V. [*Inverness.* Macbeth's *Castle.*]

Enter *Macbeth's Wife,* alone, with a letter.

   Lady. [*reads*] 'They met me in the day of success; and I have
learn'd by the perfect'st report they have more in them than mortal
knowledge. When I burn'd in desire to question them further, they
made themselves air, into which they vanish'd. Whiles I stood rapt
in the wonder of it, came missives from the King, who all-hail'd me
Thane of Cawdor, by which title, before, these Weird Sisters saluted
me, and referr'd me to the coming on of time with "Hail, King that
shalt be!" This have I thought good to deliver thee, my dearest
partner of greatness, that thou mightst not lose the dues of rejoicing
by being ignorant of what greatness is promis'd thee. Lay it to thy
heart, and farewell.'   15

Glamis thou art, and Cawdor, and shalt be—
What thou art promis'd. Yet do I fear thy nature.
It is too full o' th' milk of human kindness
To catch the nearest way. Thou wouldst be great;
Art not without ambition, but without   20
The illness should attend it. What thou wouldst highly,
That wouldst thou holily; wouldst not play false,
And yet wouldst wrongly win. Thou'ldst have, great Glamis,
That which cries 'Thus thou must do,' if thou have it;
And that which rather thou dost fear to do   25

Than wishest should be undone. Hie thee hither,
That I may pour my spirits in thine ear
And chastise with the valour of my tongue
All that impedes thee from the golden round
Which fate and metaphysical aid doth seem   30
To have thee crown'd withal.

                    Enter *Messenger*.

                              What is your tidings?
    Mess. The King comes here to-night.
    Lady.   Thou'rt mad to say it!
Is not thy master with him? who, were't so,
Would have inform'd for preparation.
    Mess. So please you, it is true. Our Thane is coming. 35
One of my fellows had the speed of him,
Who, almost dead for breath, had scarcely more
Than would make up his message.
    Lady.   Give him tending;
He brings great news.

                                        Exit Messenger.
                    The raven himself is hoarse
That croaks the fatal entrance of Duncan   40
Under my battlements. Come, you spirits
That tend on mortal thoughts, unsex me here,
And fill me, from the crown to the toe, top-full
Of direst cruelty! Make thick my blood;
Stop up th' access and passage to remorse,   45
That no compunctious visitings of nature
Shake my fell purpose nor keep peace between
Th' effect and it! Come to my woman's breasts
And take my milk for gall, you murth'ring ministers,
Wherever in your sightless substances   50
You wait on nature's mischief! Come, thick night,

And pall thee in the dunnest smoke of hell,
That my keen knife see not the wound it makes,
Nor heaven peep through the blanket of the dark
To cry 'Hold, hold!'

Enter Macbeth.

                   Great Glamis! worthy Cawdor!   55
Greater than both, by the all-hail hereafter!
Thy letters have transported me beyond
This ignorant present, and I feel now
The future in the instant.
   Macb.   My dearest love,
Duncan comes here to-night.
   Lady.   And when goes hence?   60
   Macb. To-morrow, as he purposes.
   Lady.   O, never
Shall sun that morrow see!
Your face, my Thane, is as a book where men
May read strange matters. To beguile the time,
Look like the time; bear welcome in your eye,   65
Your hand, your tongue; look like the innocent flower,
But be the serpent under't. He that's coming
Must be provided for; and you shall put
This night's great business into my dispatch,
Which shall to all our nights and days to come   70
Give solely sovereign sway and masterdom.
   Macb. We will speak further.
   Lady.   Only look up clear.
To alter favour ever is to fear.
Leave all the rest to me.   *Exeunt.*

Scene VI. [*Inverness. Before* Macbeth's *castle.*]

Hautboys and torches. Enter King [*Duncan*], Malcolm, Donalbain, Banquo, Lennox, Macduff, Ross, Angus, and *Attendants.*

King. This castle hath a pleasant seat. The air
Nimbly and sweetly recommends itself
Unto our gentle senses.
 Ban.   This guest of summer,
The temple-haunting martlet, does approve
By his lov'd mansionry that the heaven's breath   5
Smells wooingly here. No jutty, frieze,
Buttress, nor coign of vantage, but this bird
Hath made his pendent bed and procreant cradle.
Where they most breed and haunt, I have observ'd
The air is delicate.

Enter Lady [Macbeth].

 King.   See, see, our honour'd hostess!   10
The love that follows us sometime is our trouble,
Which still we thank as love. Herein I teach you
How you shall bid God 'ield us for your pains
And thank us for your trouble.
 Lady.   All our service
In every point twice done, and then done double,   15
Were poor and single business to contend
Against those honours deep and broad wherewith
Your Majesty loads our house. For those of old,
And the late dignities heap'd up to them,
We rest your hermits.
 King.   Where's the Thane of Cawdor?   20
We cours'd him at the heels and had a purpose
To be his purveyor; but he rides well,

And his great love, sharp as his spur, hath holp him
To his home before us. Fair and noble hostess,
We are your guest to-night.

    Lady.   Your servants ever   25
Have theirs, themselves, and what is theirs, in compt,
To make their audit at your Highness' pleasure,
Still to return your own.

    King.   Give me your hand;
Conduct me to mine host. We love him highly
And shall continue our graces towards him.   30
By your leave, hostess.   *Exeunt.*

Scene VII. [*Inverness*. Macbeth's *Castle*.]

Hautboys. Torches. Enter a *Sewer*, and divers *Servants* with
    dishes and service over the stage. Then enter *Macbeth*.

    Macb. If it were done when 'tis done, then 'twere well
It were done quickly. If th' assassination
Could trammel up the consequence, and catch,
With his surcease, success; that but this blow
Might be the be-all and the end-all here,   5
But here, upon this bank and shoal of time,
We'ld jump the life to come. But in these cases
We still have judgment here, that we but teach
Bloody instructions, which, being taught, return
To plague th' inventor. This even-handed justice   10
Commends th' ingredience of our poison'd chalice
To our own lips. He's here in double trust:
First, as I am his kinsman and his subject—
Strong both against the deed; then, as his host,
Who should against his murtherer shut the door,   15
Not bear the knife myself. Besides, this Duncan

Hath borne his faculties so meek, hath been
So clear in his great office, that his virtues
Will plead like angels, trumpet-tongu'd, against
The deep damnation of his taking-off;　　　　20
And pity, like a naked new-born babe,
Striding the blast, or heaven's cherubin, hors'd
Upon the sightless couriers of the air,
Shall blow the horrid deed in every eye,
That tears shall drown the wind. I have no spur　　　　25
To prick the sides of my intent, but only
Vaulting ambition, which o'erleaps itself
And falls on th' other side.

Enter Lady [Macbeth].

　　　　　　　　　　　How now? What news?
Lady. He has almost supp'd. Why have you left the chamber?
Macb. Hath he ask'd for me?
Lady.　　　　　　　Know you not he has?　　30
Macb. We will proceed no further in this business.
He hath honour'd me of late, and I have bought
Golden opinions from all sorts of people,
Which would be worn now in their newest gloss,
Not cast aside so soon.
Lady.　　　　　Was the hope drunk　　35
Wherein you dress'd yourself? Hath it slept since?
And wakes it now to look so green and pale
At what it did so freely? From this time
Such I account thy love. Art thou afeard
To be the same in thine own act and valour　　40
As thou art in desire? Wouldst thou have that
Which thou esteem'st the ornament of life,
And live a coward in thine own esteem,

Letting 'I dare not' wait upon 'I would,'
Like the poor cat i' th' adage?

   Macb.   Prithee peace!   45
I dare do all that may become a man.
Who dares do more is none.

   Lady.   What beast was't then
That made you break this enterprise to me?
When you durst do it, then you were a man;
And to be more than what you were, you would   50
Be so much more the man. Nor time nor place
Did then adhere, and yet you would make both.
They have made themselves, and that their fitness now
Does unmake you. I have given suck, and know
How tender 'tis to love the babe that milks me.   55
I would, while it was smiling in my face,
Have pluck'd my nipple from his boneless gums
And dash'd the brains out, had I so sworn as you
Have done to this.

   Macb.   If we should fail?

   Lady.   We fail?
But screw your courage to the sticking place,   60
And we'll not fail. When Duncan is asleep
(Whereto the rather shall his day's hard journey
Soundly invite him), his two chamberlains
Will I with wine and wassail so convince
That memory, the warder of the brain,   65
Shall be a fume, and the receipt of reason
A limbeck only. When in swinish sleep
Their drenched natures lie as in a death,
What cannot you and I perform upon
Th' unguarded Duncan? what not put upon   70
His spongy officers, who shall bear the guilt
Of our great quell?

 Macb.   Bring forth men-children only;
For thy undaunted mettle should compose
Nothing but males. Will it not be receiv'd,
When we have mark'd with blood those sleepy **two**   75
Of his own chamber and us'd their very daggers,
That they have done't?
 Lady.   Who dares receive it **other,**
As we shall make our griefs and clamour **roar**
Upon his death?
 Macb. I am settled and bend up
Each corporal agent to this terrible feat.   80
Away, and mock the time with fairest show;
False face must hide what the false heart doth know. *Exeunt.*

ACT II. Scene I. [*Inverness. Court of* Macbeth's *Castle.*]

Enter *Banquo*, and *Fleance* with a torch before him.

Ban. How goes the night, boy?
Fle. The moon is down; I have not heard the clock.
Ban. And she goes down at twelve.
Fle.   I take't, 'tis later, sir.
Ban. Hold, take my sword. There's husbandry in heaven;
Their candles are all out. Take thee that too.   5
A heavy summons lies like lead upon me,
And yet I would not sleep. Merciful powers,
Restrain in me the cursed thoughts that nature
Gives way to in repose!

Enter *Macbeth*, and a *Servant* with a torch.

                        Give me my sword.
Who's there?   10
    Macb. A friend.
    Ban. What, sir, not yet at rest? The King's abed.
He hath been in unusual pleasure and
Sent forth great largess to your offices.
This diamond he greets your wife withal   15
By the name of most kind hostess, and shut up
In measureless content.
    Macb.   Being unprepar'd,
Our will became the servant to defect,
Which else should free have wrought.
    Ban.   All's well.
I dreamt last night of the three Weird Sisters.   20
To you they have show'd some truth.
    Macb.   I think not of them.
Yet when we can entreat an hour to serve,

22

We would spend it in some words upon that business,
If you would grant the time.

    Ban.   At your kind'st leisure.

    Macb. If you shall cleave to my consent, when 'tis,   25
It shall make honour for you.

    Ban.   So I lose none
In seeking to augment it but still keep
My bosom franchis'd and allegiance clear,
I shall be counsell'd.

    Macb.   Good repose the while!

    Ban. Thanks, sir. The like to you!   30

                    Exeunt Banquo [and Fleance].

    Macb. Go bid thy mistress, when my drink is ready,
She strike upon the bell. Get thee to bed.

                           Exit [Servant].

Is this a dagger which I see before me,
The handle toward my hand? Come, let me clutch thee!
I have thee not, and yet I see thee still.   35
Art thou not, fatal vision, sensible
To feeling as to sight? or art thou but
A dagger of the mind, a false creation,
Proceeding from the heat-oppressed brain?
I see thee yet, in form as palpable   40
As this which now I draw.
Thou marshall'st me the way that I was going,
And such an instrument I was to use.
Mine eyes are made the fools o' th' other senses,
Or else worth all the rest. I see thee still;   45
And on thy blade and dudgeon gouts of blood,
Which was not so before. There's no such thing.
It is the bloody business which informs
Thus to mine eyes. Now o'er the one half-world
Nature seems dead, and wicked dreams abuse   50

The curtain'd sleep. Now witchcraft celebrates
Pale Hecate's offerings; and wither'd murther,
Alarum'd by his sentinel, the wolf,
Whose howl's his watch, thus with his stealthy pace,
With Tarquin's ravishing strides, towards his design   55
Moves like a ghost. Thou sure and firm-set earth,
Hear not my steps which way they walk, for fear
Thy very stones prate of my whereabout
And take the present horror from the time,
Which now suits with it. Whiles I threat, he lives;   60
Words to the heat of deeds too cold breath gives.

A bell rings.

I go, and it is done. The bell invites me.
Hear it not, Duncan, for it is a knell
That summons thee to heaven, or to hell.   *Exit.*

Scene II. [*Inverness*. Macbeth's *Castle*.]

Enter *Lady* [*Macbeth*].

Lady. That which hath made them drunk hath made me
      bold;
What hath quench'd them hath given me fire. Hark! Peace!
It was the owl that shriek'd, the fatal bellman
Which gives the stern'st good-night. He is about it.
The doors are open, and the surfeited grooms   5
Do mock their charge with snores. I have drugg'd their possets,
That death and nature do contend about them
Whether they live or die.
      Macb. [*within*] Who's there? What, ho?
      Lady. Alack, I am afraid they have awak'd,   10
And 'tis not done! Th' attempt, and not the deed,
Confounds us. Hark! I laid their daggers ready;

He could not miss 'em. Had he not resembled
My father as he slept, I had done't.

Enter Macbeth.

My husband!

    Macb. I have done the deed. Didst thou not hear a noise?
    Lady. I heard the owl scream and the crickets cry.   16
Did you not speak?
    Macb.   When?
    Lady.   Now.
    Macb.   As I descended?
    Lady. Ay.
    Macb. Hark!
Who lies i' th' second chamber?
    Lady.   Donalbain.   20
    Macb. This is a sorry sight.   [*Looks on his hands.*]
    Lady. A foolish thought, to say a sorry sight.
    Macb. There's one did laugh in's sleep, and one cried
    'Murther!'
That they did wake each other. I stood and heard them.
But they did say their prayers and address'd them   25
Again to sleep.
    Lady.   There are two lodg'd together.
    Macb. One cried 'God bless us!' and 'Amen!' the other,
As they had seen me with these hangman's hands,
List'ning their fear. I could not say 'Amen!'
When they did say 'God bless us!'
    Lady.   Consider it not so deeply.   30
    Macb. But wherefore could not I pronounce 'Amen'?
I had most need of blessing, and 'Amen'
Stuck in my throat.
    Lady.   These deeds must not be thought
After these ways. So, it will make us mad.

Macb. Methought I heard a voice cry 'Sleep no more!   35
Macbeth does murther sleep'—the innocent sleep,
Sleep that knits up the ravell'd sleave of care,
The death of each day's life, sore labour's bath,
Balm of hurt minds, great nature's second course,
Chief nourisher in life's feast.

  Lady.   What do you mean?   40

  Macb. Still it cried 'Sleep no more!' to all the house;
'Glamis hath murther'd sleep, and therefore Cawdor
Shall sleep no more! Macbeth shall sleep no more!'

  Lady. Who was it that thus cried? Why, worthy Thane,
You do unbend your noble strength to think   45
So brainsickly of things. Go get some water
And wash this filthy witness from your hand.
Why did you bring these daggers from the place?
They must lie there. Go carry them and smear
The sleepy grooms with blood.

  Macb.   I'll go no more.   50
I am afraid to think what I have done;
Look on't again I dare not.

  Lady.   Infirm of purpose!
Give me the daggers. The sleeping and the dead
Are but as pictures. 'Tis the eye of childhood
That fears a painted devil. If he do bleed,   55
I'll gild the faces of the grooms withal,
For it must seem their guilt. *Exit. Knocking within.*

  Macb.   Whence is that knocking?
How is't with me when every noise appals me?
What hands are here? Ha! they pluck out mine eyes!
Will all great Neptune's ocean wash this blood   60
Clean from my hand? No. This my hand will rather
The multitudinous seas incarnadine,
Making the green one red.

Enter *Lady* [*Macbeth*].

Lady. My hands are of your colour, but I shame
To wear a heart so white. (*Knock.*) I hear a knocking   65
At the south entry. Retire we to our chamber.
A little water clears us of this deed.
How easy is it then! Your constancy
Hath left you unattended. (*Knock.*) Hark! more knocking.
Get on your nightgown, lest occasion call us   70
And show us to be watchers. Be not lost
So poorly in your thoughts.
   Macb. To know my deed, 'twere best not know myself.
                                                    Knock.
Wake Duncan with thy knocking! I would thou couldst!
                                                    Exeunt.

Scene III. [*Inverness.* Macbeth's *Castle.*]

Enter a *Porter*. Knocking within.

Porter. Here's a knocking indeed! If a man were porter
of hell gate, he should have old turning the key. (*Knock.*)
Knock, knock, knock! Who's there, i' th' name of Belzebub?
Here's a farmer that hang'd himself on th' expectation of
plenty. Come in time! Have napkins enow about you; here
you'll sweat for't. (*Knock.*) Knock, knock! Who's there, in
th' other devil's name? Faith, here's an equivocator, that could
swear in both the scales against either scale; who committed
treason enough for God's sake, yet could not equivocate to
heaven. O, come in, equivocator! (*Knock.*) Knock, knock,
knock! Who's there? Faith, here's an English tailor come
hither for stealing out of a French hose. Come in, tailor. Here

you may roast your goose. (*Knock.*) Knock, knock! Never at quiet! What are you? But this place is too cold for hell. I'll devil-porter it no further. I had thought to have let in some of all professions that go the primrose way to th' everlasting bonfire. (*Knock.*) Anon, anon! [*Opens the gate.*] I pray you remember the porter.

Enter *Macduff* and *Lennox*.

Macd. Was it so late, friend, ere you went to bed,
That you do lie so late? 25
Port. Faith, sir, we were carousing till the second cock; and drink, sir, is a great provoker of three things.
Macd. What three things does drink especially provoke?
Port. Marry, sir, nose-painting, sleep, and urine. Lechery, sir, it provokes, and unprovokes: it provokes the desire, but it takes away the performance. Therefore much drink may be said to be an equivocator with lechery: it makes him, and it mars him; it sets him on, and it takes him off; it persuades him, and disheartens him; makes him stand to, and not stand to; in conclusion, equivocates him in a sleep, and, giving him the lie, leaves him. 40
Macd. I believe drink gave thee the lie last night.
Port. That it did, sir, i' the very throat on me; but I requited him for his lie; and, I think, being too strong for him, though he took up my legs sometime, yet I made a shift to cast him. 46
Macd. Is thy master stirring?

Enter *Macbeth*.

Our knocking has awak'd him; here he comes.
Len. Good morrow, noble sir.
Macb. Good morrow, both.

Macd. Is the King stirring, worthy Thane?

Macb.   Not yet.   50

Macd. He did command me to call timely on him;
I have almost slipp'd the hour.

Macb.   I'll bring you to him.

Macd. I know this is a joyful trouble to you;
But yet 'tis one.

Macb. The labour we delight in physics pain.   55
This is the door.

Macd.   I'll make so bold to call,
For 'tis my limited service.   *Exit.*

Len. Goes the King hence to-day?

Macb.   He does; he did appoint
so.

Len. The night has been unruly. Where we lay,
Our chimneys were blown down; and, as they say,   60
Lamentings heard i' th' air, strange screams of death,
And prophesying, with accents terrible,
Of dire combustion and confus'd events
New hatch'd to th' woful time. The obscure bird
Clamour'd the livelong night. Some say the earth   65
Was feverous and did shake.

Macb.   'Twas a rough night.

Len. My young remembrance cannot parallel
A fellow to it.

Enter *Macduff.*

Macd. O horror, horror, horror! Tongue nor heart
Cannot conceive nor name thee!

Macb. and Len.   What's the matter?   70

Macd. Confusion now hath made his masterpiece!
Most sacrilegious murther hath broke ope

The Lord's anointed temple and stole thence
The life o' th' building!

    Macb.   What is't you say? the life?

    Len. Mean you his Majesty?   75

    Macd. Approach the chamber, and destroy your sight
With a new Gorgon. Do not bid me speak.
See, and then speak yourselves.

                      Exeunt Macbeth and Lennox.
                      Awake, awake!
Ring the alarum bell. Murther and treason!
Banquo and Donalbain! Malcolm! awake!   80
Shake off this downy sleep, death's counterfeit,
And look on death itself! Up, up, and see
The great doom's image! Malcolm! Banquo!
As from your graves rise up and walk like sprites
To countenance this horror! Ring the bell!   85
                        Bell rings.

            Enter *Lady* [*Macbeth*].

    Lady. What's the business,
That such a hideous trumpet calls to parley
The sleepers of the house? Speak, speak!

    Macd.   O gentle lady,
'Tis not for you to hear what I can speak!
The repetition in a woman's ear   90
Would murther as it fell.

              Enter *Banquo.*

            O Banquo, Banquo,
Our royal master's murther'd!

    Lady.   Woe, alas!
What, in our house?

Ban.   Too cruel anywhere.
Dear Duff, I prithee contradict thyself
And say it is not so.   95

Enter *Macbeth, Lennox,* and *Ross.*

Macb. Had I but died an hour before this chance,
I had liv'd a blessed time; for from this instant
There's nothing serious in mortality;
All is but toys; renown and grace is dead;
The wine of life is drawn, and the mere lees   100
Is left this vault to brag of.

Enter *Malcolm* and *Donalbain.*

Don. What is amiss?
Macb.   You are, and do not know't.
The spring, the head, the fountain of your blood
Is stopp'd, the very source of it is stopp'd.
Macd. Your royal father's murther'd.
Mal.   O, by whom?   105
Len. Those of his chamber, as it seem'd, had done't.
Their hands and faces were all badg'd with blood;
So were their daggers, which unwip'd we found
Upon their pillows.
They star'd and were distracted. No man's life   110
Was to be trusted with them.
Macb. O, yet I do repent me of my fury
That I did kill them.
Macd.   Wherefore did you so?
Macb. Who can be wise, amaz'd, temp'rate, and furious,
Loyal and neutral, in a moment? No man.   115
The expedition of my violent love
Outrun the pauser, reason. Here lay Duncan,

His silver skin lac'd with his golden blood,
And his gash'd stabs look'd like a breach in nature
For ruin's wasteful entrance; there, the murtherers,   120
Steep'd in the colours of their trade, their daggers
Unmannerly breech'd with gore. Who could refrain
That had a heart to love and in that heart
Courage to make 's love known?
    Lady.   Help me hence, ho!
    Macd. Look to the lady.
    Mal. [*aside to Donalbain*] Why do we hold our tongues,
That most may claim this argument for ours?   126
    Don. [*aside to Malcolm*] What should be spoken here,
    where our fate,
Hid in an auger hole, may rush and seize us?
Let's away.
Our tears are not yet brew'd.
    Mal.   [*aside to Donalbain*] Nor our strong sorrow   130
Upon the foot of motion.
    Ban.   Look to the lady.
                [*Lady Macbeth is carried out.*]
And when we have our naked frailties hid,
That suffer in exposure, let us meet
And question this most bloody piece of work,
To know it further. Fears and scruples shake us.   135
In the great hand of God I stand, and thence
Against the undivulg'd pretence I fight
Of treasonous malice.
    Macd.   And so do I.
    All.   So all.
    Macb. Let's briefly put on manly readiness
And meet i' th' hall together.
    All.   Well contented.   140
        Exeunt [*all but Malcolm and Donalbain*].

Mal. What will you do? Let's not consort with them.
To show an unfelt sorrow is an office
Which the false man does easy. I'll to England.
     Don. To Ireland I. Our separated fortune
Shall keep us both the safer. Where we are,   145
There's daggers in men's smiles; the near in blood,
The nearer bloody.
     Mal.   This murtherous shaft that's shot
Hath not yet lighted, and our safest way
Is to avoid the aim. Therefore to horse!
And let us not be dainty of leave-taking   150
But shift away. There's warrant in that theft
Which steals itself when there's no mercy left.   *Exeunt.*

Scene IV. [*Inverness. Without* Macbeth's *Castle.*]

Enter *Ross* with an *Old Man.*

Old Man. Threescore and ten I can remember well;
Within the volume of which time I have seen
Hours dreadful and things strange; but this sore night
Hath trifled former knowings.
     Ross.   Ah, good father,
Thou seest the heavens, as troubled with man's act,   5
Threaten his bloody stage. By th' clock 'tis day,
And yet dark night strangles the travelling lamp.
Is't night's predominance, or the day's shame,
That darkness does the face of earth entomb
When living light should kiss it?
     Old Man.   'Tis unnatural,   10
Even like the deed that's done. On Tuesday last

A falcon, tow'ring in her pride of place,
Was by a mousing owl hawk'd at and kill'd.

   Ross. And Duncan's horses (a thing most strange and cer-
    tain),
Beauteous and swift, the minions of their race,   15
Turn'd wild in nature, broke their stalls, flung out,
Contending 'gainst obedience, as they would make
War with mankind.

   Old Man.   'Tis said they eat each other.

   Ross. They did so, to th' amazement of mine eyes
That look'd upon't.

Enter Macduff.

              Here comes the good Macduff.   20
How goes the world, sir, now?

   Macd.   Why, see you not?

   Ross. Is't known who did this more than bloody deed?

   Macd. Those that Macbeth hath slain.

   Ross.   Alas, the day!
What good could they pretend?

   Macd.   They were suborn'd.
Malcolm and Donalbain, the King's two sons,   25
Are stol'n away and fled, which puts upon them
Suspicion of the deed.

   Ross.   'Gainst nature still!
Thriftless ambition, that wilt raven up
Thine own live's means! Then 'tis most like
The sovereignty will fall upon Macbeth.   30

   Macd. He is already nam'd, and gone to Scone
To be invested.

   Ross.   Where is Duncan's body?

   Macd. Carried to Colmekill,

The sacred storehouse of his predecessors
And guardian of their bones.

    Ross.   Will you to Scone?   35

    Macd. No, cousin, I'll to Fife.

    Ross.   Well, I will thither.

    Macd. Well, may you see things well done there. Adieu,
Lest our old robes sit easier than our new!

    Ross. Farewell, father.

    Old Man. God's benison go with you, and with those   40
That would make good of bad, and friends of foes!

                                      Exeunt omnes.

Enter Banquo.

Ban. Thou hast it now—King, Cawdor, Glamis, all,
As the Weird Women promis'd; and I fear
Thou play'dst most foully for't. Yet it was said
It should not stand in thy posterity,
But that myself should be the root and father   5
Of many kings. If there come truth from them
(As upon thee, Macbeth, their speeches shine),
Why, by the verities on thee made good,
May they not be my oracles as well
And set me up in hope? But, hush, no more!   10

Sennet sounded. Enter *Macbeth, as King; Lady* [*Macbeth,
as Queen*]; *Lennox, Ross, Lords,* and *Attendants.*

Macb. Here's our chief guest.
Lady.   If he had been forgotten,
It had been as a gap in our great feast,
And all-thing unbecoming.
Macb. To-night we hold a solemn supper, sir,
And I'll request your presence.
Ban.   Let your Highness   15
Command upon me, to the which my duties
Are with a most indissoluble tie
For ever knit.
Macb.   Ride you this afternoon?
Ban. Ay, my good lord.   20
Macb. We should have else desir'd your good advice
(Which still hath been both grave and prosperous)
In this day's council; but we'll take to-morrow.
Is't far you ride?

Ban. As far, my lord, as will fill up the time   25
'Twixt this and supper. Go not my horse the better,
I must become a borrower of the night
For a dark hour or twain.
    Macb.   Fail not our feast.
    Ban. My lord, I will not.
    Macb. We hear our bloody cousins are bestow'd   30
In England and in Ireland, not confessing
Their cruel parricide, filling their hearers
With strange invention. But of that to-morrow,
When therewithal we shall have cause of state
Craving us jointly. Hie you to horse. Adieu,   35
Till you return at night. Goes Fleance with you?
    Ban. Ay, my good lord. Our time does call upon's.
    Macb. I wish your horses swift and sure of foot,
And so I do commend you to their backs.
Farewell.   40
                              Exit Banquo.

Let every man be master of his time
Till seven at night. To make society
The sweeter welcome, we will keep ourself
Till supper time alone. While then, God be with you!
            Exeunt Lords [and others. Manent Macbeth and a
                                 Servant].
Sirrah, a word with you. Attend those men   45
Our pleasure?
    Serv. They are, my lord, without the palace gate.
    Macb. Bring them before us.   *Exit Servant.*
                    To be thus is nothing,
But to be safely thus. Our fears in Banquo
Stick deep; and in his royalty of nature   50
Reigns that which would be fear'd. 'Tis much he dares,
And to that dauntless temper of his mind

He hath a wisdom that doth guide his valour
To act in safety. There is none but he
Whose being I do fear; and under him   55
My Genius is rebuk'd, as it is said
Mark Antony's was by Cæsar. He chid the Sisters
When first they put the name of King upon me,
And bade them speak to him. Then, prophet-like,
They hail'd him father to a line of kings.   60
Upon my head they plac'd a fruitless crown
And put a barren sceptre in my gripe,
Thence to be wrench'd with an unlineal hand,
No son of mine succeeding. If't be so,
For Banquo's issue have I fil'd my mind;   65
For them the gracious Duncan have I murther'd;
Put rancours in the vessel of my peace
Only for them, and mine eternal jewel
Given to the common enemy of man
To make them kings, the seed of Banquo kings!   70
Rather than so, come, Fate, into the list,
And champion me to th' utterance! Who's there?

Enter *Servant* and two *Murtherers*.

Now go to the door and stay there till we call.

Exit Servant.

Was it not yesterday we spoke together?
  Murtherers. It was, so please your Highness.
  Macb.   Well then, now 75
Have you consider'd of my speeches? Know
That it was he, in the times past, which held you
So under fortune, which you thought had been
Our innocent self. This I made good to you
In our last conference, pass'd in probation with you   80
How you were borne in hand, how cross'd; the instruments;

Who wrought with them; and all things else that might
To half a soul and to a notion craz'd
Say 'Thus did Banquo.'
   1. Mur.   You made it known to us.
   Macb. I did so; and went further, which is now   85
Our point of second meeting. Do you find
Your patience so predominant in your nature
That you can let this go? Are you so gospell'd
To pray for this good man and for his issue,
Whose heavy hand hath bow'd you to the grave   90
And beggar'd yours for ever?
   1. Mur.   We are men, my liege.
   Macb. Ay, in the catalogue ye go for men,
As hounds and greyhounds, mongrels, spaniels, curs,
Shoughs, water-rugs, and demi-wolves are clipt
All by the name of dogs. The valued file   95
Distinguishes the swift, the slow, the subtle,
The housekeeper, the hunter, every one
According to the gift which bounteous nature
Hath in him clos'd; whereby he does receive
Particular addition, from the bill   100
That writes them all alike; and so of men.
Now, if you have a station in the file,
Not i' th' worst rank of manhood, say't;
And I will put that business in your bosoms
Whose execution takes your enemy off,   105
Grapples you to the heart and love of us,
Who wear our health but sickly in his life,
Which in his death were perfect.
   2. Mur.   I am one, my liege,
Whom the vile blows and buffets of the world
Have so incens'd that I am reckless what   110
I do to spite the world.

   1. Mur.   And I another,
So weary with disasters, tugg'd with fortune,
That I would set my life on any chance,
To mend it or be rid on't.
   Macb.   Both of you
Know Banquo was your enemy.
   Murtherers.   True, my lord.   115
   Macb. So is he mine; and in such bloody distance
That every minute of his being thrusts
Against my near'st of life; and though I could
With barefac'd power sweep him from my sight
And bid my will avouch it, yet I must not,   120
For certain friends that are both his and mine,
Whose loves I may not drop, but wail his fall
Who I myself struck down. And thence it is
That I to your assistance do make love,
Masking the business from the common eye   125
For sundry weighty reasons.
   2. Mur.   We shall, my lord,
Perform what you command us.
   1. Mur.   Though our lives—
   Macb. Your spirits shine through you. Within this hour at
    most
I will advise you where to plant yourselves,
Acquaint you with the perfect spy o' th' time,   130
The moment on't; for't must be done to-night,
And something from the palace; always thought
That I require a clearness; and with him,
To leave no rubs nor botches in the work,
Fleance his son, that keeps him company,   135
Whose absence is no less material to me
Than is his father's, must embrace the fate
Of that dark hour. Resolve yourselves apart;

I'll come to you anon.

 Murtherers.   We are resolv'd, my lord.

 Macb. I'll call upon you straight. Abide within. 140

       [*Exeunt Murtherers.*]

It is concluded. Banquo, thy soul's flight,

If it find heaven, must find it out to-night.   *Exit.*

Scene II. [*Forres. The Palace.*]

Enter *Macbeth's Lady* and a *Servant.*

 Lady. Is Banquo gone from court?

 Serv. Ay, madam, but returns again to-night.

 Lady. Say to the King I would attend his leisure

For a few words.

 Serv.   Madam, I will.   *Exit.*

 Lady.   Naught's had, all's spent,

Where our desire is got without content.

'Tis safer to be that which we destroy

Than by destruction dwell in doubtful joy.

Enter *Macbeth.*

How now, my lord? Why do you keep alone,

Of sorriest fancies your companions making,

Using those thoughts which should indeed have died 10

With them they think on? Things without all remedy

Should be without regard. What's done is done.

 Macb. We have scotch'd the snake, not kill'd it.

She'll close, and be herself, whilst our poor malice

Remains in danger of her former tooth.   15

But let the frame of things disjoint, both the worlds suffer,

Ere we will eat our meal in fear and sleep

In the affliction of these terrible dreams

That shake us nightly. Better be with the dead,
Whom we, to gain our peace, have sent to peace,   20
Than on the torture of the mind to lie
In restless ecstasy. Duncan is in his grave;
After life's fitful fever he sleeps well.
Treason has done his worst. Nor steel nor poison,
Malice domestic, foreign levy, nothing,   25
Can touch him further.
    Lady.   Come on.
Gentle my lord, sleek o'er your rugged looks;
Be bright and jovial among your guests to-night.
    Macb. So shall I, love; and so, I pray, be you.
Let your remembrance apply to Banquo;   30
Present him eminence both with eye and tongue—
Unsafe the while, that we
Must lave our honours in these flattering streams
And make our faces vizards to our hearts,
Disguising what they are.
    Lady.   You must leave this.   35
    Macb. O, full of scorpions is my mind, dear wife!
Thou know'st that Banquo, and his Fleance, lives.
    Lady. But in them Nature's copy's not eterne.
    Macb. There's comfort yet! They are assailable.
Then be thou jocund. Ere the bat hath flown   40
His cloister'd flight, ere to black Hecate's summons
The shard-borne beetle with his drowsy hums
Hath rung night's yawning peal, there shall be done
A deed of dreadful note.
    Lady.   What's to be done?
    Macb. Be innocent of the knowledge, dearest chuck,   45
Till thou applaud the deed. Come, seeling night,
Scarf up the tender eye of pitiful day,
And with thy bloody and invisible hand

Cancel and tear to pieces that great bond
Which keeps me pale! Light thickens, and the crow   50
Makes wing to th' rooky wood.
Good things of day begin to droop and drowse,
Whiles night's black agents to their preys do rouse.
Thou marvell'st at my words; but hold thee still:
Things bad begun make strong themselves by ill.   55
So prithee go with me.   *Exeunt.*

Scene III. [*Forres. A park near the Palace.*]

Enter three *Murtherers.*

1. Mur. But who did bid thee join with us?
3. Mur.   Macbeth.
2. Mur. He needs not our mistrust, since he delivers
Our offices, and what we have to do,
To the direction just.
1. Mur.   Then stand with us.
The west yet glimmers with some streaks of day.   5
Now spurs the lated traveller apace
To gain the timely inn, and near approaches
The subject of our watch.
3. Mur.   Hark! I hear horses.
Ban. (*within*) Give us a light there, ho!
2. Mur.   Then 'tis he! The rest
That are within the note of expectation   10
Already are i' th' court.
1. Mur.   His horses go about.
3. Mur. Almost a mile; but he does usually,
So all men do, from hence to th' palace gate
Make it their walk.

Enter *Banquo*, and *Fleance* with a torch.

2. Mur.　　　　　A light, a light!

3. Mur.　　　　　　　　'Tis he.

1. Mur. Stand to't.　　　　　　　　　　　　15

Ban. It will be rain to-night.

1. Mur.　　　　　Let it come down!

　　　　　　　　[They fall upon Banquo.]

Ban. O, treachery! Fly, good Fleance, fly, fly, fly!
Thou mayst revenge. O slave!

　　　　　　　　[Dies. Fleance escapes.]

3. Mur. Who did strike out the light?

1. Mur.　　　　　　　　Was't not the way?

3. Mur. There's but one down; the son is fled.

2. Mur.　　　　　　　　We have lost　20
Best half of our affair.

1. Mur. Well, let's away, and say how much is done.

　　　　　　　　　　　　　　Exeunt.

Scene IV. *[Forres. Hall in the Palace.]*

Banquet prepar'd. Enter *Macbeth*, *Lady* [*Macbeth*], *Ross*,
Lennox, *Lords*, and *Attendants*.

Macb. You know your own degrees, sit down. At first
And last the hearty welcome.

Lords.　　　　　　Thanks to your Majesty.

Macb. Ourself will mingle with society
And play the humble host.
Our hostess keeps her state, but in best time　　5
We will require her welcome.

Lady. Pronounce it for me, sir, to all our friends,
For my heart speaks they are welcome.

Enter *First Murtherer* [to the door].

Macb. See, they encounter thee with their hearts' thanks.
Both sides are even. Here I'll sit i' th' midst.   10
Be large in mirth; anon we'll drink a measure
The table round. [*Goes to the door.*] There's blood upon thy
   face.

Mur. 'Tis Banquo's then.

Macb. 'Tis better thee without than he within.
Is he dispatch'd?   15

Mur. My lord, his throat is cut. That I did for him.

Macb. Thou art the best o' th' cutthroats! Yet he's good
That did the like for Fleance. If thou didst it,
Thou art the nonpareil.

Mur.   Most royal sir,
Fleance is scap'd.   20

Macb. [*aside*] Then comes my fit again. I had else been
   perfect;
Whole as the marble, founded as the rock,
As broad and general as the casing air.
But now I am cabin'd, cribb'd, confin'd, bound in
To saucy doubts and fears.—But Banquo's safe?   25

Mur. Ay, my good lord. Safe in a ditch he bides,
With twenty trenched gashes on his head,
The least a death to nature.

Macb.   Thanks for that!
There the grown serpent lies; the worm that's fled
Hath nature that in time will venom breed,   30
No teeth for th' present. Get thee gone. To-morrow
We'll hear ourselves again.

                                              Exit Murderer.

Lady.   My royal lord,
You do not give the cheer. The feast is sold
That is not often vouch'd, while 'tis a-making,

'Tis given with welcome. To feed were best at home. 35
From thence, the sauce to meat is ceremony;
Meeting were bare without it.

Enter the *Ghost of Banquo*, and sits in *Macbeth's* place.

Macb.   Sweet remembrancer!
Now good digestion wait on appetite,
And health on both!
    Len.   May't please your Highness sit.
    Macb. Here had we now our country's honour, roof'd, 40
Were the grac'd person of our Banquo present;
Who may I rather challenge for unkindness
Than pity for mischance!
    Ross.   His absence, sir,
Lays blame upon his promise. Please't your Highness
To grace us with your royal company?   45
    Macb. The table's full.
    Len.   Here is a place reserv'd, sir.
    Macb. Where?
    Len. Here, my good lord. What is't that moves your High-
        ness?
    Macb. Which of you have done this?
    Lords.   What, my good lord?
    Macb. Thou canst not say I did it. Never shake 50
Thy gory locks at me.
    Ross. Gentlemen, rise. His Highness is not well.
    Lady. Sit, worthy friends. My lord is often thus,
And hath been from his youth. Pray you keep seat.
The fit is momentary; upon a thought   55
He will again be well. If much you note him,
You shall offend him and extend his passion.
Feed, and regard him not.—Are you a man?

Macb. Ay, and a bold one, that dare look on that
Which might appal the devil.

Lady.   O proper stuff!   60
This is the very painting of your fear.
This is the air-drawn dagger which you said
Led you to Duncan. O, these flaws and starts
(Impostors to true fear) would well become
A woman's story at a winter's fire,   65
Authoriz'd by her grandam. Shame itself!
Why do you make such faces? When all's done,
You look but on a stool.

Macb. Prithee see there! behold! look! lo! How say you?
Why, what care I? If thou canst nod, speak too.   70
If charnel houses and our graves must send
Those that we bury back, our monuments
Shall be the maws of kites.

                                          [*Exit Ghost.*]
Lady.   What, quite unmann'd in folly?
Macb. If I stand here, I saw him.
Lady.   Fie, for shame!
Macb. Blood hath been shed ere now, i' th' olden time,   75
Ere humane statute purg'd the gentle weal;
Ay, and since too, murthers have been perform'd
Too terrible for the ear. The time has been
That, when the brains were out, the man would die,
And there an end! But now they rise again,   80
With twenty mortal murthers on their crowns,
And push us from our stools. This is more strange
Than such a murther is.
Lady.   My worthy lord,
Your noble friends do lack you.
Macb.   I do forget.
Do not muse at me, my most worthy friends.   85

I have a strange infirmity, which is nothing
To those that know me. Come, love and health to all!
Then I'll sit down. Give me some wine, fill full.

Enter *Ghost*.

I drink to th' general joy o' th' whole table,
And to our dear friend Banquo, whom we miss.   90
Would he were here! To all, and him, we thirst,
And all to all.
    Lords.   Our duties, and the pledge.
    Macb. Avaunt, and quit my sight! Let the earth hide thee!
Thy bones are marrowless, thy blood is cold;
Thou hast no speculation in those eyes   95
Which thou dost glare with!
    Lady.   Think of this, good peers,
But as a thing of custom. 'Tis no other.
Only it spoils the pleasure of the time.
    Macb. What man dare, I dare.
Approach thou like the rugged Russian bear,   100
The arm'd rhinoceros, or th' Hyrcan tiger;
Take any shape but that, and my firm nerves
Shall never tremble. Or be alive again
And dare me to the desert with thy sword.
If trembling I inhabit then, protest me   105
The baby of a girl. Hence, horrible shadow!
Unreal mock'ry, hence!
                                 [Exit Ghost.]
             Why, so! Being gone,
I am a man again. Pray you sit still.
    Lady. You have displac'd the mirth, broke the good meeting
With most admir'd disorder.
    Macb.   Can such things be,   110

And overcome us like a summer's cloud
Without our special wonder? You make me strange
Even to the disposition that I owe,
When now I think you can behold such sights
And keep the natural ruby of your cheeks   115
When mine is blanch'd with fear.
   Ross.   What sights, my lord?
   Lady. I pray you speak not. He grows worse and worse;
Question enrages him. At once, good night.
Stand not upon the order of your going,
But go at once.
   Len.   Good night, and better health   120
Attend his Majesty!
   Lady.   A kind good night to all!
               Exeunt Lords [and Attendants].
   Macb. It will have blood, they say; blood will have blood.
Stones have been known to move and trees to speak;
Augures and understood relations have
By maggot-pies and choughs and rooks brought forth   125
The secret'st man of blood. What is the night?
   Lady. Almost at odds with morning, which is which.
   Macb. How say'st thou that Macduff denies his person
At our great bidding?
   Lady.   Did you send to him, sir?
   Macb. I hear it by the way; but I will send.   130
There's not a one of them but in his house
I keep a servant fee'd. I will to-morrow
(And betimes I will) unto the Weird Sisters.
More shall they speak; for now I am bent to know
By the worst means the worst. For mine own good   135
All causes shall give way. I am in blood
Stepp'd in so far that, should I wade no more,
Returning were as tedious as go o'er.

Strange things I have in head, that will to hand,
Which must be acted ere they may be scann'd.　　　　140
　　Lady. You lack the season of all natures, sleep.
　　Macb. Come, we'll to sleep. My strange and self-abuse
Is the initiate fear that wants hard use.
We are yet but young in deed.　　　　　　　　*Exeunt.*

Scene V. [*A heath.*]

　　Thunder. Enter the three *Witches*, meeting *Hecate*.

　　1. Witch. Why, how now, Hecate? You look angerly.
　　Hec. Have I not reason, beldams as you are,
Saucy and overbold? How did you dare
To trade and traffic with Macbeth
In riddles and affairs of death;　　　　　　　5
And I, the mistress of your charms,
The close contriver of all harms,
Was never call'd to bear my part
Or show the glory of our art?
And, which is worse, all you have done　　　　10
Hath been but for a wayward son,
Spiteful and wrathful, who, as others do,
Loves for his own ends, not for you.
But make amends now. Get you gone
And at the pit of Acheron　　　　　　　15
Meet me i' th' morning. Thither he
Will come to know his destiny.
Your vessels and your spells provide,
Your charms and everything beside.
I am for th' air. This night I'll spend　　　　20
Unto a dismal and a fatal end.
Great business must be wrought ere noon.

Upon the corner of the moon
There hangs a vap'rous drop profound.
I'll catch it ere it come to ground; 25
And that, distill'd by magic sleights,
Shall raise such artificial sprites
As by the strength of their illusion
Shall draw him on to his confusion.
He shall spurn fate, scorn death, and bear 30
His hopes 'bove wisdom, grace, and fear;
And you all know security
Is mortals' chiefest enemy.
    Music and a song within. 'Come away, come away,' &c.
Hark! I am call'd. My little spirit, see,
Sits in a foggy cloud and stays for me.   [*Exit.*] 35
   1. Witch. Come, let's make haste. She'll soon be back again.
                         Exeunt.

Scene VI. [*Forres. The Palace.*]

Enter *Lennox* and another *Lord.*

   Len. My former speeches have but hit your thoughts,
Which can interpret farther. Only I say
Things have been strangely borne. The gracious Duncan
Was pitied of Macbeth. Marry, he was dead!
And the right valiant Banquo walk'd too late; 5
Whom, you may say (if't please you) Fleance kill'd,
For Fleance fled. Men must not walk too late.
Who cannot want the thought how monstrous
It was for Malcolm and for Donalbain
To kill their gracious father? Damned fact! 10
How it did grieve Macbeth! Did he not straight,
In pious rage, the two delinquents tear,

That were the slaves of drink and thralls of sleep?
Was not that nobly done? Ay, and wisely too!
For 'twould have anger'd any heart alive   15
To hear the men deny't. So that I say
He has borne all things well; and I do think
That, had he Duncan's sons under his key
(As, an't please heaven, he shall not), they should find
What 'twere to kill a father. So should Fleance.   20
But peace! for from broad words, and 'cause he fail'd
His presence at the tyrant's feast, I hear
Macduff lives in disgrace. Sir, can you tell
Where he bestows himself?

Lord.   The son of Duncan,
From whom this tyrant holds the due of birth,   25
Lives in the English court, and is receiv'd
Of the most pious Edward with such grace
That the malevolence of fortune nothing
Takes from his high respect. Thither Macduff
Is gone to pray the holy King upon his aid   30
To wake Northumberland and warlike Siward;
That by the help of these (with Him above
To ratify the work) we may again
Give to our tables meat, sleep to our nights,
Free from our feasts and banquets bloody knives,   35
Do faithful homage and receive free honours—
All which we pine for now. And this report
Hath so exasperate the King that he
Prepares for some attempt of war.

Len.   Sent he to Macduff?

Lord. He did; and with an absolute 'Sir, not I!'   40
The cloudy messenger turns me his back
And hums, as who should say, 'You'll rue the time
That clogs me with this answer.'

Len.   And that well might
Advise him to a caution t' hold what distance
His wisdom can provide. Some holy angel   45
Fly to the court of England and unfold
His message ere he come, that a swift blessing
May soon return to this our suffering country
Under a hand accurs'd!
Lord.   I'll send my prayers with him.
                                        Exeunt.

ACT IV. Scene I. [*A cavern. In the middle, a cauldron boiling.*]

Thunder. Enter the three *Witches*.

1. Witch. Thrice the brinded cat hath mew'd.
2. Witch. Thrice and once the hedge-pig whin'd.
3. Witch. Harpier cries; 'tis time, 'tis time.
1. Witch. Round about the cauldron go;
In the poison'd entrails throw. 5
Toad, that under cold stone
Days and nights has thirty-one
Swelt'red venom sleeping got,
Boil thou first i' th' charmed pot.
All. Double, double, toil and trouble; 10
Fire burn, and cauldron bubble.
2. Witch. Fillet of a fenny snake,
In the cauldron boil and bake;
Eye of newt, and toe of frog,
Wool of bat, and tongue of dog, 15
Adder's fork, and blindworm's sting,
Lizard's leg, and howlet's wing;
For a charm of pow'rful trouble
Like a hell-broth boil and bubble.
All. Double, double, toil and trouble; 20
Fire burn, and cauldron bubble.
3. Witch. Scale of dragon, tooth of wolf,
Witch's mummy, maw and gulf
Of the ravin'd salt-sea shark,
Root of hemlock, digg'd i' th' dark; 25
Liver of blaspheming Jew,
Gall of goat, and slips of yew
Sliver'd in the moon's eclipse;

54

Nose of Turk and Tartar's lips;
Finger of birth-strangled babe   30
Ditch-deliver'd by a drab:
Make the gruel thick and slab.
Add thereto a tiger's chaudron
For th' ingredience of our cauldron.
   All. Double, double, toil and trouble;   35
Fire burn, and cauldron bubble.
   2. Witch. Cool it with a baboon's blood,
Then the charm is firm and good.

      Enter *Hecate* to the other three *Witches.*

   Hec. O, well done! I commend your pains,
And every one shall share i' th' gains.   40
And now about the cauldron sing
Like elves and fairies in a ring,
Enchanting all that you put in.
        Music and a song, 'Black spirits,' &c.
            [*Exit Hecate.*]
   2. Witch. By the pricking of my thumbs,
Something wicked this way comes.   45
         Open locks,
         Whoever knocks!

         Enter *Macbeth.*

   Macb. How now, you secret, black, and midnight hags?
What is't you do?
   All.   A deed without a name.
   Macb. I conjure you by that which you profess   50
(Howe'er you come to know it), answer me.
Though you untie the winds and let them fight
Against the churches; though the yesty waves
Confound and swallow navigation up;

Though bladed corn be lodg'd and trees blown down;　　55
Though castles topple on their warders' heads;
Though palaces and pyramids do slope
Their heads to their foundations; though the treasure
Of nature's germens tumble all together,
Even till destruction sicken—answer me　　　　　　60
To what I ask you.
　　1. Witch.　　　　Speak.
　　2. Witch.　　　　　　Demand.
　　3. Witch.　　　　　　　　We'll answer.
　　1. Witch. Say, if th' hadst rather hear it from our mouths
Or from our masters.
　　Macb.　　　　Call 'em! Let me see 'em.
　　1. Witch. Pour in sow's blood, that hath eaten
Her nine farrow; grease that's sweaten　　　　　65
From the murderer's gibbet throw
Into the flame.
　　All.　　　Come, high or low;
Thyself and office deftly show!

Thunder. First Apparition, an Armed Head.

　　Macb. Tell me, thou unknown power—
　　1. Witch.　　　　　　　　He knows thy
　　thought.
Hear his speech, but say thou naught.　　　　　70
　　1. Appar. Macbeth! Macbeth! Macbeth! Beware Macduff;
Beware the Thane of Fife. Dismiss me. Enough.
　　　　　　　　　　　　　　He descends.
　　Macb. Whate'er thou art, for thy good caution thanks!
Thou hast harp'd my fear aright. But one word more—
　　1. Witch. He will not be commanded. Here's another, 75
More potent than the first.

Thunder. Second Apparition, a Bloody Child.

2. Appar. Macbeth! Macbeth! Macbeth!
Macb. Had I three ears, I'ld hear thee.
2. Appar. Be bloody, bold, and resolute; laugh to scorn
The pow'r of man, for none of woman born   80
Shall harm Macbeth.   *Descends.*
    Macb. Then live, Macduff. What need I fear of thee?
But yet I'll make assurance double sure
And take a bond of fate. Thou shalt not live!
That I may tell pale-hearted fear it lies   85
And sleep in spite of thunder.

Thunder. Third Apparition, a Child Crowned, with a tree in his hand.

                              What is this
That rises like the issue of a king
And wears upon his baby-brow the round
And top of sovereignty?
    All.   Listen, but speak not to't.
    3. Appar. Be lion-mettled, proud, and take no care   90
Who chafes, who frets, or where conspirers are.
Macbeth shall never vanquish'd be until
Great Birnam Wood to high Dunsinane Hill
Shall come against him.   *Descends.*
    Macb.   That will never be.
Who can impress the forest, bid the tree   95
Unfix his earth-bound root? Sweet bodements, good!
Rebellion's head rise never till the Wood
Of Birnam rise, and our high-plac'd Macbeth
Shall live the lease of nature, pay his breath
To time and mortal custom. Yet my heart   100

Throbs to know one thing. Tell me, if your art
Can tell so much—shall Banquo's issue ever
Reign in this kingdom?
    All.   Seek to know no more.
    Macb. I will be satisfied. Deny me this,
And an eternal curse fall on you! Let me know.   105
Why sinks that cauldron? and what noise is this?
                                   Hautboys.

    1. Witch. Show!
    2. Witch. Show!
    3. Witch. Show!
    All. Show his eyes, and grieve his heart!   110
Come like shadows, so depart!
        *A show of eight Kings, [the eighth] with a glass in
                      his hand, and Banquo last.*
    Macb. Thou art too like the spirit of Banquo. Down!
Thy crown does sear mine eyeballs. And thy hair,
Thou other gold-bound brow, is like the first.
A third is like the former. Filthy hags!   115
Why do you show me this? A fourth? Start, eyes!
What, will the line stretch out to th' crack of doom?
Another yet? A seventh? I'll see no more.
And yet the eighth appears, who bears a glass
Which shows me many more; and some I see   120
That twofold balls and treble sceptres carry.
Horrible sight! Now I see 'tis true;
For the blood-bolter'd Banquo smiles upon me
And points at them for his. [*Apparitions vanish.*] What? Is
    this so?
    1. Witch. Ay, sir, all this is so. But why   125
Stands Macbeth thus amazedly?
Come, sisters, cheer we up his sprites
And show the best of our delights.

I'll charm the air to give a sound
While you perform your antic round,   130
That this great king may kindly say
Our duties did his welcome pay.

                  Music. The Witches dance, and vanish.

   Macb. Where are they? Gone? Let this pernicious hour
Stand aye accursed in the calendar!
Come in, without there!

                  Enter Lennox.

   Len.   What's your Grace's will?   135
   Macb. Saw you the Weird Sisters?
   Len.   No, my lord.
   Macb. Came they not by you?
   Len.   No indeed, my lord.
   Macb. Infected be the air whereon they ride,
And damn'd all those that trust them! I did hear
The galloping of horse. Who was't came by?   140
   Len. 'Tis two or three, my lord, that bring you word
Macduff is fled to England.
   Macb.   Fled to England?
   Len. Ay, my good lord.
   Macb. [*aside*] Time, thou anticipat'st my dread exploits.
The flighty purpose never is o'ertook   145
Unless the deed go with it. From this moment
The very firstlings of my heart shall be
The firstlings of my hand. And even now,
To crown my thoughts with acts, be it thought and done!
The castle of Macduff I will surprise,   150
Seize upon Fife, give to the edge o' th' sword
His wife, his babes, and all unfortunate souls
That trace him in his line. No boasting like a fool!

This deed I'll do before this purpose cool.
But no more sights!—Where are these gentlemen?   155
Come, bring me where they are.   *Exeunt.*

Scene II. [*Fife.* Macduff's *Castle.*]

Enter *Macduff's Wife,* her *Son,* and *Ross.*

Wife. What had he done to make him fly the land?
Ross. You must have patience, madam.
Wife.   He had none.
His flight was madness. When our actions do not,
Our fears do make us traitors.
Ross.   You know not
Whether it was his wisdom or his fear.   5
Wife. Wisdom? To leave his wife, to leave his babes,
His mansion, and his titles, in a place
From whence himself does fly? He loves us not,
He wants the natural touch. For the poor wren,
(The most diminitive of birds) will fight,   10
Her young ones in her nest, against the owl.
All is the fear, and nothing is the love,
As little is the wisdom, where the flight
So runs against all reason.
Ross.   My dearest coz,
I pray you school yourself. But for your husband,   15
He is noble, wise, judicious, and best knows
The fits o' th' season. I dare not speak much further;
But cruel are the times, when we are traitors
And do not know ourselves; when we hold rumour
From what we fear, yet know not what we fear,   20
But float upon a wild and violent sea
Each way and none. I take my leave of you.

Shall not be long but I'll be here again.
Things at the worst will cease, or else climb upward
To what they were before.—My pretty cousin,   25
Blessing upon you!

   Wife. Father'd he is, and yet he's fatherless.

   Ross. I am so much a fool, should I stay longer,
It would be my disgrace and your discomfort.
I take my leave at once.   *Exit.*

   Wife.   Sirrah, your father's dead;   30
And what will you do now? How will you live?

   Son. As birds do, mother.

   Wife.   What, with worms and flies?

   Son. With what I get, I mean; and so do they.

   Wife. Poor bird! thou'dst never fear the net nor lime,
The pitfall nor the gin.   35

   Son. Why should I, mother? Poor birds they are not set for.
My father is not dead, for all your saying.

   Wife. Yes, he is dead. How wilt thou do for a father?

   Son. Nay, how will you do for a husband?

   Wife. Why, I can buy me twenty at any market.   40

   Son. Then you'll buy 'em to sell again.

   Wife. Thou speak'st with all thy wit; and yet, i' faith,
With wit enough for thee.

   Son. Was my father a traitor, mother?

   Wife. Ay, that he was!   45

   Son. What is a traitor?

   Wife. Why, one that swears, and lies.

   Son. And be all traitors that do so?

   Wife. Every one that does so is a traitor and must be
hang'd.   50

   Son. And must they all be hang'd that swear and lie?

   Wife. Every one.

   Son. Who must hang them?

Wife. Why, the honest men.   55

Son. Then the liars and swearers are fools; for there are
liars and swearers enow to beat the honest men and hang up
them.

Wife. Now God help thee, poor monkey!
But how wilt thou do for a father?   60

Son. If he were dead, you'ld weep for him. If you would
not, it were a good sign that I should quickly have a new
father.

Wife. Poor prattler, how thou talk'st!

Enter a *Messenger.*

Mess. Bless you, fair dame! I am not to you known,   65
Though in your state of honour I am perfect.
I doubt some danger does approach you nearly.
If you will take a homely man's advice,
Be not found here. Hence with your little ones!
To fright you thus methinks I am too savage;   70
To do worse to you were fell cruelty,
Which is too nigh your person. Heaven preserve you!
I dare abide no longer.   *Exit.*
Wife.   Whither should I fly?
I have done no harm. But I remember now
I am in this earthly world, where to do harm   75
Is often laudable, to do good sometime
Accounted dangerous folly. Why then, alas,
Do I put up that womanly defence
To say I have done no harm?—What are these faces?

Enter *Murtherers.*

Mur. Where is your husband?   80
Wife. I hope, in no place so unsanctified
Where such as thou mayst find him.

Mur.   He's a traitor.
Son. Thou liest, thou shag-ear'd villain!
Mur.   What, you egg!
                                            [*Stabs him.*]
Young fry of treachery!
Son.   He has kill'd me, mother.
Run away, I pray you!   [*Dies.*] 85
        Exit [*Wife*], *crying* 'Murther!' [*and pursued by the
                                            Murtherers*].

Scene III. [*England. Before* King Edward's *Palace.*]

Enter *Malcolm and Macduff.*

Mal. Let us seek out some desolate shade, and there
Weep our sad bosoms empty.
Macd.   Let us rather
Hold fast the mortal sword and, like good men,
Bestride our downfall'n birthdom. Each new morn
New widows howl, new orphans cry, new sorrows   5
Strike heaven on the face, that it resounds
As if it felt with Scotland and yell'd out
Like syllable of dolour.
Mal.   What I believe, I'll wail;
What know, believe; and what I can redress,
As I shall find the time to friend, I will.   10
What you have spoke, it may be so perchance.
This tyrant, whose sole name blisters our tongues,
Was once thought honest; you have lov'd him well;
He hath not touch'd you yet. I am young; but something
You may deserve of him through me, and wisdom   15
To offer up a weak, poor, innocent lamb
T' appease an angry god.
Macd. I am not treacherous.

Mal.   But Macbeth is.
A good and virtuous nature may recoil
In an imperial charge. But I shall crave your pardon.   20
That which you are, my thoughts cannot transpose.
Angels are bright still, though the brightest fell.
Though all things foul would wear the brows of grace,
Yet grace must still look so.

    Macd.   I have lost my hopes.

    Mal. Perchance even there where I did find my doubts. 25
Why in that rawness left you wife and child,
Those precious motives, those strong knots of love,
Without leave-taking? I pray you,
Let not my jealousies be your dishonours,
But mine own safeties. You may be rightly just,   30
Whatever I shall think.

    Macd.   Bleed, bleed, poor country!
Great tyranny, lay thou thy basis sure,
For goodness dare not check thee! Wear thou thy wrongs;
The title is affeer'd! Fare thee well, lord.
I would not be the villain that thou think'st   35
For the whole space that's in the tyrant's grasp
And the rich East to boot.

    Mal.   Be not offended.
I speak not as in absolute fear of you.
I think our country sinks beneath the yoke,
It weeps, it bleeds, and each new day a gash   40
Is added to her wounds. I think withal
There would be hands uplifted in my right;
And here from gracious England have I offer
Of goodly thousands. But, for all this,
When I shall tread upon the tyrant's head   45
Or wear it on my sword, yet my poor country
Shall have more vices than it had before,

More suffer and more sundry ways than ever,
By him that shall succeed.

 Macd.   What should he be?

 Mal. It is myself I mean; in whom I know   50
All the particulars of vice so grafted
That, when they shall be open'd, black Macbeth
Will seem as pure as snow, and the poor state
Esteem him as a lamb, being compar'd
With my confineless harms.

 Macd.   Not in the legions   55
Of horrid hell can come a devil more damn'd
In evils to top Macbeth.

 Mal.   I grant him bloody,
Luxurious, avaricious, false, deceitful,
Sudden, malicious, smacking of every sin
That has a name. But there's no bottom, none,   60
In my voluptuousness. Your wives, your daughters,
Your matrons, and your maids could not fill up
The cistern of my lust; and my desire
All continent impediments would o'erbear
That did oppose my will. Better Macbeth   65
Than such an one to reign.

 Macd.   Boundless intemperance
In nature is a tyranny. It hath been
Th' untimely emptying of the happy throne
And fall of many kings. But fear not yet
To take upon you what is yours. You may   70
Convey your pleasures in a spacious plenty,
And yet seem cold—the time you may so hoodwink.
We have willing dames enough. There cannot be
That vulture in you to devour so many
As will to greatness dedicate themselves,   75
Finding it so inclin'd.

Mal.   With this there grows
In my most ill-composed affection such
A stanchless avarice that, were I King,
I should cut off the nobles for their lands,
Desire his jewels, and this other's house,   80
And my more-having would be as a sauce
To make me hunger more, that I should forge
Quarrels unjust against the good and loyal,
Destroying them for wealth.
    Macd.   This avarice
Sticks deeper, grows with more pernicious root   85
Than summer-seeming lust; and it hath been
The sword of our slain kings. Yet do not fear.
Scotland hath foisons to fill up your will
Of your mere own. All these are portable,
With other graces weigh'd.   90
    Mal. But I have none. The king-becoming graces,
As justice, verity, temp'rance, stableness,
Bounty, perseverance, mercy, lowliness,
Devotion, patience, courage, fortitude,
I have no relish of them, but abound   95
In the division of each several crime,
Acting it many ways. Nay, had I pow'r, I should
Pour the sweet milk of concord into hell,
Uproar the universal peace, confound
All unity on earth.
    Macd.   O Scotland, Scotland!   100
    Mal. If such a one be fit to govern, speak.
I am as I have spoken.
    Macd.   Fit to govern?
No, not to live. O nation miserable,
With an untitled tyrant bloody-scept'red,
When shalt thou see thy wholesome days again,   105

Since that the truest issue of thy throne
By his own interdiction stands accurs'd
And does blaspheme his breed? Thy royal father
Was a most sainted king; the queen that bore thee,
Oft'ner upon her knees than on her feet,   110
Died every day she liv'd. Fare thee well!
These evils thou repeat'st upon thyself
Have banish'd me from Scotland. O my breast,
Thy hope ends here!
   Mal.   Macduff, this noble passion,
Child of integrity, hath from my soul   115
Wip'd the black scruples, reconcil'd my thoughts
To thy good truth and honour. Devilish Macbeth
By many of these trains hath sought to win me
Into his power; and modest wisdom plucks me
From over-credulous haste; but God above   120
Deal between thee and me! for even now
I put myself to thy direction and
Unspeak mine own detraction, here abjure
The taints and blames I laid upon myself
For strangers to my nature. I am yet   125
Unknown to woman, never was forsworn,
Scarcely have coveted what was mine own,
At no time broke my faith, would not betray
The devil to his fellow, and delight
No less in truth than life. My first false speaking   130
Was this upon myself. What I am truly,
Is thine and my poor country's to command;
Whither indeed, before thy here-approach,
Old Siward with ten thousand warlike men
Already at a point was setting forth.   135
Now we'll together; and the chance of goodness
Be like our warranted quarrel! Why are you silent?

Macd. Such welcome and unwelcome things at once
'Tis hard to reconcile.

Enter a *Doctor.*

Mal. Well, more anon. Comes the King forth, I pray you?
Doct. Ay, sir. There are a crew of wretched souls   141
That stay his cure. Their malady convinces
The great assay of art; but at his touch,
Such sanctity hath heaven given his hand,
They presently amend.
Mal.   I thank you, doctor.   145

Exit [*Doctor*]

Macd. What's the disease he means?
Mal.   'Tis call'd the evil:
A most miraculous work in this good king,
Which often since my here-remain in England
I have seen him do. How he solicits heaven
Himself best knows; but strangely-visited people,   150
All swol'n and ulcerous, pitiful to the eye,
The mere despair of surgery, he cures,
Hanging a golden stamp about their necks,
Put on with holy prayers; and 'tis spoken,
To the succeeding royalty he leaves   155
The healing benediction. With this strange virtue,
He hath a heavenly gift of prophecy,
And sundry blessings hang about his throne
That speak him full of grace.

Enter *Ross.*

Macd.   See who comes here.
Mal. My countryman; but yet I know him not.   160
Macd. My ever gentle cousin, welcome hither.
Mal. I know him now. Good God betimes remove
The means that makes us strangers!

Ross.   Sir, amen.
Macd. Stands Scotland where it did?
Ross.   Alas, poor country,
Almost afraid to know itself! It cannot   165
Be call'd our mother, but our grave; where nothing,
But who knows nothing, is once seen to smile;
Where sighs and groans, and shrieks that rent the air,
Are made, not mark'd; where violent sorrow seems
A modern ecstasy. The dead man's knell   170
Is there scarce ask'd for who; and good men's lives
Expire before the flowers in their caps,
Dying or ere they sicken.
Macd.   O, relation
Too nice, and yet too true!
Mal.   What's the newest grief?
Ross. That of an hour's age doth hiss the speaker;   175
Each minute teems a new one.
Macd.   How does my wife?
Ross. Why, well.
Macd.   And all my children?
Ross.   Well too.
Macd. The tyrant has not batter'd at their peace?
Ross. No; they were well at peace when I did leave 'em.
Macd. Be not a niggard of your speech. How goes't? 180
Ross. When I came hither to transport the tidings
Which I have heavily borne, there ran a rumour
Of many worthy fellows that were out;
Which was to my belief witness'd the rather
For that I saw the tyrant's power afoot.   185
Now is the time of help. Your eye in Scotland
Would create soldiers, make our women fight
To doff their dire distresses.
Mal.   Be't their comfort

We are coming thither. Gracious England hath
Lent us good Siward and ten thousand men.   190
An older and a better soldier none
That Christendom gives out.
    Ross.   Would I could answer
This comfort with the like! But I have words
That would be howl'd out in the desert air,
Where hearing should not latch them.
    Macd.   What concern they? 195
The general cause? or is it a fee-grief
Due to some single breast?
    Ross.   No mind that's honest
But in it shares some woe, though the main part
Pertains to you alone.
    Macd.   If it be mine,
Keep it not from me, quickly let me have it.   200
    Ross. Let not your ears despise my tongue for ever,
Which shall possess them with the heaviest sound
That ever yet they heard.
    Macd.   Humh! I guess at it.
    Ross. Your castle is surpris'd; your wife and babes
Savagely slaughter'd. To relate the manner,   205
Were, on the quarry of these murther'd deer,
To add the death of you.
    Mal.   Merciful heaven!
What, man! Ne'er pull your hat upon your brows.
Give sorrow words. The grief that does not speak
Whispers the o'erfraught heart and bids it break.   210
    Macd. My children too?
    Ross.   Wife, children, servants, all
That could be found.
    Macd.   And I must be from thence?
My wife kill'd too?

Ross.   I have said.
Mal.   Be comforted.
Let's make us med'cines of our great revenge
To cure this deadly grief.   215
    Macd. He has no children. All my pretty ones?
Did you say all? O hell-kite! All?
What, all my pretty chickens and their dam
At one fell swoop?
    Mal. Dispute it like a man.
    Macd.   I shall do so;   220
But I must also feel it as a man.
I cannot but remember such things were
That were most precious to me. Did heaven look on
And would not take their part? Sinful Macduff,
They were all struck for thee! Naught that I am,   225
Not for their own demerits, but for mine,
Fell slaughter on their souls. Heaven rest them now!
    Mal. Be this the whetstone of your sword. Let grief
Convert to anger; blunt not the heart, enrage it.
    Macd. O, I could play the woman with mine eyes   230
And braggart with my tongue! But, gentle heavens,
Cut short all intermission. Front to front
Bring thou this fiend of Scotland and myself.
Within my sword's length set him. If he scape,
Heaven forgive him too!
    Mal.   This tune goes manly.   235
Come, go we to the King. Our power is ready;
Our lack is nothing but our leave. Macbeth
Is ripe for shaking, and the pow'rs above
Put on their instruments. Receive what cheer you may.
The night is long that never finds the day.   240
                                            Exeunt.

Enter a Doctor of Physic *and a* Waiting Gentlewoman.

Doct. I have two nights watch'd with you, but can perceive no truth in your report. When was it she last walk'd?

Gent. Since his Majesty went into the field I have seen her rise from her bed, throw her nightgown upon her, unlock her closet, take forth paper, fold it, write upon't, read it, afterwards seal it, and again return to bed; yet all this while in a most fast sleep. 9

Doct. A great perturbation in nature, to receive at once the benefit of sleep and do the effects of watching! In this slumb'ry agitation, besides her walking and other actual performances, what (at any time) have you heard her say?

Gent. That, sir, which I will not report after her.

Doct. You may to me, and 'tis most meet you should.

Gent. Neither to you nor any one, having no witness to confirm my speech. 21

Enter Lady [*Macbeth*], *with a taper.*

Lo you, here she comes! This is her very guise, and, upon my life, fast asleep! Observe her; stand close.

Doct. How came she by that light? 25

Gent. Why, it stood by her. She has light by her continually. 'Tis her command.

Doct. You see her eyes are open.

Gent. Ay; but their sense is shut.

Doct. What is it she does now? Look how she rubs her hands. 31

Gent. It is an accustom'd action with her, to seem thus washing her hands. I have known her continue in this a quarter of an hour.

Lady. Yet here's a spot. 35

Doct. Hark, she speaks! I will set down what comes from her, to satisfy my remembrance the more strongly.

Lady. Out, damned spot! out, I say! One; two. Why then 'tis time to do't. Hell is murky. Fie, my lord, fie! a soldier, and afeard? What need we fear who knows it, when none can call our pow'r to accompt? Yet who would have thought the old man to have had so much blood in him? 45

Doct. Do you mark that?

Lady. The Thane of Fife had a wife. Where is she now? What, will these hands ne'er be clean? No more o' that, my lord, no more o' that! You mar all with this starting. 50

Doct. Go to, go to! You have known what you should not.

Gent. She has spoke what she should not, I am sure of that. Heaven knows what she has known. 55

Lady. Here's the smell of the blood still. All the perfumes of Arabia will not sweeten this little hand. Oh, oh, oh!

Doct. What a sigh is there! The heart is sorely charg'd. 60

Gent. I would not have such a heart in my bosom for the dignity of the whole body.

Doct. Well, well, well.

Gent. Pray God it be, sir. 64

Doct. This disease is beyond my practice. Yet I have known those which have walk'd in their sleep who have died holily in their beds.

Lady. Wash your hands, put on your nightgown, look not so pale! I tell you yet again, Banquo's buried. He can not come out on's grave. 71

Doct. Even so?

Lady. To bed, to bed! There's knocking at the gate. Come, come, come, come, give me your hand! What's done cannot be undone. To bed, to bed, to bed! *Exit.*

Doct. Will she go now to bed?

Gent. Directly.

Doct. Foul whisp'rings are abroad. Unnatural deeds
Do breed unnatural troubles. Infected minds   80
To their deaf pillows will discharge their secrets.
More needs she the divine than the physician.
God, God forgive us all! Look after her;
Remove from her the means of all annoyance,
And still keep eyes upon her. So good night.   85
My mind she has mated, and amaz'd my sight.
I think, but dare not speak.

Gent.   Good night, good doctor.

Exeunt.

Scene II. [*The country near Dunsinane.*]

Drum and Colours. Enter *Menteith, Caithness, Angus,*
Lennox, Soldiers.

Ment. The English pow'r is near, led on by Malcolm,
His uncle Siward, and the good Macduff.
Revenges burn in them; for their dear causes
Would to the bleeding and the grim alarm
Excite the mortified man.

Ang.   Near Birnam Wood   5
Shall we well meet them; that way are they coming.

Caith. Who knows if Donalbain be with his brother?

Len. For certain, sir, he is not. I have a file
Of all the gentry. There is Siward's son
And many unrough youths that even now   10
Protest their first of manhood.

Ment.   What does the tyrant?

Caith. Great Dunsinane he strongly fortifies.
Some say he's mad; others, that lesser hate him,
Do call it valiant fury; but for certain
He cannot buckle his distemper'd cause   15
Within the belt of rule.
    Ang.   Now does he feel
His secret murthers sticking on his hands.
Now minutely revolts upbraid his faith-breach.
Those he commands move only in command,
Nothing in love. Now does he feel his title   20
Hang loose about him, like a giant's robe
Upon a dwarfish thief.
    Ment.   Who then shall blame
His pester'd senses to recoil and start,
When all that is within him does condemn
Itself for being there?
    Caith.   Well, march we on   25
To give obedience where 'tis truly ow'd.
Meet we the med'cine of the sickly weal;
And with him pour we in our country's purge
Each drop of us.
    Len.   Or so much as it needs
To dew the sovereign flower and drown the weeds.   30
Make we our march towards Birnam.
                                        Exeunt, marching.

Scene III. [*Dunsinane. A room in the Castle.*]

Enter *Macbeth, Doctor,* and *Attendants.*

Macb. Bring me no more reports. Let them fly all!
Till Birnam Wood remove to Dunsinane,
I cannot taint with fear. What's the boy Malcolm?

Was he not born of woman? The spirits that know
All mortal consequences have pronounc'd me thus: 5
'Fear not, Macbeth. No man that's born of woman
Shall e'er have power upon thee.' Then fly, false thanes,
And mingle with the English epicures.
The mind I sway by and the heart I bear
Shall never sag with doubt nor shake with fear.   10

                   Enter *Servant.*

The devil damn thee black, thou cream-fac'd loon!
Where got'st thou that goose look?
   Serv. There is ten thousand—
   Macb.   Geese, villain?
   Serv.   Soldiers, sir.
   Macb. Go prick thy face and over-red thy fear,
Thou lily-liver'd boy. What soldiers, patch?   15
Death of thy soul! Those linen cheeks of thine
Are counsellors to fear. What soldiers, whey-face?
   Serv. The English force, so please you.
   Macb. Take thy face hence.

                             [*Exit Servant.*]
             Seyton!—I am sick at heart,
When I behold—Seyton, I say!—This push   20
Will cheer me ever, or disseat me now.
I have liv'd long enough. My way of life
Is fallen into the sere, the yellow leaf;
And that which should accompany old age,
As honour, love, obedience, troops of friends,   25
I must not look to have; but, in their stead,
Curses not loud but deep, mouth-honour, breath,
Which the poor heart would fain deny, and dare not.
Seyton!

Enter *Seyton*.

Sey. What's your gracious pleasure?

Macb.   What news more?   30

Sey. All is confirm'd, my lord, which was reported.

Macb. I'll fight, till from my bones my flesh be hack'd.
Give me my armour.

Sey.   'Tis not needed yet.

Macb. I'll put it on.
Send out moe horses, skirr the country round;   35
Hang those that talk of fear. Give me mine armour.
How does your patient, doctor?

Doct.   Not so sick, my lord,
As she is troubled with thick-coming fancies
That keep her from her rest.

Macb.   Cure her of that!
Canst thou not minister to a mind diseas'd,   40
Pluck from the memory a rooted sorrow,
Raze out the written troubles of the brain,
And with some sweet oblivious antidote
Cleanse the stuff'd bosom of that perilous stuff
Which weighs upon the heart?

Doct.   Therein the patient   45
Must minister to himself.

Macb. Throw physic to the dogs, I'll none of it!—
Come, put mine armour on. Give me my staff.—
Seyton, send out.—Doctor, the thanes fly from me.—
Come, sir, dispatch.—If thou couldst, doctor, cast   50
The water of my land, find her disease,
And purge it to a sound and pristine health,
I would applaud thee to the very echo,
That should applaud again.—Pull't off, I say.—

What rhubarb, senna, or what purgative drug,   55
Would scour these English hence? Hear'st thou of them?
 Doct. Ay, my good lord. Your royal preparation
Makes us hear something.
 Macb.   Bring it after me!
I will not be afraid of death and bane
Till Birnam Forest come to Dunsinane.   60
      [Exeunt all but the Doctor.]
 Doct. Were I from Dunsinane away and clear,
Profit again should hardly draw me here.   *Exit.*

Scene IV. *[Country near Birnam Wood.]*

Drum and Colours. Enter *Malcolm, Siward, Macduff, Siward's
Son, Menteith, Caithness, Angus,* [*Lennox, Ross,*] and *Soldiers,* marching.

 Mal. Cousins, I hope the days are near at hand
That chambers will be safe.
 Ment.   We doubt it nothing.
 Siw. What wood is this before us?
 Ment.   The Wood of Birnam.
 Mal. Let every soldier hew him down a bough
And bear't before him. Thereby shall we shadow   5
The numbers of our host and make discovery
Err in report of us.
 Soldiers. It shall be done.
 Siw. We learn no other but the confident tyrant
Keeps still in Dunsinane and will endure
Our setting down before't.
 Mal.   'Tis his main hope;   10
For where there is advantage to be given,
Both more and less have given him the revolt;

And none serve with him but constrained things,
Whose hearts are absent too.
    Macd.   Let our just censures
Attend the true event, and put we on   15
Industrious soldiership.
    Siw.   The time approaches
That will with due decision make us know
What we shall say we have, and what we owe.
Thoughts speculative their unsure hopes relate,
But certain issue strokes must arbitrate;   20
Towards which advance the war.
                        Exeunt, marching.

Scene V. [*Dunsinane. Within the Castle.*]

Enter *Macbeth*, *Seyton*, and *Soldiers*, with *Drum* and *Colours*.

    Macb. Hang out our banners on the outward walls.
The cry is still, 'They come!' Our castle's strength
Will laugh a siege to scorn. Here let them lie
Till famine and the ague eat them up.
Were they not forc'd with those that should be ours,   5
We might have met them dareful, beard to beard,
And beat them backward home.
                   A cry within of women.
                   What is that noise?
    Sey. It is the cry of women, my good lord.   [*Exit.*]
    Macb. I have almost forgot the taste of fears.
The time has been, my senses would have cool'd   10
To hear a night-shriek, and my fell of hair
Would at a dismal treatise rouse and stir
As life were in't. I have supp'd full with horrors.
Direness, familiar to my slaughterous thoughts,
Cannot once start me.

[Enter *Seyton*.]

      Wherefore was that cry?   **15**
 Sey. The Queen, my lord, is dead.
  Macb. She should have died hereafter;
There would have been a time for such a word.
To-morrow, and to-morrow, and to-morrow
Creeps in this petty pace from day to day   **20**
To the last syllable of recorded time;
And all our yesterdays have lighted fools
The way to dusty death. Out, out, brief candle!
Life's but a walking shadow, a poor player,
That struts and frets his hour upon the stage   **25**
And then is heard no more. It is a tale
Told by an idiot, full of sound and fury,
Signifying nothing.

Enter a *Messenger*.

Thou com'st to use thy tongue. Thy story quickly!
 Mess. Gracious my lord,   **30**
I should report that which I say I saw,
But know not how to do't.
  Macb.   Well, say, sir!
 Mess. As I did stand my watch upon the hill,
I look'd toward Birnam, and anon methought
The wood began to move.
  Macb.   Liar and slave!   **35**
 Mess. Let me endure your wrath if't be not so.
Within this three mile may you see it coming;
I say, a moving grove.
  Macb.   If thou speak'st false,
Upon the next tree shalt thou hang alive,

Till famine cling thee. If thy speech be sooth,   40
I care not if thou dost for me as much.
I pull in resolution, and begin
To doubt th' equivocation of the fiend,
That lies like truth. 'Fear not, till Birnam wood
Do come to Dunsinane!' and now a wood   45
Comes toward Dunsinane. Arm, arm, and out!
If this which he avouches does appear,
There is nor flying hence nor tarrying here.
I gin to be aweary of the sun,
And wish th' estate o' th' world were now undone.   50
Ring the alarum bell! Blow wind, come wrack,
At least we'll die with harness on our back!

Exeunt.

Scene VI. [*Dunsinane. Before the Castle.*]

Drum and Colours. Enter *Malcolm, Siward, Macduff,* and
their *Army*, with boughs.

Mal. Now near enough. Your leavy screens throw down
And show like those you are. You, worthy uncle,
Shall with my cousin, your right noble son,
Lead our first battle. Worthy Macduff and we
Shall take upon 's what else remains to do,   5
According to our order.
Siw.   Fare you well.
Do we but find the tyrant's power to-night,
Let us be beaten if we cannot fight.
Macd. Make all our trumpets speak, give them all breath,
Those clamorous harbingers of blood and death.   10

Exeunt. Alarums continued.

Scene VII. [*Another part of the field.*]

Enter *Macbeth*.

Macb. They have tied me to a stake. I cannot fly,
But bear-like I must fight the course. What's he
That was not born of woman? Such a one
Am I to fear, or none.

Enter *Young Siward*.

Y. Siw. What is thy name?
Macb.   Thou'lt be afraid to hear it. 5
Y. Siw. No; though thou call'st thyself a hotter name
Than any is in hell.
Macb.   My name's Macbeth.
Y. Siw. The devil himself could not pronounce a title
More hateful to mine ear.
Macb.   No, nor more fearful.
Y. Siw. Thou liest, abhorred tyrant! With my sword   10
I'll prove the lie thou speak'st.
                              Fight, and Young Siward slain.
Macb.   Thou wast born of woman.
But swords I smile at, weapons laugh to scorn,
Brandish'd by man that's of a woman born.   *Exit.*

Alarums. Enter *Macduff*.

Macd. That way the noise is. Tyrant, show thy face!
If thou beest slain and with no stroke of mine,   15
My wife and children's ghosts will haunt me still.
I cannot strike at wretched kerns, whose arms
Are hir'd to bear their staves. Either thou, Macbeth,
Or else my sword with an unbattered edge
I sheathe again undeeded. There thou shouldst be.   20

By this great clatter one of greatest note
Seems bruited. Let me find him, Fortune!
And more I beg not.   *Exit. Alarums.*

           Enter *Malcolm* and *Siward.*

  Siw. This way, my lord. The castle's gently rend'red:
The tyrant's people on both sides do fight;   25
The noble thanes do bravely in the war;
The day almost itself professes yours,
And little is to do.
  Mal.   We have met with foes
That strike beside us.
  Siw.   Enter, sir, the castle.
                         Exeunt. Alarum.

      Scene VIII. [*Another part of the field.*]

              Enter *Macbeth.*

  Macb. Why should I play the Roman fool and die
On mine own sword? Whiles I see lives, the gashes
Do better upon them.

              Enter *Macduff.*

  Macd.   Turn, hellhound, turn!
  Macb. Of all men else I have avoided thee.
But get thee back! My soul is too much charg'd   5
With blood of thine already.
  Macd.   I have no words;
My voice is in my sword, thou bloodier villain
Than terms can give thee out!
                        Fight. Alarum.
  Macb.   Thou losest labour.
As easy mayst thou the intrenchant air
With thy keen sword impress as make me bleed.   10

Let fall thy blade on vulnerable crests.
I bear a charmed life, which must not yield
To one of woman born.
 Macd.   Despair thy charm!
And let the angel whom thou still hast serv'd
Tell thee, Macduff was from his mother's womb 15
Untimely ripp'd.
 Macb. Accursed be that tongue that tells me so,
For it hath cow'd my better part of man!
And be these juggling fiends no more believ'd,
That palter with us in a double sense, 20
That keep the word of promise to our ear
And break it to our hope! I'll not fight with thee!
 Macd. Then yield thee, coward,
And live to be the show and gaze o' th' time!
We'll have thee, as our rarer monsters are, 25
Painted upon a pole, and underwrit
'Here may you see the tyrant.'
 Macb.   I will not yield,
To kiss the ground before young Malcolm's feet
And to be baited with the rabble's curse.
Though Birnam Wood be come to Dunsinane, 30
And thou oppos'd, being of no woman born,
Yet I will try the last. Before my body
I throw my warlike shield. Lay on, Macduff,
And damn'd be him that first cries 'Hold, enough!'
      Exeunt fighting. Alarums.

Retreat and flourish. Enter, with *Drum* and *Colours*, *Malcolm*,
  Siward, *Ross*, *Thanes*, and *Soldiers*.

 Mal. I would the friends we miss were safe arriv'd. 35
 Siw. Some must go off; and yet, by these I see,
So great a day as this is cheaply bought.

Mal. Macduff is missing, and your noble son.

Ross. Your son, my lord, has paid a soldier's debt.
He only liv'd but till he was a man,   40
The which no sooner had his prowess confirm'd
In the unshrinking station where he fought
But like a man he died.

Siw.   Then he is dead?

Ross. Ay, and brought off the field. Your cause of sorrow
Must not be measur'd by his worth, for then   45
It hath no end.

Siw.   Had he his hurts before?

Ross. Ay, on the front.

Siw.   Why then, God's soldier be he!
Had I as many sons as I have hairs,
I would not wish them to a fairer death.
And so his knell is knoll'd.

Mal.   He's worth more sorrow,   50
And that I'll spend for him.

Siw.   He's worth no more.
They say he parted well and paid his score,
And so, God be with him! Here comes newer comfort.

Enter *Macduff*, with *Macbeth's* head.

Macd. Hail, King! for so thou art. Behold where stands
Th' usurper's cursed head. The time is free.   55
I see thee compass'd with thy kingdom's pearl,
That speak my salutation in their minds;
Whose voices I desire aloud with mine—
Hail, King of Scotland!

All.   Hail, King of Scotland!   *Flourish.*

Mal. We shall not spend a large expense of time   60
Before we reckon with your several loves
And make us even with you. My Thanes and kinsmen,

Henceforth be Earls, the first that ever Scotland
In such an honour nam'd. What's more to do
Which would be planted newly with the time—   65
As calling home our exil'd friends abroad
That fled the snares of watchful tyranny,
Producing forth the cruel ministers
Of this dead butcher and his fiendlike queen,
Who (as 'tis thought) by self and violent hands   70
Took off her life—this, and what needful else
That calls upon us, by the grace of Grace
We will perform in measure, time, and place.
So thanks to all at once and to each one,
Whom we invite to see us crown'd at Scone.   75

Flourish. Exeunt omnes.

NOTES

The tragedy plunges, as usual, *in medias res*. The Weird Sisters are at the close of a consultation and about to separate. We infer that they have some design that involves Macbeth; but not until scene ii do we learn who Macbeth is, or what is meant by 'the battle.' The place of the scene is not indicated in the Folios. We may imagine any wild and desolate region— not, however, the blasted heath where the Sisters meet Macbeth in scene iii, since that is mentioned as a different place in l. 6. For the nature of the Weird Sisters, see Introduction, pp. xvi ff. They are not mortal witches, but supernatural beings—great powers or ministers of fate, as their name denotes. Their entry at the outset is highly significant; for they are the ruling forces of the tragedy: it is Macbeth's trust in them that is the immediate cause of his first crime and that determines his final downfall. In this scene, as elsewhere, we note a gradation in the knowledge of the Weird Sisters. The first asks questions; the second answers; the third gives definite information about the future—namely, that the battle will be over before sunset and that Macbeth will cross a certain heath.

1, 2. When ... rain? When shall we meet again in a storm? Witches and demons were supposed to be particularly active in boisterous weather, which, indeed, was often thought to be caused by their spells (cf. i, 3, 10–25; iv, 1, 52–60). The storm at the outset is symbolic of the whole course of this tempestuous drama. There is a storm on the night of Duncan's murder, and the next day is dark and gloomy (ii, 3, 59–68; ii, 4, 1–10). When Banquo is attacked (iii, 3, 16) a storm is brewing. Thunder ushers in the Weird Sisters in iv, 1.

3. hurlyburly. The battle described in the next scene is now raging.

8, 9. Graymalkin, etc. The Weird Sisters are summoned by their 'familiars' (attendant spirits), who have been instructed to call when the time comes for their mistresses to depart, each

87

on her own evil errand. One of these demons has the shape of
a grey cat, another that of a paddock or toad. The name and
shape of the Third Sister's familiar are not mentioned; but he
calls, like the others, and she answers 'Anon!' i.e., 'In a moment!' In iv, 1, 3, he is styled 'Harpier.' *Graymalkin* means
'little grey Mall' (a form of *Moll*, i.e., 'Mary'). A cat appears
as a familiar spirit in the first of the really notable Elizabethan
witch-trials, at Chelmsford in 1566. It was a white-spotted
creature named Sathan, which sucked blood; it took the form
of a toad and caused the death of a man who touched it; it
helped its mistress to an unsatisfactory husband. For other
examples of cats and toads as familiar spirits and of witches
that took the shape of cats or toads, see Kittredge, *Witchcraft in
Old and New England*, pp. 177–179, 181–183.

10, 11. **Fair is foul,** etc. Fair weather and good deeds are
foul to the Weird Sisters, and only foul things are beautiful.
Their principle is that of Milton's Satan—'Evil, be thou my
good.'

Scene II.

This scene is purely expository. It takes place on the same
day as scene i. We hear full details of the double victory won
by Macbeth, the king's near kinsman, assisted by Banquo. He
has defeated the rebels under Macdonwald and slain their
leader with his own hand. King Sweno, the Norwegian in-
vader, has attacked the Scots while still in the disorder of this
victory, but has been routed in his turn. The news is told in
part by a wounded Sergeant, and finished by the Thane of
Ross. Thus we have a complete account of Macbeth's valorous
deeds, and learn of the high esteem in which he is held by
the army, as well as by his fellow nobles. To this is added the
King's tribute of honour to Macbeth, his brave and devoted
cousin and chief general. The whole scene, then, leaves us
with the highest opinion of Macbeth as a great warrior and a
loyal subject (see i, 7, 33, note). The place of the scene is not

exactly indicated, but appears to be a camp not far from the battlefield, for the Sergeant is on his way to the rear to have his wounds dressed. The *alarum* (or trumpet call) in the stage direction may be a sound from the conflict or quite as probably an incident of the camp. From scene iii it appears that the King is now at or near Forres (i, 3, 39), and this town is nearly a hundred miles north of County Fife, where the battle is fought (l. 48). However, neither Shakespeare nor his audience felt any concern about details of Scottish geography.

Stage direction. **Alarum**: properly, a call to arms (*all' arme*); then, a trumpet call to the onset or to any muster.

3. **sergeant** (three syllables): an officer of much higher rank than a modern sergeant. The Folio calls him a 'Captaine' in the stage direction. He may best be described, somewhat vaguely, as an officer of the guard.

4. **hardy**: stout, valiant.

5. **my captivity.** Malcolm has been in the thick of the fight and would have been captured but for the Sergeant. The Prince has returned to the King's camp with a report, but he now calls upon the Sergeant for later news. The suggestion for Malcolm's adventure comes from Holinshed, where another Malcolm (one of Duncan's captains) is taken prisoner and put to death by the rebels.—**Hail**: the vowel is prolonged with a change of pitch, so as to give the effect of two syllables. Cf. i, 6, 30.—**brave.** Less restricted in sense than in the modern idiom. It includes brilliant service and fine qualities in general—not merely valour. Cf. l. 16.

8. **spent**: exhausted.

9. **choke their art**: hamper each other's movements so that neither can make use of his skill as a swimmer.—**Macdonwald**: a Scottish noble who, according to Holinshed, 'tooke vpon him to be chiefe capteine of all such rebels as would stand against the king.' Holinshed calls him Makdowald.

10. **to that**: as if for the very purpose (of making him a perfect rebel). Davenant substitutes 'to which end.' To the loyal Sergeant rebellion is the worst of crimes, and it therefore

seems only appropriate that Macdonwald should embody all the villany of which human nature is capable.

12. **swarm:** emphatic.—**Western Isles:** the Hebrides. Holinshed says that 'a great multitude of people' came from the Western Isles to aid Makdowald, and adds that 'no small number of Kernes and Galloglasses' from Ireland joined his army 'in hope of the spoile.'

13. **Of:** with.—**kerns and gallowglasses:** two kinds of Irish soldiers well known to the Elizabethans. John Dymmok, in *A Treatice of Ireland, ca.* 1600 (ed. Irish Archæological Society, p. 7), describes the kern as 'a kinde of footeman, sleightly armed with a sworde, a targett of woode, or a bow and sheafe of arrows with barbed heades, or els 3 dartes, which they cast with wonderfull facillity and nearnes.' They were wild freebooters rather than regular troops. King Richard II (ii, 1, 156–158) calls them

> rough rug-headed kerns,
> Which live like venom where no venom else
> But only they have privilege to live.

The *gallowglasses* were picked men and much more formidable. Spenser describes the 'galloglass' as a footsoldier 'armed in a long shirt of mayle downe to the calfe of his legg, with a long brode axe in his hand' (*Present State of Ireland*, Globe ed., p. 640).

14. **his damned quarrel:** the accursed cause for which Macdonwald fought; 'that rebellious quarell,' as Holinshed calls it. The Folio reads *Quarry*. The emendation is Hanmer's. *Quarry* means 'the game slaughtered in any hunt,' and so is common in the sense of 'prey.' *His damned quarry* might mean 'the loyal Scottish army, damned (condemned, doomed) in Macdonwald's mind to be his prey'; but *smiling* does not suit this interpretation, for it implies *favour*, and Fortune was not at that moment favourable to the King's men. For *quarrel* cf. iv, 3, 137.

15. **Show'd,** etc.: appeared to have taken Macdonwald as her lover; seemed to have granted him her favour. Fortune is often regarded as a harlot, because she shows favour to all men

but is constant to none. Cf. Chaucer, *Troilus*, i, 841–854.—**all:** everything that Macdonwald and Fortune can do.

16. **brave.** Cf. l. 5, note.

19. **minion:** darling, favourite (French *mignon*). Macdonwald appeared to be Fortune's favourite, but Macbeth was the chosen darling of Valour—'Bellona's bridegroom.' Cf. *King John*, ii, 1, 390–394:

> Turn face to face and bloody point to point.
> Then in a moment Fortune shall cull forth
> Out of one side her happy minion,
> To whom in favour she shall give the day
> And kiss him with a glorious victory.

20. **slave:** villain, rascal—as a general term of abuse.

21, 22. **Which . . . chaps:** Who was not able to part with Macbeth (to get rid of him) until Macbeth had ripped him up from the navel to the jaws. The form of expression is intentionally grotesque. *Which* refers to the *slave* (Macdonwald). *Shook hands* means 'shook hands at parting.' Cf. *Hamlet*, i, 5, 128: 'I hold it fit that we shake hands and part.' Some editors make *which* refer to Macbeth, and this may be right. Steevens quotes Marlowe and Nashe, *Dido*, ii, 1, 550, 551 (ed. Tucker Brooke, p. 407):

> Then from the nauell to the throat at once,
> He ript old Priam.

That Shakespeare was familiar with this old play would be a matter of course. He seems to have remembered the lines that immediately precede those quoted by Steevens:

> Which he [Pyrrhus] disdaining whiskt his sword about,
> And with the wind thereof the King fell downe—

when he wrote, in *Hamlet*, ii, 2, 494–496:

> Pyrrhus at Priam drives, in rage strikes wide;
> But with the whiff and wind of his fell sword
> Th' unnerved father falls.

24. **cousin.** According to Holinshed, Malcolm II had two daughters; and Duncan was the son of the elder, Macbeth of

the younger. This is the genealogy adopted by Shakespeare. In fact, however, Macbeth was not so nearly related to Duncan.—**worthy**: noble. The word has none of its modern condescending suggestion.

25–28. As whence ... swells: As from the east, whence comes the sunrise, storms often break forth, so from the seeming source of comfort (the victory over Macdonwald) a disadvantage came to the Scottish army—for the King of Norway attacked them with fresh troops while still in the disorder of victory.—**gins his reflection**: begins his shining.—**spring**: source.

30. skipping kerns. Cf. *The Life and Death of Captain Thomas Stukeley*, ca. 1596, printed 1605 (ed. Simpson, *The School of Shakspere*, I, 191):

> Tomorrow comes O'Kane with Gallinglasse
> And Teague Magennies with his lightfoot kerne.

In *Soliman and Perseda*, i, 3, 94–96 (Kyd, ed. Boas, p. 171), Basilisco the braggart boasts—

> Vpon a Time in Ireland I fought
> On horseback with an hundred Kernes
> From Titans Easterne vprise to his Western downefall.

Skipping expresses the scorn of the professional soldier for these irregular marauders, but does not necessarily imply cowardice.

31. the Norweyan lord: Sweno (Svend), King of Norway. In Holinshed the invasion of Scotland by Sweno is distinct from Macdonwald's rebellion, and the defeat of Sweno is followed by another invasion of Danes sent by King Canute. Shakespeare's treatment of the material is a good example of dramatic condensation.—**surveying vantage**: noting an opportune moment for attack. Cf. *Richard III*, v, 3, 15: 'Let us survey the vantage of the ground.'

34. captains: generals, commanders—trisyllabic, as if *capitains* (an older form of the word).—**Yes.** The irony of the Sergeant's reply is meant to fit his blunt, soldierly manner.

36. **sooth**: truth.

37. **cracks**: charges. Regularly used of any thunderous sound, as in iv, 1, 117: 'th' crack of doom.' Cf. *Taming of the Shrew*, i, 2, 95, 96:

> Though she chide as loud
> As thunder when the clouds in autumn crack;

and *Titus Andronicus*, ii, 1, 3: 'Secure of thunder's crack or lightning flash.' Cf. Greene, *Mamillia*, 1583 (ed. Grosart, II, 124): 'The coward that feareth ẙ crack of ẙ canon, will neuer proue a couragious captaine.' Here transferred from the sound to that which causes the sound.

38. **Doubly redoubled.** Cf. *Richard II*, i, 3, 80–82:

> And let thy blows, doubly redoubled,
> Fall like amazing thunder on the casque
> Of thy adverse pernicious enemy.

39. **Except**: unless. *Bathe* is emphatic.

40. **memorize ... Golgotha:** make the place memorable as a second Golgotha, or field of the dead. Cf. *Richard II*, iv, 1, 136 ff.:

> And if you crown him, let me prophesy,
> The blood of English shall manure the ground;
> . . . .
> Disorder, horror, fear, and mutiny
> Shall here inhabit, and this land be call'd
> The field of Golgotha and dead men's skulls.

Golgotha is Calvary (*Matthew*, xxviii, 33; *Mark*, xv, 22; *Luke*, xxiii, 33; *John*, xix, 17). Shakespeare has adopted the explanation usual in his time, that Golgotha was so called ('the place of a skull') from the many skulls of executed persons that lay about. Cf. Marston, *The Malcontent*, iv, 2, 141, 142 (ed. Bullen, I, 290): 'This earth is the only grave and Golgotha wherein all things that live must rot'; Davenant, *Albovine*, ii (ed. Maidment and Logan, I, 45):

> But my nuptial the king did celebrate
> In Golgotha, where skulls and dusty bones
> Inhabit.

41. **I cannot tell:** I do not know what their purpose was.

43. **become thee.** Duncan sees nothing unbecoming in the Sergeant's language, nor did the Elizabethan audience. He uses the style then conventionally expected of the typical soldier—a mixture of bombast and homeliness.

45. **worthy.** Cf. l. 24.—**Thane:** an old title of nobility in Scotland (Anglo-Saxon *thegn*), roughly corresponding to the English *Earl*. See v, 8, 63.

47. **seems to speak:** looks as if he were about to speak.

48. **Fife.** A county on the east coast, north of the Firth of Forth. Here Sweno was defeated, according to Holinshed. The defeat of Macdonwald took place, some time before, in Lochaber, on the other side of Scotland.

49, 50. **Norweyan:** Norwegian.—**flout . . . cold:** The Norwegian banners are still flying proudly and insulting (*flouting*) the Scottish sky, as they did at the beginning of the fight, but now they serve merely to cool off our soldiers, heated by the victorious battle. The grotesque hyperbole is intentional, expressing the speaker's triumphant contempt for the vanquished foe.—**cold,** for 'pleasantly cool,' occurs in Lyly's *Euphues* (ed. Bond, II, 170): 'To lye in the parching Sunne, when he may sleepe in the colde shadow.'—**Norway:** the King of Norway. Ross takes up the story where the Sergeant dropped it.

52. Ross does not say that the Thane of Cawdor was present at the battle. There are ways of 'assisting' the enemy besides fighting in his ranks. Later we learn that the help was secretly furnished. Cf. i, 3, 111–114. Holinshed gives no details about Cawdor's treason and does not bring it into connection with either the rebels or Sweno.

53. **dismal:** threatening disaster (to the Scots). The original meaning of *dismal* was 'ill-omened.' Cf. *Sir John Oldcastle*, ii, 2, 77: 'Friday quoth a! Dismall day!'

54. **Bellona's bridegroom.** So splendid a fighter is Macbeth that Ross speaks of Bellona, the goddess of war, as taking him for her husband. Contrast ll. 14, 15.—**lapp'd in proof:** wrapped (clad) in armour of proof, i.e., well-tested armour.

55. **Confronted ... comparisons:** met him face to face and encountered each of his movements with one that matched it.

56. **Point ... arm:** Macbeth's sword point contending against Sweno's sword point, and the rebellious arm of Sweno contending against Macbeth's arm. Sweno is not a rebel, but his arm is called *rebellious* because he is opposing the lawful monarch. Most editors shift the comma (which follows *point* in the Folios), putting it after *rebellious*; but the old punctuation makes excellent sense.

57. **lavish:** unbridled, over-confident.

58. **That:** so that.

59. **Norways':** Norwegians'.—**craves composition:** asks for a truce, or for terms of peace. *Composition* is often used in the general sense of 'agreement.'

61. **Saint Colme's Inch:** St. Columba's Island; Inchcolm in the Firth of Forth.

62. **dollars.** Spanish dollars and German thalers were well known to the Elizabethans. The anachronism of mentioning them in the time of Macbeth (the eleventh century) need not worry us.

63, 64. **deceive ... interest:** play me false in my most important and confidential concerns. *Our* is the so-called plural of majesty (the royal *we*).—**present:** instant.—The verse is an alexandrine (of six feet).

66. **I'll see it done.** Between this speech and the entrance of Ross at i, 3, 88, he has communicated the King's orders to the commissioners in charge of Cawdor. See i, 4, 1, 2.

Scene III.

This scene takes place before sunset (i, 1, 5) on the day of the battle, while Macbeth and Banquo are marching towards Forres to join the King after their double victory. They are accompanied by some of their troops (l. 30), but these are far enough in the rear to be out of the way during the interview with the Weird Sisters. The place is indicated by Macbeth's words in l. 77: 'this blasted heath.' Holinshed puts the meeting with the Sisters in a 'laund,' or open space in the woods, while Macbeth and Banquo journeyed towards Forres 'without other companie, saue onelie themselues.' The incident, according to him, took place some time after the defeat of Sweno. Here again Shakespeare practises dramatic condensation.

2. **swine.** Witches were thought to show their malice by causing the death of domestic animals, usually by disease. Swine were often the victims, not because witches had any special enmity for them, but merely because they were a common possession, even with the poorest.

5. **mounch'd:** munched.

6. **Aroint thee:** Begone! Off with you! Cf. *Lear*, iii, 4, 129. Shakespeare adopts an incident very frequent in his time. An old woman, suspected of witchcraft, begs for something to eat or drink or for a bit of money, but is driven away with insults. She goes off, muttering threats or curses. Soon after, sickness or misfortune visits the household. Such was the evidence given at many witch trials. In the present case the sordid and pitiful incident is ennobled by a touch of the romance and mystery of the sea.—**rump-fed:** fat-rumped. Cf. *Troilus and Cressida*, v, 2, 55, 56.—**ronyon:** literally, scab; scabby person; but usually (as here) a mere term of abuse or contempt. Cf. *Merry Wives*, iv, 2, 194, 195: 'You baggage, you polecat, you runnion!'

7. **th' Tiger.** A well-known name for ships in Shakespeare's time. Cf. *Twelfth Night*, v, 1, 65.

8. **in a sieve.** It was believed that witches could use sieves as boats. In an historical case (reported in *Newes from Scotland*, 1591) which made a great noise in Scotland, and in which King James was personally interested, several witches, and among them one Dr. Fian, a schoolmaster, were convicted of having gone to sea in a sieve, raised a storm, and caused a frightful wreck.

9. **like:** in the shape of. Witches were thought to change themselves into the forms of animals. Often, however, the animal had some defect, for the devil's creatures should not be perfect like God's. In rat shape it would be easy for the witch to slip on board the Tiger from the wharf at Aleppo. Once on board, she could work her will in bewitching the vessel on the return voyage. See Kittredge, *Witchcraft in Old and New England*, Chap. x. For *like* cf. i, 7, 21; ii, 3, 84; iii, 4, 100; iv, 1, 87.

10. **I'll do.** What the witch means to do she describes fully in ll. 18-25. By raising storms she will drive the Tiger off her course and keep her tossing about at sea for months, until water and food are exhausted and the captain (the ronyon's husband) is almost dead from hunger, thirst, and lack of sleep. She cannot sink the ship, or cast her away, for the Tiger is fated to reach the home port; but she will make the voyage one long torture. Cf. Kittredge, *Witchcraft*, pp. 12-15, 174 ff.

11. **a wind.** Witches were supposed to govern wind and weather. Sailors frequently paid them for favourable winds or bribed them not to let ill winds blow. Ovid's Medea can 'calm the rough waves by her charms or stir them up when they are at rest; can drive away the clouds or spread them over the sky, and can banish or summon the winds at will' (*Metamorphoses*, vii, 200-202). See Kittredge, *Witchcraft*, Chap. viii.

14. **all the other:** all the others, i.e., all the other winds. By causing now this wind to blow, now that, she means to keep the Tiger tempest-tossed and far from home.

15. **ports they blow:** the harbours to which they blow. She controls the *directions* of the various winds and so can keep the Tiger away from any port.

17. **card:** compass—properly, the part of the compass on which the points are marked and over which the needle plays. The Mariner in Lyly's *Gallathea*, i, 4, boasts of his knowledge of the 'Carde' and 'the two and thirty poynts for the winde.'

18. **drain ... hay:** keep him at sea till all the water on board shall be exhausted and he shall be parched with thirst.

20. **penthouse lid.** A penthouse is a shed or lean-to attached to a building and having but one slope to its roof. The eyelid with its fringe of eyelash is compared to such a roof. Cf. Dekker, *Satiromastix*, 1602 (Pearson ed., I, 239):

> The haires that like a lace
> Are sticht vnto the liddes, borrow those formes,
> Like Pent-houses to saue the eyes from stormes.

21. **forbid:** under a ban or spell. To *forbid* means, literally, 'to pray *against*.'

22. **sev'nights:** se'nnights, weeks. Our Teutonic ancestors counted time by *nights* and *winters*. Cf. *fortnight.*—**nine.** Three and its multiple nine were magic numbers. Cf. ll. 35, 36; iv, 1, 1. See Karl Weinhold, *Die mystische Neunzahl bei den Deutschen* (Berlin Academy, *Abhandlungen*, 1897). Cf. the anonymous play *Looke About You* (Malone Society, ll. 2125-2130), printed in 1600 (sig. H 2 rº):

> Then nyne times like northen laplanders,
> He backward circled the sacred Font,
> And nyne times backward sayd his Orisons,
> As often curst the glorious hoast of heauen,
> As many times inuocke[d] the fiends of hell,
> And so turn'd witch, for Gloster is a witch.

23. **dwindle, peak, and pine.** All three verbs mean the same thing—'waste away.' Cf. the old-fashioned word *peakèd* for 'thin,' 'emaciated.' Witches were thought to cause emaciation by melting a waxen image of their victim (see Kittredge, *Witchcraft*, Chap. iii), but this is not a case of image magic: the shipmaster is to be brought to the point of death from weariness, hunger, and thirst.

24. **cannot be lost:** since fate has decreed that it shall come safe to harbour at last.

28. **thumb.** Fragments of dead bodies were used in evil magic, and were thought to be especially powerful if the person had died a violent death (see iv, 1, 30). Since the pilot

had been wrecked on the homeward passage, his thumb would work as a powerful charm to keep the Tiger away from port. See Kittredge, *Witchcraft*, Chap. vii.

32. **Weird Sisters:** misprinted *weyward* in the Folio here and in i, 5 (letter), ii, 1, 20, but spelled *weyard* in all other places (iii, 1, 2; iii, 4, 133; iv, 1, 136). These forms at all events indicate dissyllabic pronunciation. The phrase 'Weird Sisters' was adopted by Shakespeare from Holinshed, where it is explained as equivalent to 'the goddesses of destinie.' His adoption of the phrase shows that he also adopted the interpretation, and that therefore his witches are the representatives or agents of fate. We shall find that this is the case throughout the play. See Introduction, pp. xvi–xx.

33. **Posters ... land:** travellers who ride through the air, posthaste, over sea and land.

35. **Thrice to thine,** etc.: three times round (hand-in-hand in the magic dance) for thy turn, and three times for my turn. See l. 22, note.

38. Macbeth and Banquo enter, on their way to Forres (see scene iv). They are talking about the battle and the weather. They are separated by a slight interval from their troop, so that the Weird Sisters meet them alone. The day is *foul* because of the bad weather, *fair* because of the glorious victory. So King Henry, speaking of the stormy morning on the day of the Battle of Shrewsbury, says: 'Nothing can seem foul to those that win' (*1 Henry IV*, v, 1, 8). Macbeth's casual remark carries our minds back to the last speech in scene i ('Fair is foul, and foul is fair') and thus suggests a mysterious relation, unsuspected by Macbeth himself, between him and the Weird Sisters.

40–43. The Weird Sisters, though masquerading as witches, appear far more unearthly than any mortal hags with whom Macbeth and the Elizabethans were familiar. This is one of the passages that sharply distinguish these great ministers of fate from the ordinary witch of Macbeth's or Shakespeare's time.—**wild in their attire.** From Holinshed: 'There met them three women in strange and wild apparell, resembling creatures of elder world,' i.e., of ancient times.[1] How the Weird Sisters were attired on Shakespeare's stage we cannot tell; but manifestly they were not dressed like the witches of everyday life, with whose appearance Macbeth (and the audience as well) would be perfectly familiar.—**question**: hold converse with.

44. **choppy**: chapped.

45. **should be women**: ought to be women (to judge by your general appearance).

46. **beards**. Witches were often thought to be bearded, and, indeed, the haggard old women who passed for witches must often have had some beard. Compare the famous scene in *The Merry Wives* (iv, 2) where Falstaff is disguised as Mother Prat, a reputed witch, and Evans, catching sight of his beard, exclaims: 'I think the oman is a witch indeed. I like not when a oman has a great peard.'

53. **fantastical**: imaginary; creatures of the deluded imagination.

54. **show**: seem, appear to be. Cf. i, 2, 15.

55, 56. **with ... hope**: with present honour of noble possession (the two thaneships) and great prediction of royal hope (the crown). Banquo emphasizes the distinction between the mere greeting of the First and the Second Sister, on the one hand, and the actual prediction of the Third Sister, on the other.

57. **That ... withal**: so that he seems carried out of himself (as in a trance) by it (your salutation). Macbeth uses almost the same words in describing his feelings in the letter to his wife (i, 5): 'Whiles I stood rapt in the wonder of it.'

58. **seeds**. Future events are contained (in embryo) in time's seeds; their occurrence, if they come to pass, will be the sprouting of the seeds. Cf. *Winter's Tale*, iv, 4, 489, 490:

> Let nature crush the sides o' th' earth together
> And mar the seeds within!

[1] 'Thre wemen, clothit in elrage and uncouth weid,' i.e., in unearthly and strange attire (Bellenden); 'tres apparuere muliebri specie, insolita vestitus facie' (Boece).

Eggs are sometimes substituted for seeds in this metaphor, as in ii, 3, 63, 64. Both figures are combined in *2 Henry IV*, iii, 1, 82–86:

> A man may prophesy,
> With a near aim, of the main chance of things
> As yet not come to life, which in their seeds
> And weak beginnings lie intreasured.
> Such things become the hatch and brood of time.

60, 61. **neither beg . . . hate:** neither beg your favours nor fear your hate. For the order of words cf. ll. 55, 56.

67. **get:** beget. Banquo was the mythical ancestor of the royal Stuarts.

71. Macbeth's father Finlaeg (Finlay), Thane of Glamis, had died shortly before. Holinshed (following Boece and Bellenden) calls him *Sinell*.

72, 73. Macbeth, who has been absent from court on an arduous campaign, knows nothing of Cawdor's treason. Banquo is similarly uninformed. It is clear that the 'assistance' given by Cawdor (i, 2, 52) was secret and that Cawdor was not present in the battle. His treason had been discovered after Macbeth left the court, and he was under arrest when the battle took place. Cf. ll. 109 ff., below.

74. **the prospect of belief:** the farthest look into the future that belief can take.

75, 76. **from whence . . . intelligence:** from what source you have this strange information. Manifestly the prophesy is supernatural: is it derived from good spirits or from demons? Macbeth balances the same question in ll. 130–137.—**owe:** own, possess, have.

79, 80. **bubbles.** In Holinshed both Macbeth and Banquo make light of the predictions: 'This was reputed at the first but some vaine fantasticall illusion by Mackbeth and Banquho, insomuch that Banquho would call Mackbeth in iest, king of Scotland; and Mackbeth againe would call him in sport likewise, the father of manie kings.' In Shakespeare, there is a marked contrast between them in both words and demeanour. Macbeth is deeply impressed and intensely serious; Banquo takes the incident rather lightly, though later it assumes importance in his mind (ii, 1, 20, 21; iii, 1, 1–10). The difference is one of temperament. For Banquo's mildly humorous style cf. l. 107; i, 4, 32, 33; ii, 1, 4, 5; iii, 1, 26–28.—**are of them:** belong to that category. *Of* (emphatic) is partitive.

81. **corporal:** corporeal, material.

84. **the insane root:** probably hemlock root (one of the ingredients in the hell-broth in iv, 1, 25), though other roots were known to have a similar effect. Steevens quotes Greene, *Francesco's Fortunes*, 1590 (ed. Grosart, VIII, 195): 'You haue eaten of the rootes of Hemlock, that makes mens eyes conceipt [i.e., imagine] vnseene obiects.'—**insane:** causing insanity. The accent is thrown back upon the penult since the next syllable in the verse bears the ictus. Such dissyllabic adjectives had a variable accent in Shakespeare's time: e.g., *human(e)*, *divine*, *complete*, *profound*, *obscure* (ii, 3, 64). See Schmidt's *Shakespeare-Lexicon*, pp. 1413–1415.

86. **Your children,** etc. Macbeth repeats the part of the prediction that concerns Banquo in order to prompt Banquo to repeat 'You shall be king.' Thus he assures himself that he has heard aright.

89–97. Ross refers particularly to both parts of the double victory, as the Sergeant had done (i, 2)—to the battle with the rebels (including the single combat with Macdonwald) and to the defeat of the Norwegian king.

92, 93. **His wonders . . . his:** The wonder he feels (which tends to make him speechless—dumb with admiration) vies with the wish he has to utter thy praises. If the wonder remains *his* (i.e., if he continues to feel it to its full extent), he will be unable to speak, and therefore the praises (being unuttered) will not be *thine*. On the other hand, if the praises win the day and insist on being uttered, then he will no longer be *dumb* with wonder. The result of the contention is *silence* on the King's part: his wonder wins the contest.—**with that:** by that contest between dumb wonder and the wish to utter praise.

96. **Nothing afeard:** not at all afraid.

97. **Strange images of death:** death in strange and dreadful forms. Ross suggests that it is natural for so great a warrior as Macbeth to feel no fear of suffering death when he was so fully occupied in inflicting it on the foe.—**tale:** count—'as fast as they could be counted' (Johnson). *Hail* is substituted for the Folio reading *tale* by many editors.—For *Came* the Folio misprints *Can* (corrected by Rowe). See Textual Notes, p. 231, below.

98. **post with post:** one messenger riding post after another.

104. **earnest:** a small payment in advance to bind a bargain; hence, a specimen and assurance of what is to come.

106. **addition:** title. Ross unwittingly repeats the salutation of the Second Sister.—**worthy:** noble. Cf. i, 2, 24.

107. **What . . . true?** Cf. note on l. 79.

108. **lives.** See note on l. 72.—**dress me.** Shakespeare is remarkably fond of metaphors from clothing. The same figure occurs in ll. 144–146 and in v, 2, 20–22.

109. Angus shows no surprise at Macbeth's remark about Cawdor. He was well aware that the report of the thane's treason had probably not reached Macbeth's ears (see note on l. 72). He himself was not informed about all the details. His companion, Ross, knew rather more (see i, 2, 52, 53), but had not told Angus everything.

111. **combin'd:** secretly allied.

112, 113. **line the rebel:** support Macdonwald.—**hidden help.** Clearly he was not present and fighting in the battle. Macbeth knew nothing about his treason. Cf. note on i, 2, 52.—**vantage:** opportunity.—**both:** i.e., both the rebel Macdonwald and the king of Norway.

115. **confess'd.** Cf. i, 4, 5, and note.

117. **is behind:** remains, to follow in due succession. Cf. Lyly, *Euphues* (ed. Bond, I, 279): 'But the greatest thinge is yet behinde.'

120. **home:** to the full; to its logical conclusion.

121. **enkindle you unto:** fire you with hope for (not, en-

courage you to try to win). Banquo has no thought of warning
Macbeth against action, for it never occurs to him that his
friend can be disloyal to Duncan. His warning is rather
against trusting dubious prophecies and thus entertaining false
hopes.

125, 126. Win us: gain our confidence.—**betray's ... consequence:** disappoint our hopes in something of great importance that was to follow.

127. Cousins. A common greeting among noblemen, most
of whom were in fact related on account of frequent intermar-
riages. Banquo steps aside to converse with Ross and Angus,
and thus an opportunity is given for Macbeth's soliloquy.

128. swelling: stately. Cf. *Henry V*, Prologue, 3, 4:

> A kingdom for a stage, princes to act,
> And monarchs to behold the swelling scene!

130. soliciting: attempt to influence me.

131. good: from a good source.—**ill:** from an evil source;
diabolical in origin. Cf. ll. 75, 76.

132. earnest of success: an assurance or pledge of what is to
follow (that is, of the promised kingship). Cf. l. 104. *Success*
does not mean 'prosperity in my efforts,' but merely 'what is
to follow,' 'the future.' Cf. *Much Ado*, iv, 1, 235-237:

> Doubt not but success
> Will fashion the event in better shape
> Than I can lay it down in likelihood.

The fulfilment of the prophecy about the thaneship of Cawdor
is the *earnest*, since it shows that the Weird Sisters tell the
truth. Macbeth argues that, since Satan is the father of lies (cf.
l. 107), a truthful prophecy can hardly be of diabolical origin.

134. yield to: give access to, allow it to enter my mind.—
suggestion: evil thought, temptation.

135. image. Macbeth has a visualizing imagination. What
to most men would be a vague idea, is to him a *thing seen* in
all the colours of reality. When it occurs to him that the

quickest way to get the crown would be to kill the King, in a
flash he sees himself actually committing the murder.—**unfix
my hair.** Cf. v, 5, 10–13.

136. **seated:** firm and intrepid; not easily agitated.

137. **Against the use of nature:** contrary to my natural habit
(for Macbeth is not accustomed to feel fear).—**Present fears:**
actual objects of fear; frightful things that are before one's
eyes. Cf. ll. 95–97.

139. **fantastical:** imaginary. Cf. l. 53. This soliloquy is certainly meant to mark the moment when the thought of murdering Duncan first enters Macbeth's mind. To infer from
Lady Macbeth's words in i, 7, 47–52, that Macbeth had plotted
the murder before the action of the play begins, destroys the
whole effect of the present passage.

140–142. **my single state of man:** my weak human condition; my nature as a poor, feeble human creature. *Single* for
'weak' is common. Perhaps there is a suggestion of the metaphor which represents a man's nature as a state or kingdom.
Cf. *Julius Cæsar*, ii, 1, 63–69 (cited by Staunton):

> Between the acting of a dreadful thing
> And the first motion [i.e., the first thought of it], all the interim is
> Like a phantasma or a hideous dream.
> The genius and the mortal instruments
> Are then in council, and *the state of man,*
> *Like to a little kingdom,* suffers then
> The nature of an insurrection.

The genius is the man's guiding spirit: that is (practically),
his *ego.* This is now considering the deadly means of carrying out the plan—personified as 'the mortal instruments' or
agents. The result is a mutiny of the unruly passions of human
nature against the orderly forces that should control one's mind
and actions. Cf. also *King John*, iv, 2, 245–248 (cited by Liddell):

> Nay, in the body of this fleshly land,
> This kingdom, this confine of blood and breath,
> Hostility and civil tumult reigns
> Between my conscience and my cousin's death.

—**function ... not:** all my senses and faculties (my powers of mind and body) are absorbed and brought into a state of trance by my vision of a future deed (the murder of Duncan), so that I am unconscious of my actual surroundings in the present, and see and feel only the unreal future.—**Look ... rapt.** Banquo and his friends have finished their private conference and observe the abstraction of Macbeth.—**rapt.** Cf. l. 57.

143, 144. **If chance ... stir:** I leave the fulfilment of the prophecy to chance. I will make no effort to win the crown myself. Macbeth belongs to the royal family; Duncan is old and cannot live long; the princes are young and hardly fit to reign; the crown is elective. It is possible enough that he may become king in the natural order of events. Thus he puts out of his mind that thought of murder which had so horrified him. It returns later, and hardens into a purpose (i, 4, 48–53).—**may:** in the permissive sense.

145. **cleave ... mould:** do not fit or adapt themselves comfortably to the wearer's form. Cf. ll. 108, 109.

146. **use:** habit, custom.

147. **Time ... day:** Time, advancing steadily hour by hour, brings even the roughest day to an end. Macbeth is still determined to leave the fulfilment of the prophecy to chance—or, as we sometimes say, 'to time.' Nothing could better express his dismissal of the subject from his mind than his resort to a commonplace reflection. Other forms of the saying are: 'The longest day must have an end' (*Roxburghe Ballads*, II, 241; VI, 344); and Hawes's couplet (*Pastime of Pleasure*, xlii, 10):

> For though the day be never so longe,
> At last the belles ringeth to evensonge.

148. **Worthy:** noble. Cf. l. 106; i, 2, 24, 45, 48.—**stay upon your leisure:** await your convenience.

149. **Give ... favour:** Pardon me.—**wrought:** disturbed, agitated. Macbeth courteously excuses his fit of abstraction as due to his suddenly remembering important business that had slipped his mind.

151. **regist'red:** i.e., 'within the book and volume of my brain' (*Hamlet*, i, 5, 103).

152. **Let us toward the King.** The omission of a verb of motion is a common Elizabethan idiom.

153. **at more time:** when we have more leisure.

154. **The interim . . . it:** when we have thought it over in the meantime. The *interim* or *interval* is personified, and is represented as itself considering the matter.

155. **Our free hearts:** our thoughts and feelings freely. When this scene closes, Macbeth has no intention of murdering Duncan: he has put the thought out of his mind, so he thinks, forever.

Scene IV.

This scene takes place on the day after the events of scenes i–iii. In the meantime Ross has dispatched the commissioners with the King's order for the execution of Cawdor (i, 2, 64–66), and the report of his penitence and death has reached Malcolm's ears.

1. **Are not?** See Textual Notes, p. 231, below.

2. **Those in commission:** the royal commissioners appointed to attend to Cawdor's trial and execution.

5. **confess'd his treasons.** This shows that Cawdor did not actually take arms against the King. If he had fought on the side of the enemy, there would be no sense in saying that he had confessed his treasons very frankly. Cf. i, 3, 111–114.

9–11. **had been . . . trifle:** had learned the lesson how, at death, to part with his dearest possession (life) easily.—**ow'd:** owned.—**As:** as if.—**careless:** uncared-for, worthless, insignificant.

12. **construction:** interpretation, meaning. Cf. *Twelfth Night*, ii, 3, 188–191: 'I will plant you . . . where he shall find the letter. Observe his construction of it.' Duncan has barely uttered these words when another trusted vassal enters, whose face also he has no art to construe.

16. Duncan uses the familiar and affectionate *thou* instead of the more formal *you* in speaking to his near kinsman.

19, 20. **the proportion:** the larger proportion; the preponderance.—**mine** (emphatic): on *my* side of the account—so that the balance might stand in my favour (as having paid more than I owed).

21. **More . . . pay:** And so, even if I should give thee all I possess, the balance would still stand against me.

22 ff. The formality of Macbeth's language here, as elsewhere, is often thought to show hypocrisy; but this is merely the Elizabethan fashion in complimentary addresses. The same formality appears in Ross's address to Macbeth (i, 3, 89–93).

23. **pays itself:** is its own recompense.

24–27. **our duties . . . everything:** Our duties are in the same situation with reference to your throne and royal position (*state*) in which children are with reference to their parents and servants with reference to their masters; for, like children and servants, we can do no more than we ought, no matter how much we may do.—**everything . . . honour:** everything that tends to safeguard and fulfil our obligation to love and honour you.

28. **to plant thee:** i.e., by making thee Thane of Cawdor.

32. **grow.** Banquo speaks in his accustomed half-jesting vein (cf. i, 3, 79, note), echoing the word *grow* just used by the King: 'If I take root when you press me to your heart, and grow there like a tree, whatever fruit I bear shall be yours.'

34. **Wanton:** perverse, contrary, since tears are the natural expression rather of sorrow than of joy. Cf. *Romeo and Juliet*, iii, 2, 102–104:

> Back, foolish tears, back to your native spring!
> Your tributary drops belong to woe,
> Which you, mistaking, offer up to joy.

Cf. also *Tempest*, iii, 1, 73, 74; *All's Well*, iv, 3, 76–79; *Winter's Tale*, v, 2, 49–51; *King John*, v, 7, 108, 109; *Lear*, i, 4, 191–194.

37, 38. **We will:** it is our royal purpose. Duncan changes from the singular *I* to the royal *we*.—**establish . . . Malcolm:** settle my royal rank upon Malcolm as my recognized successor.

39. **Prince of Cumberland.** The throne of Scotland was elective within the limits of the royal family. When Duncan died, the electors were not unlikely to prefer Macbeth, Duncan's cousin, to a young and inexperienced prince like Malcolm. But Duncan's expressed purpose of making Malcolm Prince of Cumberland would, if it were carried out, involve his recognition as heir apparent by all the nobility, and they would thus pledge themselves to elect him when his father should die. It is the 'irony of fate' that Duncan takes occasion to signalize his joy over Macbeth's victories by nominating Malcolm Prince of Cumberland, thus signing his own death warrant. Cf. Holinshed: 'The same night after, at supper, Banquho iested with him [Macbeth] and said; "Now Mackbeth thou hast obteined those things which the two former sisters prophesied, there remaineth onelie for thee to purchase that which the third said should come to passe." Wherevpon Mackbeth reuoluing the thing in his mind, began euen then to deuise how he might atteine to the kingdome: but yet he thought with himselfe that he must tarie a time, which should aduance him thereto (by the diuine prouidence) as it had come to passe in his former preferment [cf. i, 3, 143, 144]. But shortlie after it chanced that king Duncane, hauing two sonnes . . ., he made the elder of them, called Malcolme prince of Cumberland, as it were thereby to appoint him his successor in the kingdome, immediatlie after his deceasse. Mackbeth sore troubled herewith, for that he saw by this means his hope sore hindered (where by the old lawes of the realme, the ordinance was, that if he that should succeed were not of able age to take the charge vpon himselfe, he that was next of bloud vnto him should be admitted) he began to take counsell how he might vsurpe the kingdome by force, hauing a iust quarell so to doo (as he tooke the matter) for that Duncane did what in him lay to defraud him of all maner of title and claime, which he might in time to come, pretend vnto the crowne.'

41. There is to be a general distribution of honours when the Prince is formally invested with his new title.

42. **From hence,** etc. Addressed to Macbeth: 'Let us go hence.'—**Inverness:** where Macbeth's castle is.

43. **bind ... you:** oblige me still further by receiving me as a guest.

44. **The rest ... you:** Even repose, when not used in your service, ceases to be rest and becomes toil. Hence Macbeth will not tarry, but will hasten home to prepare for Duncan's visit.

45. **harbinger:** an officer sent ahead (when a king intends to visit a place) to arrange for proper lodgings (*harbourage*) for him and his suite.

47. **worthy:** noble. Cf. i, 2, 24.

48. Having taken his leave, Macbeth retires to the back of the stage, and Duncan turns to converse with Banquo. Macbeth's soliloquy, then, is spoken just before he goes out of the door. He is in full sight of the audience, but has made his exit from the royal presence. During the soliloquy Duncan is listening to Banquo, who is talking of the battle and praising Macbeth, as appears from ll. 54–56.—**a step:** an advance in honour (for Malcolm).

49. **fall down ... o'erleap:** i.e., if Malcolm is Prince of Cumberland I must either give up all hope of kingship, or must win the crown by my own efforts, in spite of his being the acknowledged successor. Here the thought of murdering Duncan recurs and hardens into a purpose; for it looks as if fate were declining to 'crown' him 'without his stir' (i, 3, 143, 144).

52. **The eye wink at the hand:** Let my eyes not see the deed that my hand commits. Cf. i, 5, 51–55; ii, 2, 50–52.—**let that be.** The sudden but resolute purpose of murder here expressed differs utterly from the horrified imagining in i, 3, 134–142.

56. **Let's after him.** Cf. i, 3, 152.

58. **It:** common in the familiar style to express affection, as here, or contempt, as in *As You Like It*, i, 1, 148: 'It is the stubbornest young fellow of France.'

Scene V.

This scene takes place on the same day as scene iv,—the second day of the action. Lady Macbeth reads only the last part of the letter aloud. What she omits contained matters with which we are already familiar—an account of the battle, of the meeting with the Weird Sisters, of their greeting and prophecy. The letter was written and dispatched in the interval between scene iii and scene iv, before Duncan had invited himself to Macbeth's castle (i, 4, 42, 43). When he wrote it, Macbeth had put the thought of murder out of his mind and had not yet allowed it to reënter his thoughts as a purpose, for Malcolm had not been nominated Prince of Cumberland.

1. **in the day of success:** on my lucky day (the day on which I had won the battle), so that I may put greater faith in their prophecy.

2. **the perfect'st report.** This is often interpreted as 'experience,' which is, of course, the best kind of testimony. But the plain meaning is the best. Macbeth had made inquiries (between scene iii and scene iv) and had learned that the Weird Sisters had a reputation for supernatural knowledge. The fact that he gives them their correct name (Weird Sisters) in the letter shows that he has found out something about them since the interview on the heath. Davenant's version reads: 'I have been told they have,' etc.

4. **made themselves air.** Cf. i, 3, 81, 82. Holinshed's words are: 'the foresaid women vanished immediatlie out of their sight.'—**Whiles:** while.—**I stood rapt.** Once more a repetition of the language of the third scene: 'Look how our partner's rapt' (i, 3, 142).

5-14. **missives:** messengers.—**deliver thee:** report to thee.—**partner of greatness.** Macbeth and his wife are so deeply attached to each other that neither can think of any division or individuality in their interests. Cf. ll. 55–59, 70, 71.

16. **shalt be.** *Shalt* does not express Lady Macbeth's determination. It merely repeats the words of the Third Sister as

quoted in the letter: 'Hail, King that shalt be!' But she instinctively checks herself at the word *king* and substitutes, after a moment's pause, a reticent phrase: 'Glamis thou art, and Cawdor, and shalt be—*What thou art promis'd.*' Cf. l. 56.

18. **th' milk of human kindness.** *Milk* is often used metaphorically for the kindly and gentle qualities in human nature (l. 49). Cf. iv, 3, 98: 'the sweet milk of concord.' Goneril scorns her husband's 'milky gentleness' (*King Lear*, i, 4, 364; cf. iv, 2, 50). See *1 Henry IV*, ii, 3, 35; *Coriolanus*, v, 4, 30, 31; *Titus Andronicus*, ii, 3, 144. Since Lady Macbeth is soliloquizing, we know that she is expressing her real opinion. That she is mistaken in her husband is an inadmissible notion: she knows him thoroughly. Clearly, then, Shakespeare wishes us to believe that Macbeth, like many great soldiers, was personally of a gentle disposition. This quality comes out sharply in the great soliloquy in scene vii, where the 'pity of it' is the last and convincing argument against the murder (ll. 21-25). Shakespeare thus departs significantly from Holinshed, who describes Macbeth as 'somewhat cruell of nature.'

19. **the nearest way.** Like Macbeth, she thinks at once, as anybody would have done in those wild times, of murder as the nearest way. Unlike him, however, she does not try to banish the thought, but entertains it as a definite purpose in which she never falters. This is characteristic of Lady Macbeth: her mind works with directness and intense simplicity, and her will is of steel. The nearest way becomes, in the lines that follow, the only way, for she has no patience with any but the shortest route to any destination.

21. **The illness should attend it:** the evil quality (ruthlessness) which should always accompany ambition. The omission of the relative pronoun, now confined (except in rapid colloquial speech) to the objective case, was once common in the nominative as well.

22, 23. **holily.** The word has a tinge of scorn: 'You wish to do nothing in furthering your aspirations that a *saint* might not do.' Ambition and saintliness are, in her opinion, incompatible.—**wouldst wrongly win:** You are like a gambler who is unwilling to cheat, and yet is eager to win a stake that cannot be won without false play.

24–26. The cry is merely '*Thus* thou must do.' The rest of the sentence is Lady Macbeth's own comment: 'You wish to have the crown; and the crown, if you're to have it at all, demands of you one particular deed: it cries "*Thus* thou must do!" And your reluctance so to act comes rather from a weak fear of sinning than from any strong wish that the deed should not be done. You would not mourn for the King if he were to be killed by accident, or by some third party, without any guilt of yours.' There are no quotation marks in the Folios. Davenant's version paraphrases:

> Thou willingly, Great Glamis, wouldst enjoy
> The end without the means!

27. **my spirits:** my resolution and energy of will. The figure of pouring into the ear must be a reminiscence of the poison in *Hamlet* (i, 5, 63). Cf. also *Othello*, ii, 3, 362: 'I'll pour this pestilence into his ear.' With ll. 27–31 Coad compares *2 Henry VI*, i, 2, 3–12, 63–67, where the Duchess of Gloucester foreshadows the rôle of Lady Macbeth in this scene.

28. **chástise:** rebuke and suppress.

29. **All that impedes thee:** i.e., gentleness of nature and scruples of conscience.—**golden round.** Cf. iv, 1, 88, 89: 'the round And top of sovereignty.'

30, 31. **metaphysical:** supernatural.—**seem ... withal:** seem to intend to cause thee to be crowned with. *Have* is emphatic. For *seem* referring to the future, cf. i, 2, 47. *Withal* means simply 'with,' as often at the end of a phrase.

32. **The King comes here to-night.** Fate advances with rapid steps, as in the entrance of the messengers 'all-hailing' Macbeth Thane of Cawdor immediately after the disappearance of the Weird Sisters (i, 3).—**Thou'rt mad to say it!** To the messenger this sounds merely like a strong expression of surprise, but the audience understands the excitement with which the

Lady greets what seems to her like 'fate and metaphysical aid.'
So in l. 39 'great news' means one thing to the innocent messenger, another to the audience.

34. inform'd: sent me information of the visit.

36. had the speed of: outstripped.

39. The raven. There are ravens flying about the castle, and
their croak, now heard by Lady Macbeth, seems to her even
hoarser than usual, as if they were predicting the King's death.
Some editors, rather prosaically, think that she is alluding to
the breathless messenger. Birds of ill omen play a considerable
part in this tragedy. See ii, 2, 3, 4, 16; ii, 3, 64, 65; ii, 4, 12,
13; iii, 2, 50, 51; iii, 4, 124–126.

40. entrance: trisyllabic. *Fatal* has a double meaning—'di-
rected by fate' and 'fatal to Duncan.' Cf. Lyly, *Sapho and
Phao*, iii, 3: 'The owle hath not shrikte at the window, or the
night Rauen croked, both being fatall.'

41. you spirits. A direct invocation to those evil spirits, whatever they may be, that are always ready to foster murderous
thoughts—'the instruments of darkness,' as Banquo calls them
in i, 3, 124. Shirley, in *The Maid's Revenge*, v, 2 (I 2 r⁰),
imitates the invocation:

> If there be
> Those furies which doe waite on desperate men,
> As some have thought, and guide their hands to mischiefe:
> Come from the wombe of night, assist a maide
> Ambitious to be made a monster like you;
> I will not dread your shapes, I am dispos'd
> To be at friendship with you, and want nought
> But your blacke aide to seale it.

42. mortal: deadly, murderous.

44. Make thick my blood. Blood thickened by melancholy
was thought to cause gloomy ferocity of disposition. Cf. *King
John*, iii, 3, 42–47.

45. th' accéss ... remorse: every way of approach by which
compassion can come to my heart.

46. compunctious ... nature: natural instincts of compassion.

47. fell: cruel, savage.

47, 48. **keep peace ... it:** come between my cruel purpose and its fulfilment (*effect*), so as to prevent that fulfilment and thus to keep the peace.

49. **for:** in exchange for. Take away milk (which signifies gentleness: see l. 18) and substitute gall (which signifies bitter resentment or enmity). Cf. *The Returne from Pernassus*, Part II, v, 4 (ed. Macray, p. 153):

> For had not Cambridge bin to me vnkinde,
> I had not turn'd to gall a milkye minde.

The *murth'ring ministers* (i.e., agents, assistants) are the 'spirits that tend on mortal thoughts.'

50. **sightless:** invisible.

51. **wait on ... mischief:** are on the watch to help forward any of the evil deeds to which our nature is prone.

52. **pall:** cover as with a pall or mantle, enshroud.—**dunnest:** darkest. Cf. ii, 4, 5-11.

53. **my keen knife.** Lady Macbeth so identifies herself with her husband's acts that she thinks of the deed as her own (cf. ii, 2, 13, 14).—**see not.** Cf. i, 4, 52: 'The eye wink at the hand.' But Lady Macbeth's expression is the stronger: even the knife is not to see the wound.

54. **peep:** as with the eye of one single star. Cf. *Lucrece*, 788.—**blanket.** Davenant substituted *curtains*. McPeek (*Modern Language Notes*, XLVI [1931], 391) compares Munday, *Downfall of Robert Earl of Huntington*, v, 1:

> Muffle the eye of day,
> Ye gloomy clouds (and darker than my deeds,
> That darker be than pitchy sable night)
> Muster together on these high-topp'd trees,
> That not a spark of light thorough their sprays
> May hinder what I mean to execute.

See ii, 2, 62, note.

56. See l. 16, and note.

57, 58. **transported me:** swept me forward as in a vision.—**ignorant.** The present is *ignorant* because the substantial fulfilment of one's hopes and fears is known only to the future.

59. the instant: the present moment.

60. Macbeth does not know that his wife has heard of Duncan's visit. His letter was dispatched before he had seen the King (see note, p. 111).

61. as he purposes. Macbeth speaks without sinister emphasis and in as matter-of-fact a tone as he can command, but his face betrays him.

64. the time: the people of the time. 'If you wish to delude people, you must look like the rest of the world, not as if you had something on your mind.' Lady Macbeth goes on to describe the normal expression and demeanour expected of a host.

66, 67. look ... serpent under't. Cf. *Romeo and Juliet*, iii, 2, 73: 'O serpent heart, hid with a flow'ring face!' For other varieties of the Virgilian 'latet anguis in herba' (*Eclogues*, iii, 93) see Tilley, *Elizabethan Proverb Lore*, No. 570.

69. great business. Lady Macbeth, whose eye is on the object to be attained, thinks and speaks of the murder as a glorious deed. The splendour of the prize is reflected in her mind on the action itself.—**dispatch:** management.

71. A stately and sonorous verse, splendidly expressive of Lady Macbeth's enthusiasm for the dominion that is to come. For the use of alliteration cf. iii, 2, 6, 7; iii, 4, 24; iv, 1, 123; iv, 3, 188.

72. We will speak further. In this further conference on the subject, which must be imagined to take place between this scene and the next (before Duncan's arrival), Macbeth declares his resolution to kill the King. Lady Macbeth repeats the upshot of it in i, 7, 49–52, 58, 59.—**clear:** with an unruffled countenance. Cf. iii, 2, 27, 28:

> Gentle my lord, sleek o'er your rugged looks;
> Be bright and jovial among your guests to-night.

73. To alter ... fear: When a person shows a disturbed countenance, it is always inferred that he has something on his mind—and that may rouse suspicion among our guests.—**favour:** countenance, expression.

Scene VI.

This scene takes place toward night on the same day as scene v (see i, 5, 60). Sir Joshua Reynolds, writing of 'repose' in painting, remarks 'that the most ornamental style requires repose, to set off even its ornaments to advantage.' He cites as a parallel 'an instance of repose in that faithful and accurate painter of nature, Shakspeare,' namely, the dialogue between Duncan and Banquo in this scene. 'The subject of this quiet and easy conversation gives that repose so necessary to the mind, after the tumultuous bustle of the preceding scenes, and perfectly contrasts the scene of horrour that immediately succeeds' (*Eighth Discourse at the Royal Academy*, 1778, *Works*, ed. Malone, 1798, I, 252, 253). The relief, however, is merely that which comes from a change of style and from the surface consideration of pleasant objects, not the relief of change in mood. Indeed, the horror of the situation is only increased by the cheerful confidence which Duncan shows in approaching the place of slaughter.

1. **seat:** situation, site.

2, 3. **The air ... senses:** The air, by its freshness and sweetness, appeals pleasantly to our senses and makes them gentle— i.e., soothes them. *Gentle* is proleptic. Dr. Johnson felicitously remarks that it 'intimates the peaceable delight of a fine day.' Banquo repeats the idea in the phrase 'smells wooingly' (l. 6).

4. **martlet:** the house martin, called 'temple-haunting' because it often builds about churches. Davenant has 'Martin.' The Folio misprint—'Barlet'—was corrected by Rowe. Cf. *Merchant of Venice*, ii, 9, 28, 29:

> Like the martlet,
> Builds in the weather on the outward wall.

—**approve:** prove.

5. **By ... mansionry:** by the fact that he has chosen this as a favourite site for his mansions. *Mansionry* (Theobald's cor-

rection for the Folio reading *Mansonry*) is collective, implying many nests—as explained in the graphic details that follow.

6. **wooingly:** so as to appeal to the senses by its delightful freshness.—**jutty:** out-jutting place in the building.

7. **coign of vantage:** advantageous corner or angle.

8. **procreant cradle:** 'cradle where he breeds' (Davenant).

10. Lady Macbeth has been on the watch and meets the King at the castle gate with gracefully ceremonious hospitality. Perhaps we are to suppose that Macbeth distrusts his own self-control and therefore delegates this duty to his wife. Perhaps, on the other hand, it is she who has arranged the matter, fearing that Macbeth will not 'look up clear.' The question is of little moment—for Macbeth must have greeted Duncan soon after. For dramatic purposes Shakespeare's adjustment is manifestly the best that could be devised.

11–14. Duncan begins with a general statement: 'We sometimes find that the love which others feel for us actually gives us trouble, because they follow us about and force their attentions on us; yet we always (*still*) are grateful for such affection, because it is *love*, of which one cannot have too much.' Then he makes a particular application of this principle to the present circumstances. 'Herein (i.e., in making this remark) I am teaching you, Lady Macbeth, how to pray God to reward me for the efforts I am causing you to make in receiving me as your guest, and also how to thank me for the trouble I am giving you by my visit—for the visit is due to my love for you and your husband.' Cf. *Winter's Tale*, v, 3, 9: 'We honour you with trouble.'—**'ield:** yield, i.e., repay.

14. **All our service,** etc. Duncan has paid Lady Macbeth a formal but skilfully turned compliment in the taste of the Elizabethan time. Her reply is equally graceful. Her ceremonious style is in fine contrast to Duncan's gracious badinage. It must not be regarded as intended by Shakespeare to suggest hypocrisy, for the Lady is a good actor: she would have spoken quite as formally if she had harboured no designs on the King's life. See note on i, 4, 22.

16, 17. **single:** feeble, insignificant—here in special antithesis to *double*.—**contend against:** vie with, offset.

19. **late dignities:** the thaneships of Glamis and Cawdor.

20. **We rest your hermits:** we remain your grateful beads-men. A beadsman was a poor dependent supported by some patron, for whom he was bound to pray in return for bounties received. Among the beadsmen attached to noble houses were frequently hermits—that is, persons under a vow to live a solitary life devoted to prayer and to subsist upon alms. A hermitage was not necessarily in a deserted place: it might be near a castle or even in a city. Cf. *Titus Andronicus*, iii, 2, 40, 41: 'as perfect As begging hermits in their holy prayers.'

21. **We:** plural for *I* (the 'royal *we*').—**cours'd him:** rode rapidly after him.

22. **púrveyor:** literally, an officer who precedes a king or a great noble when on a journey and makes arrangements for provisions and other supplies. See note on **i, 4, 45:** 'I'll be myself the harbinger.'

23. **holp:** old form for *helped*.

26. **theirs:** their vassals and dependents (Lat. *suos*).—**what is theirs:** all their possessions (Lat. *sua*).—**in compt:** on ac-count, on deposit (not as their own property, but as something entrusted to them by you).

27. **make their audit:** render their account (as an agent or banker must do).

28. **Still:** always, at any moment. She means that everything she and her husband have is really the King's, and that he has the right to call for it, or any part of it, at any time.

30. **our.** Prolonged, and so dissyllabic on account of the change of pitch involved. Cf. i, 2, 5.—**graces:** royal favours. Cf. i, 4, 28, 29.

31. **By your leave:** Allow me! A courteous remark as Dun-can takes her by the hand and escorts her in.—**hostess.** Dun-can's manner is still that of gracious playfulness. Compare Banquo's report of the King's message to Lady Macbeth in ii, 1, 15, 16.

Scene VII.

This scene takes place on the same day as scenes iv–vi. Supper is in progress in the great hall of Macbeth's castle at Inverness. The Sewer is the butler who has charge of serving the supper; *service* means 'viands,' 'a course.' The King and the nobles, with Lady Macbeth, are at table; Macbeth has left the company and now appears in a corridor or anteroom. His feelings have become too much for him and he wishes to be alone with his thoughts.

1–24. The three dissuading reasons form a climax. The lowest stands first—mere prudence; then, on a higher plane, comes loyalty, in its threefold aspect of kinship, allegiance, and hospitality; and finally, most powerful of all, there is 'human kindness': to murder so gracious a king will be horrible; the whole world will be overcome with pity for the victim. In short, to kill Duncan would be unwise, disloyal, and monstrously cruel. I can find no incitement, then, but reckless ambition—and unrestrained ambition ruins itself. The upshot of the matter is expressed in l. 31: 'We will proceed no further in this business.' It is characteristic of Macbeth's nature (as described by his wife in i, 5, 18) that pity comes at the acme of the climax. Cf. *Othello*, iv, 1, 206: 'But yet the pity of it, Iago! O Iago, the pity of it, Iago!'

1, 2. If it were done when 'tis done, etc. The first *done* and *'tis* are both emphatic: If the whole business were *over and done with* as soon as the mere deed had been done, then it would be well to act without delay. The next sentence repeats the same thought in outspoken terms and full detail. Note the shrinking vagueness of the *it* as compared with the plain-speaking *assassination* that follows. Cf. the soliloquy in iii, 4, 122–126, which begins in precisely the same way (with *it*): 'It will have blood, they say; blood will have blood.'

3. Could ... consequence: could catch (as in a trammel or net) that which may follow (and so prevent its occurrence).

4. his surcease: Duncan's death; his ceasing to exist. So

Davenant understood the phrase: he substituted 'his Death.'
Cf. *Lucrece*, 1766: 'If they surcease to be that should sur-
vive.'—**success:** the future (as in i, 3, 132)—not (as in modern usage) a successful outcome. Macbeth, dwelling on the
thought, expresses it twice in almost identical terms; for 'catch
success' is synonymous with 'trammel up the consequence.'
Many scholars take *his* in the sense of *its* and interpret *his surcease* as 'the surcease of the consequence'; but this is harder
and less likely.—**that:** so that.

5. **the be-all and the end-all:** all there is to the matter, and
the end of the whole affair.

6. **But here:** only *here* (emphatic), i.e., in this world only.—
bank and shoal of time. A man's lifetime is a mere sandbank
or bar, soon to be covered by the sea of eternity. Cf. *Henry V*,
iv, 1, 100, 101: 'Even as men wrack'd upon a sand, that look
to be washed off the next tide'; *3 Henry VI*, v, 4, 31: 'Bestride
the rock—the tide will wash you off.' *Shoal* is spelled *Schoole*
or *School* in the Folios. Some critics would read *school* and
interpret *bank* as the bench on which the pupil sits; but (1) the
figure is much less impressive; (2) *upon this school* is not
English; (3) Shakespeare never uses *bank* for 'bench.'

7. **jump the life to come:** risk eternity; take a leap in the
dark so far as the next world is concerned.

8-10. **still:** always.—**here:** in this world.—**that ... inventor:**
so that he who murders a king in order to get the crown is
teaching others how to murder *him* for the same purpose.
Cf. Seneca, *Thyestes*, 310, 311:

> In patre facient quicquid in patruo doces:
> Saepe in magistrum scelera redierunt sua.

11. **Commends:** puts, applies. The metaphor of the chalice
is in Holinshed: 'The pricke of conscience ... caused him euer
to feare, least he should be serued of the same cup, as he had
ministred to his predecessor.' Doubtless Shakespeare also remembered *Hamlet*, v, 2, 336-339.—**th' ingredience** (collective): the elements composing the draught in the chalice.

17. **borne ... meek:** exercised his powers and privileges with so mild a sway. Holinshed describes Duncan as 'soft and gentle of nature' and having 'too much of clemencie.'

18. **clear:** free from blame; void of reproach.

20. **taking-off.** Cf. iii, 1, 105.

21, 22. **like:** in the form of (as in i, 3, 9; ii, 3, 84; iii, 4, 100; iv, 1, 87).—**babe.** Such an infant is a fit object for human tenderness and therefore an apt emblem for Compassion. Or Pity (as Macbeth's imagination, roused to full activity by his emotions, conceives) may take the form of an angelic messenger (*cherubin*) sent from heaven to spread the tidings. So Patience is personified by Othello as a 'young and rose-lipp'd cherubin' (iv, 2, 63).—**Striding the blast:** riding the wind—because the feeling of compassion will spread through the realm as if borne 'on the wings of all the winds.' Cf. *Psalms,* xviii, 10.

23. **sightless:** invisible (i, 5, 50).—**couriers:** coursers, steeds.

25. **That:** so that.—**drown the wind:** as heavy rain is said to do. Cf. *Troilus and Cressida*, iv, 4, 55: 'Where are my tears? Rain, to lay this wind' (Liddell).

25–28. Ambition, first thought of as a *spur*, becomes the horseman who, meaning to vault into the saddle, springs too high and falls disgracefully. *Side* (not in the Folios) was supplied by Hanmer. Sense and metre both favour it. Some editors follow Rowe and put a dash after *th' other*, supposing Macbeth's speech to be interrupted by the sudden entrance of his wife. But this is a soliloquy, representing *thought*, not utterance, and the thought cannot be thus interrupted. The mixture of metaphors is above criticism. The figures are not confused by a feeble vision; they are rather welded together by the white-hot imagination of the speaker; or, to express the fact differently, they crowd into Macbeth's mind too fast for one to be fully expressed before the other begins. Cf. Gabriel Harvey, *Foure Letters*, 1592 (ed. Grosart, I, 193): 'How many millions of greene youthes, haue in ouermounting, most ruefully dismounted, and left behinde them full-lamentable

Histories?' Compare the scene between Duke Humphrey of Gloucester and the Duchess in *2 Henry VI* (i, 2), and the Duchess's recourse to sorcery (i, 4), which present striking parallels to *Macbeth*.

29. Lady Macbeth, worried by her husband's absence from the table, and fearing for his resolution, has come to seek him. —**supp'd:** finished supper.—**chamber:** the dining room, hall.

30. **Know you not he has?** Of course he has! You might know that well enough without asking!

33. **all sorts of people.** In i, 2, Shakespeare has taken pains to show how high Macbeth stands with 'all sorts of people' from the Sergeant, who expresses the feelings of the army, to the highest nobility and the King himself. The present speech proves the deliberate expository purpose of that scene.

34. **would be:** wish to be, demand to be—and so practically equivalent to 'ought to be' or 'must be.'

35–37. **Was the hope,** etc.: Was the hope that you expressed to me a little while ago like a reveller, who wakes next morning sallow of face and is nauseated by the mere thought of his last night's debauch?—**dress'd.** Shakespeare is fond of metaphors from clothing. Macbeth has just used such a figure, and his wife picks it up and gives it a scornful turn. With the metaphor of 'dressing one's self in hope' (for entertaining hope) cf. 'attir'd in wonder' (*Much Ado*, iv, 1, 145); 'attir'd in discontent' (*Lucrece*, 1601); 'dress'd myself in such humility' (*1 Henry IV*, iii, 2, 51); 'clothe me in a forc'd content'(*Othello*, iii, 4, 120).—**green:** sallow. Cf. Chaucer, *Troilus*, iv, 1154, 1155:

> And thus she lith with hewes pale and grene
> That whilom fressh and fairest was to sene;

Romeo and Juliet, ii, 2, 8: 'sick and green.'

39. **Such:** just as fickle as your resolution has proved.

42. **the ornament of life:** life's chief adornment—the crown.

43. **And live a coward:** i.e., do without it, and always accuse yourself of cowardice when you think of the opportunity you have lost.—**esteem:** opinion.

44. **wait upon:** constantly attend, always follow.

45. **th' adage.** The proverb takes many forms. Thus, John Heywood, *Dialogue*, 1562, Pt. i, Chap. xi (Spenser Society ed., p. 28): 'The cat would eate fyshe, and would not wet her feete'; *Piers the Ploughman's Crede*, l. 405: 'Thou woldest not weten thy fote and woldest fich kacchen'; Gower, *Confessio Amantis*, iv, 1108, 1109:

> And as a cat wold ete fisshes
> Withoute wettinge of his cles;

Mabbe, *Celestina*, Act vii (Tudor Translations, p. 126): 'Trowtes cannot be taken with drie breeches. And if the Cat will have fish, she must wet her foote.' Mediæval Latin forms are 'Cattus amat pisces, sed non vult crura madere' (Egbert of Lüttich, *Fecunda Ratis*, l. 336; ed. Voigt, p. 74); 'Catus wult piscem, sed non wult tangere flumen' (Wyclif, *De Blasphemia*, cap. 15; Wyclif Society ed., p. 222); 'Modus iste catinus, Vult piscem sed non piscari' (Geoffrey de Vinsauf, *Poetria Nova*, ll. 2021, 2022; ed. Leyser, *Historia Poetarum*, 1721, p. 974); 'Catus amat piscem, sed non vult tingere plantas.' See Hazlitt, *English Proverbs*, 1907, p. 412; Skeat, *Early English Proverbs*, pp. 87, 88; Apperson, *English Proverbs*, p. 88.

47. **do more.** The Folios misprint 'no more.' Corrected by Rowe. Davenant has 'he who dares more, is none.'—**none:** no man, but a wild beast. Cf. *Measure for Measure*, ii, 4, 134, 135:

> Be that you are;
> That is, a woman. If you be more, you're none.

Lady Macbeth picks up her husband's phrase and carries it out with scornful logic: 'If you were not prompted by a man's spirit when you broke this enterprise to me, then you must have been ruled by a *beast*!'

48. **break:** broach, propose. Macbeth had not, in strictness, broached the plan to his wife, but in her taunting mood she chooses to interpret his letter (with its 'promised greatness' and its 'lay it to thy heart') as such an opening of the subject.

Her words are quite precise enough for anger. If they were more accurate, they would be less true to nature.

49. Lady Macbeth is referring to what Macbeth had said in a conversation implied in his remark 'We will speak further,' at the end of scene v. This conversation of course took place in the interval between scenes v and vi, and was in reality a continuation of that in scene v. What Macbeth then said is made clear by the Lady's résumé in the present speech.

50–52. **And to be . . . man:** And by being more daring than you were then—by daring to *do* what you then dared to *resolve*—you would be even more the man than you then were.—**Nor . . . both:** When we had that conversation, Duncan (though expected) was not at our castle. Neither time nor place, therefore, was consistent with action at that moment. Yet you were quite ready to *make* an opportunity in case he should not come after all. You were brave enough when there was no chance to act. Now that the moment has come, its presence unmans you. There is no allusion here to any plot formed before the beginning of the play. It is clear that the thought of murder did not enter Macbeth's mind until after the prediction on the heath. See i, 3, 130–144, and notes.

53. **have made themselves:** i.e., by Duncan's visit, which puts him in our power.—**that their fitness:** that very fitness of time and place.

54. **unmake:** unnerve, unman.

55. **the babe.** See note on iv, 3, 216.

58. **sworn.** In the interview in question (between scene v and scene vi), then, the Lady had won from her husband a promise that she calls an oath.

59. Here Macbeth drops the question of scruples, beaten from that posture of defence by his wife's reproaches. But he instantly opposes the act on another ground—risk of failure. His opposition is now weak, however, and soon overborne.— **We fail?** Since all Lady Macbeth's speeches in this dialogue begin with a scornful question, this is best taken in the same

way, as an exclamatory question indicating impossibility, not merely as a statement ('If we fail, we fail'). The Folios have a question mark. Davenant's version uses an exclamation point: 'How fail!'

60. **But:** only.—**screw your courage.** The figure is from a crossbow or arbalest. The bow was made of steel, and a mechanical device, sometimes worked with a crank, was attached to the barrel of the gun, by means of which the bow was bent. When fully screwed up, the bowstring would catch in a notch (the *sticking place*) and the weapon was ready to discharge. Lady Macbeth says that all her husband has to do is to get his courage screwed up to the point at which it will remain ready for action without slipping back like an arbalest only partly wound up. Cf. l. 79 and note.

61. **we'll.** Not 'we shall,' but 'we will,' expressing determination—'We'll have no failing. I will see to that!'

62, 63. **Whereto . . . him:** and his hard journey will make him all the readier to sleep, and to sleep soundly.—**chamberlains:** grooms of the bedchamber; officers who had charge of the King's chamber and slept by his bed as a bodyguard.

64. **wassail:** carousal. — **convince:** overpower completely (Latin *convinco*).

65–67. **memory . . . only.** According to the old physiology, memory resided in the base of the brain at the back of the skull, just above the neck, and reason in the upper part below the dome of the head. The fumes of wine were thought to rise from the stomach to the brain and thus to cause drunkenness. Cf. Bacon, *Sylva Sylvarum*, §726. The memory is first overcome, being the warder (the guard at the entrance); then the *receipt* (receptacle, container) of reason is invaded by the fumes. Memory is properly called the *warder* because, as Brunetto Latini writes, it 'records and retains whatever comes into it' (*Tesoretto*, vii, 258–260). Cf. Tomkis, *Lingua* (1607), v, 3:

> By this time Appetite is at the Table,
> And with a lowly Cringe presents the Wine,
> To his olde Master Gustus; now he takes it,

> And drinkes perchance to Lingua, she craftily
> Kisses the Cup, but lets not downe a drop,
> And giues it to the rest; 'tis sweet, theile swallow it,
> But when 'tis once descended to the stomack,
> And sends vp noisome vapours to the braine,
> 'Twill make them swagger gallantly, theile rage
> Most strangely, or Acrasias Art deceiues her.

—**limbeck:** the alembic, or cap of the still, into which the fumes rise in the process of distillation. Cf. Whitlock, *Zootomia*, 1654, p. 249: 'The foulnesse of the *stomack* filleth the *head*, (the top of the *Alembick*).' Boyle, in *The Usefulnesse of Experimental Natural Philosophy* (Part II, Essay 2, ed. 1664, p. 34), remarks that the Galenical physicians 'compare the Stomach to a Seething pot, and the Head to an Alembick' into which the vapours ascend. Cf. Lyly, *Euphues* (ed. Bond, I, 248): 'The first draught of wine doth comfort [i.e., strengthen] the stomacke, the seconde inflame the lyuer, the thirde fume into the heade.'

68. **drenched:** drowned.

70. **put upon:** impute to; charge to, as a crime.

71. **spongy:** drunken (literally, soaking, absorbent).

72. **quell:** killing. Lady Macbeth exalts the murder as a splendid deed, precisely as she had spoken when she bade her husband 'put this night's great business into my dispatch' (i, 5, 68, 69).

73. **mettle** (the same word as *metal*): substance, quality.

74. **receiv'd:** accepted as true, believed. Macbeth (as men have a way of doing) accepts his wife's suggestion and puts it forward as if it were his own. Lady Macbeth (as wise wives do) is satisfied to have him adopt her idea and does not dispute his originating it.

77. **receive it other:** take it otherwise.

78. **As:** in view of the way in which. *Roar* is emphatic.

79. **settled:** determined, resolute.—**bend up:** stretch to its utmost tension, make quite ready for instant action. The metaphor (from a bow or crossbow) is suggested by Lady Macbeth's words in l. 60.

80. **corporal:** bodily.

81. **mock the time:** beguile the world. Here Macbeth returns to his wife the counsel she had given him near the end of scene v: 'to beguile the time, Look like the time.'—**show:** appearance, looks and bearing. Macbeth and his wife return to the table and rejoin the royal party.

ACT II. Scene I.

Banquo, having attended the King to his chamber, has taken leave of him for the night and is on his way to bed. Fleance, his son, acts as his squire.

3. **at twelve.** It is past midnight, then, and very dark. The murder, as we shall see later, was committed soon after two o'clock in the morning. Cf. notes on ii, 3, 26, and v, 1, 39.

4. **Hold:** a mere interjection, like 'here!' (cf. French *tiens*). —**take my sword.** While in attendance on the King, Banquo has worn his sword, as a matter of ceremony (a part of his uniform, so to speak). Being now off duty, he hands it to his squire. Some theorists have tried to find a deep meaning in all this; but it is a simple incident that merely shows that everybody feels safe in Macbeth's castle.—**husbandry:** economy, frugality. Another instance of Banquo's mildly humorous way of speaking. Cf. i, 4, 32.

5. **candles.** Cf. *Romeo and Juliet*, iii, 5, 9: 'Night's candles are burnt out.'—**that too:** his dagger.

6. **heavy summons:** a summons to sleep; a feeling of heavy drowsiness.

7. **would not sleep.** A vague presentiment makes him reluctant to go to bed; but he has no definite suspicion, whether of Macbeth or of anybody else.

8, 9. **nature . . . repose:** to which human nature gives admission in sleep—dreams which we cannot control. On Banquo's dreams (l. 20) cf. ll. 50, 51: 'wicked dreams abuse The curtain'd sleep.' Banquo's prayer was of the kind common enough in old days. Disagreeable and evil thoughts were supposed to be put into men's minds by demons during the helplessness of the will in slumber. Compare the prayers of Donalbain and his chamberfellow in ii, 2, 25. The same idea underlies the child's petition 'I pray to God my soul to keep' (i.e., 'to guard'). So in Bishop Patrick's prayer for Wednesday night: 'Defend us from all the powers of darkness.' In a prayer to the Virgin we read: 'Sende me grace for to slepe, and good dremys for to mete [i.e., dream]' (Brand, *Popular Antiquities*, ed. Hazlitt, III, 150). *Gives way to* means simply 'gives access to,' 'allows to enter the mind.' Banquo has dreamt of the Weird Sisters (whom he regards as evil spirits) and he prays to be spared such dreams to-night. Some critics have laboured to complicate the tragedy by making Banquo a half-accomplice, or a passive sympathizer—albeit more or less without his being aware of it himself—in Macbeth's plans, but this is quite unwarranted. For Shakespeare to represent Banquo (King James's supposed ancestor and the founder of the Stuart dynasty) as other than upright and loyal would have been extraordinary indeed.

9. Banquo is startled by the sudden sight of the torch. As soon as he hears Macbeth's voice, his nervous start passes, and he returns his sword to Fleance.

14. **largess:** gifts, gratuities.—**offices:** the kitchen, buttery, and other rooms or buildings in which the servants of a great establishment did their work; hence—the servants of the house.

15. **withal:** with.

16, 17. **hostess:** Duncan continues the pleasant humour in which he addresses the Lady in i, 6, 10 ('our honour'd hostess') and 31 ('By your leave, hostess'). This is his last word, and it carries our minds back to the light and cheerful temper of sc. vi, with telling effect.—**shut up . . . content:** He [Duncan] concluded what he had to say with expressions of unmeasured satisfaction at your hospitality. For *shut up* in the sense of 'conclude' cf. Dekker, *A Rod for Run-awayes* (ed. Grosart,

IV, 297, 298): 'I will now shut vp my Discourse'; Coryat, *Crudities*, 1611, p. 492: 'Thus finally I shut vp the description of this strange Vessell with a certaine admirable thing that I heard reported of it.'

18, 19. **Our will . . . wrought.** Our wish to entertain the King sumptuously (which otherwise would have had free play) was hampered by lack of due preparation.

22. **entreat . . . serve:** induce the busy times to grant us a little leisure for the purpose. *We* is not the 'royal *we*,' unconsciously adopted by anticipation: it means simply 'you and I.' —**serve:** serve our turn.

24. **At your kind'st leisure:** It is very kind of you! Any time when you are at leisure will suit me.

25. **cleave to my consent:** join my party; espouse my interests.—**when 'tis:** when the time comes. Macbeth intends Banquo to suppose that he means to wait patiently for the old King's death and then to become a candidate for the crown. This was, indeed, his intention before the nomination of the Prince of Cumberland (i, 4, 37 ff.). Davenant makes Macbeth express himself rather more clearly: 'If when the Prophesie begins to look like truth You will adhere to me.'

26. **So:** provided that.

27. **still:** ever, always.

28. **franchis'd:** free from blame; void of reproach.—**clear:** untarnished, stainless.

29. **I shall be counsell'd:** I shall be ready to follow your suggestion. Thus even the loyal Banquo admits the possibility that Macbeth may someday become a candidate for the crown without injustice to Duncan or his family. In making Banquo unflinchingly loyal to Duncan, Shakespeare varies from Holinshed, who says that Macbeth, 'communicating his purposed intent with his trustie friends, amongst whome Banquho was the chiefest, vpon confidence of their promised aid, slue the king.'

31. **drink:** the regular draught of warm spiced wine or the like which every Elizabethan or mediæval gentleman and

lady took just before going to bed. Such a draught was thought to be eminently wholesome.

32. **the bell:** a signal that all is ready for the murder (cf. l. 62; ii, 2, 5–14).

33–49. This famous soliloquy shows once more the highly imaginative nature of Macbeth, which visualizes to the verge of delirium. Cf. i, 3, 130 ff.

36. **fatal:** showing what is fated; sent by fate to lead me to Duncan (cf. iii, 4, 62, 63).—**sensible:** perceptible.

44, 45. **Mine eyes ... rest:** My eyes have become fools (because they are deluded and see what does not exist) in comparison with my other senses (which are under no such delusion); or else, if the dagger is real, my eyes (which alone perceive it) are worth all my other senses together. For *fool* cf. *King Lear*, ii, 2, 131, 132:

> None of these rogues and cowards
> But Ajax is their fool;

i.e., 'a fool in comparison with them,' 'vastly their inferior.'

46. **dudgeon:** haft made of dudgeon, which was a kind of fine-grained wood (probably boxwood) much used for this purpose. Macbeth sees and notes each minute detail—so vivid is the vision, so keen his imaginative eye.—**gouts:** big drops.

48. **informs:** gives [false] information (not, takes shape). Cf. Davenant: 'that thus informs my eye-sight.'

50. **wicked dreams.** This sentence is a good commentary on Banquo's prayer in ll. 7–9.—**abuse:** deceive, delude.

51. **The curtain'd sleep:** the sleeper in his curtained bed.— **Now.** Omitted in the Folios, but imperatively demanded by metre and stylistic principles. Inserted by Davenant and Rowe.

52. **Hecate:** the classical goddess of witchcraft. Witches were still believed, in the seventeenth and eighteenth centuries, to make sacrifices, sometimes even of human victims, to the devil or the infernal powers. See Kittredge, *Witchcraft in Old and New England*, pp. 93 ff., 148.

53. **Alarum'd:** summoned to action (*all' arme*, 'to arms').

54. **watch.** When the wolf howls, the murderer knows that the time has come for him to act. Hence the howl of the wolf is the murderer's timepiece, striking the hour. Watches (which struck the hours) were large, costly, and elaborate articles of luxury in Shakespeare's time. They had not become so common and cheap as to seem prosaic. Davenant takes *watch* to mean 'watchword' and, in his version of *Macbeth*, changes the figure: 'Whose howling seems the watch-word to the dead' (perhaps a misprint for *deed*).—**thus.** With this word Macbeth begins to walk stealthily toward the staircase leading to Duncan's chamber.

55. **strides:** long steps (so as to make as few footfalls as may be). The Folios read 'sides'—corrected by Pope. Cf. *Lucrece*, 365: 'Into the chamber wickedly he stalks.'

57. **which way they.** The Folios read 'which they may.' Corrected by Rowe.

58. **prate of my whereabout.** There is a reminiscence of *Luke*, xix, 40: 'If these should hold their peace, the stones would immediately cry out.' Cf. *Habakkuk*, ii, 11: 'For the stone shall cry out of the wall, and the beam out of the timber shall answer it.'

59. **the present horror:** the dreadful silence which suits the time and the purpose, and which Macbeth wishes should not be disturbed by the sound of his steps. Cf. Dryden's phrase 'an horrid stillness' (*Astræa Redux*, 7; the *dira quies* of Tacitus, *Annals*, i, 65).

60, 61. **Whiles ... gives:** Talking tends to postpone action that should be carried out in the heat of resolution. Probably an interpolation. See Introduction, p. vii. Line 60 is broken (and filled out) by the sound of the bell, Lady Macbeth's signal that all is ready (l. 32; ii, 2, 5–14). Cf. *Lear*, i, 1, 312: 'We must do something, and i' th' heat'; *Othello*, i, 2, 40: 'It is a business of some heat'; *3 Henry VI*, v, 1, 49: 'Strike now, or else the iron cools.' The mediæval proverb is, 'Dum fuerit calidum, debetur cudere ferrum' (*Romanische Forschungen*, III, 639). For English examples (from Chaucer to the present time) see

Apperson, *English Proverbs*, pp. 605, 606.—**gives.** Such plurals are common, especially when the subject has a collective sense.

62. **done.** Cf. i, 7, 1, 2; iii, 2, 12.—**The bell invites me.** See ll. 31, 32. Cf. *Merry Wives*, iii, 2, 46: 'The clock gives me my cue.'

Scene II.

Lady Macbeth is waiting in an inner court or small roofed entry at the foot of the staircase leading up to the corridor on which Duncan's chamber opens. His chamber seems to be the third from the head of the stairs. In this same part of the castle, which is separated from the rest of the building by a gate, are the apartments of Macbeth and his wife. The two young Princes have chambers in the same corridor as their father. Donalbain sleeps in the second chamber from the head of the stairs, that next to the King's; Malcolm doubtless has the room nearest the staircase on the same floor. Thus the King and his sons, with their personal attendants, are lodged in the best and safest part of the castle—that wing or tower occupied by Macbeth and Lady Macbeth. Banquo, Macduff, and the rest are lodged in another part of the castle and cannot enter that portion of the building just described (after the gate has been shut for the night) without being admitted by the Porter. His lodge is at some distance from the court or roofed entry where Lady Macbeth is waiting.

1, 2. Lady Macbeth has taken her night-draught, like the grooms and everybody else in the castle. She feels a slight exhilaration. No Elizabethan would have found this unbecoming, but some modern critics have taken great pains to explain away the obvious meaning. Cf. Shirley, *Love's Cruelty*, iii, 1 (E 2 v⁰):

> Hee's drunke already.
> That which has raisd me but to noble anger
> Is his distraction.

3. the fatal bellman. It was custom in London for the bell-man or town-crier to visit condemned prisoners on the night before their execution. Aldis Wright aptly quotes Webster, *The Duchess of Malfi*, iv, 2, 173–175 (ed. Lucas, II, 98):

> I am the common Bell-man,
> That usually is sent to condemn'd persons
> The night before they suffer.

Cf. Middleton, *Blurt, Master Constable*, iii, 1, 104, 105 (ed. Bullen, I, 54):

> The owl, whose voice
> Shrieks like the bellman in the lover's ears.

In 1604 Robert Dow, a citizen of London, gave a fund 'vnto Saint Sepullcher's parish . . . for some especiall man, by them to be appoynted to come to the saide Prison [Newgate], the midnight before execution, and then distinctly and solemnly to ring a hand bell: then to pronounce with a loud voice at the prison grate, a godly, and Christian remembrance or exhortation, appoynted by the Lorde Bishoppe' (Stow's *Annales*, ed. Howes, 1615, p. 862; cf. Andrew Knapp and William Baldwin, *The New Newgate Calendar*, I, 259, 260).—**fatal:** sent by the Fates and foretelling death. Cf. ii, 1, 36.

4. the stern'st good-night. The owl's hoot portends death, according to a superstition not yet extinct. Cf. *1 Henry VI*, iv, 2, 15: 'Thou ominous and fatal owl of death'; *Richard III*, iv, 4, 507: 'Out on ye, owls! Nothing but songs of death?'; Spenser, *Faerie Queene*, i, 5, 30: 'The messenger of death, the ghastly owle'; Lyly, *Sapho and Phao*, iii, 3: 'The owle hath not shrikte at the window, or the night Rauen croked, both being fatall'; Webster, *The Duchess of Malfi*, iv, 2, 181–183 (ed. Lucas, II, 98):

> The Schritch-Owle, and the whistler shrill,
> Call upon our Dame, aloud,
> And bid her quickly don her shrowd.

See note on i, 5, 39.

5. **The doors:** all the doors through which Macbeth would have to pass, including that of the King's chamber.—**grooms:** the two chamberlains, the grooms of the chamber.

6. **mock their charge:** make a mockery of their duty (of guarding the King).—**possets.** A posset was a curdled drink made of spiced wine or ale, hot milk, grated biscuit, pulp of apples, etc.

7. **That:** so that.—**nature:** their natural vitality; their vital forces.

8. **live or die.** Lady Macbeth does not mean that there is any danger that the chamberlains will not recover, but merely that they are drugged, as we might say, 'within an inch of their lives.' Holinshed writes that the two chamberlains of King Duff 'fell to banketting with Donwald and his wife, who had prepared diuerse delicate dishes, and sundrie sorts of drinks for their reare supper or collation, wherat they sate vp so long, till they had charged their stomachs with such full gorges, that their heads were no sooner got to the pillow, but asleepe they were so fast, that a man might haue remooued the chamber ouer them, sooner than to haue awaked them out of their droonken sleepe.'

9. Macbeth, as he is descending the staircase after the murder, is startled by an imaginary voice (l. 35), and calls out, though we are not to suppose that he loses his self-control so completely as to shout. The Folios, however, have *Enter Macbeth* before 'Who's there?' and it is possible that, in Shakespeare's theatre, Macbeth was at this point visible to the audience (though not to his wife) as he passed over the upper stage, which they were to imagine was the staircase or a landing halfway down.

11, 12. **Th' attempt...us.** *Confounds* means 'ruins.' Two interpretations are possible: (1) 'If he has made the attempt and failed, then we are ruined.' (2) 'We are ruined, it seems—and that too not by a crime, but by a bungling attempt to commit a crime!' The former is much the better; for what follows shows that Lady Macbeth still hopes that her husband has succeeded in killing Duncan without rousing anybody. Davenant's version reads: 'the attempt without the deed Would ruin us.'

13, 14. Had he not, etc. An amazing touch—utterly unexpected, yet perfectly true to nature; for Lady Macbeth had strong affections as well as a will of steel and an eye which never left the object until it was attained.

19. Hark! Macbeth does not answer his wife's question, because he is startled by an imaginary noise. After listening for a moment, and finding that it is nothing, he passes over to a different subject.

20. th' second chamber: the second from the head of the staircase, Duncan's being the third.

21. sorry: wretched, miserable.

23. There's one, etc. Macbeth goes on to tell of what he heard as he was passing the second chamber (Donalbain's) on his way back from Duncan's room after committing the murder. He heard two persons speaking, and he had to stand there, waiting outside their door with his bloody hands, until they were quiet again and he could creep by without being heard. Incredible as it seems, many readers, and some critics, have supposed these two persons to be the heavily drugged grooms!

23-25. in's: in his.—**That:** so that.—**say their prayers.** Cf. Banquo's prayer against bad dreams (ii, 1, 7-9).—**address'd them:** applied themselves.

26. two lodg'd together. 'Yes,' the Lady answers, 'there are two persons lodged in that second chamber, Donalbain and another.' The second person may have been an attendant or (perhaps more likely) a young nobleman. It was common for guests to have crowded quarters, even in great houses.

27, 28. God bless us! and **Amen!** marked the conclusion of the prayers just mentioned.—**As:** as if.—**hangman's:** executioner's.

29. List'ning their fear: listening to the prayers they uttered in their alarm at their bad dreams and sudden awaking.—

I could not say 'Amen!' To say 'amen' when one heard another utter a blessing was so habitual as to have become instinctive. Macbeth follows his habit, without conscious thought,
and finds that for the first time in his life he cannot pronounce
the word. His panic at the experience is natural, not naïve.
He feels as if his inability were an assurance of damnation.

30. **it:** not 'the murder,' but 'this trivial incident' (his inability to say 'amen').

33, 34. **thought:** thought upon, regarded.—**After these ways:**
in such a fashion as this (with an agonized dwelling on every
little detail, and perplexity as to what it means).—**So:** if we
do so.—**mad:** a kind of premonition of Lady Macbeth's final
collapse.

35. There are no quotation marks in the Folios. It is clear,
however, that 'the innocent sleep . . . feast' is Macbeth's
imagination dwelling on the idea and not a part of the cry of
the voice. Cf. Tomkis, *Lingua* (printed in 1607), v, 10:

> Soft son of night, right heir to quietness,
> Labour's repose, life's best restorative,
> Digestion's careful nurse, blood's comforter,
> Wit's help, thought's charm, the stay of microcosm,
> Sweet Somnus, chiefest enemy to care.

37. **knits up:** untangles and straightens out.—**ravell'd:**
tangled, snarled.—**sleave:** skein (as of silk thread).

38. **bath:** because it cures weariness, like a warm bath after
toil. Cf. Glapthorne, *Albertus Wallenstein*, iv, 3:

>   Natural rest
> Is, like a wholesome bath to limbs oppress'd
> With gouts and aches, to a troubled mind
> A most excelling medicine.

Of course Shakespeare read Ovid at school and he cannot have
forgotten the beautiful invocation to Sleep in the *Metamorphoses*, xi, 623–625 (cited by Rushton):

> Somne, quies rerum, placidissime, Somne, deorum,
> Pax animi, quem cura fugit, qui corpora duris
> Fessa ministeriis mulces reparasque labori!

40. **Life's feast** has two courses—food and sleep. Macbeth regards the second as even more sustaining to our nature than the first. The second course was the most substantial part of an Elizabethan dinner.—**What do you mean?** A scornful protest against Macbeth's wild talk.

42, 43. The various titles show that this imagined cry is in part a mental echo of the Weird Sisters' greeting.

45, 46. **unbend:** relax. It is weak and ignoble of you to harbour such crazy notions. *Brainsick* was a somewhat contemptuous synonym for 'insane.'

47. **witness:** evidence.

53–55. **The sleeping ... pictures:** The sleeping and the dead are only pictures of living men, and pictures cannot hurt you. *Childhood* and *painted* are emphatic: 'Only a *child* is afraid of a devil that is not real but only *painted*!' Cf. *Selimus* (1594), ll. 425, 426 (Malone Society):

> A tale to terrifie yoong babes:
> Like diuels faces scor'd on painted poasts;

Webster, *The White Devil*, iii, 2, 151: 'Terrify babes, my lord, with painted devils'; *Lucrece*, 244, 245:

> Who fears a sentence or an old man's saw
> Shall by a painted cloth be kept in awe.

56. **gild** in the sense of 'stain' or 'smear' (with blood) was common in Shakespeare's time, as in *King John*, ii, 1, 316: 'all gilt with Frenchmen's blood'; and *Edward III*, iv, 4, 97, 98 (ed. Brooke, *Shakespeare Apocrypha*, p. 94):

> For I will staine my horse quite ore with bloud,
> And double guild my spurs, but I will catch him.

Cf. 'golden blood' (ii, 3, 118) and 'red gold.' For the pun cf. *2 Henry IV*, iv, 5, 129; *Henry V*, ii, Chorus, 26. Its use here has a somewhat savage effect (quite intentional), but was not so startling to the Elizabethans as to us; for they were accustomed to punning on the most serious occasions.

57. **within:** behind the scenes. The knocking is outside the

gate which separates this tower or wing of the castle from the rest of the building. See De Quincey's essay 'On the knocking at the gate in Macbeth' for a splendid fantasia on this incident.

59, 60. Steevens compares Seneca's *Phædra*, 715-718 (a tragedy which is quoted in Latin in *Titus Andronicus*, ii, 1, 135; iv, 1, 81, 82):

> Quis eluet me Tanais aut quae barbaris
> Maeotis undis Pontico incumbens mari?
> Non ipse toto magnus Oceano pater
> Tantum expiarit sceleris.

62. **The multitudinous seas:** all the seas of the world with their multitude of tumbling waves. Cf. Munday and Chettle, *The Death of Robert Earl of Huntington*, ii, 2: 'The multitudes of seas dyed red with blood.' See note on i, 5, 54.— **incarnadine:** turn blood-red.

63. **Making the green one red:** turning the green colour of the seas into one universal red, or 'total gules' (*Hamlet*, ii, 2, 479). Cf. *The Two Noble Kinsmen*, v, 1, 49, 50 (cited by Aldis Wright). By a misprint in the Folio a comma is put after *one*. Davenant's version reads:

> No, they would sooner add a tincture to
> The Sea, and turn the green into a red.

66. **entry:** entrance.

68, 69. **Your constancy . . . unattended:** Your customary firmness has abandoned you.

70, 71. **nightgown:** dressing gown (such as would be thrown on by one called from sleep in haste).—**to be watchers:** not to have gone to bed.—**Be not lost.** Macbeth is once more 'rapt,' as in i, 3, 130.

72. **So poorly:** so weakly; in such a poor-spirited way.

73. Shaking off his fit of abstraction, Macbeth replies: 'It would be well for me to be unconscious forever, if consciousness means that I must always look my crime in the face.' **To know my deed** is equivalent to a conditional clause: 'If I must know my deed'; 'must feel my crime to the full.'

Scene III.

The Porter, with just enough wine and wassail left in his
brains to make him slow-motioned and whimsical, enters, rub-
bing the sleep from his eyes. He grumbles professionally at
having so much to do, and the fancy occurs to him that he is
after all not so hard-worked as Satan's gate-keeper. Instantly
he begins to play the part, specifying certain proverbial types
of sinners, whom he pretends to let in. Every one of these
types was instantly recognized by the audience as a stock
character in the talk of the day. His soliloquy has been much
attacked as poor fooling and probably therefore not genuine;
but there is nothing about it that is un-Shakespearean. When
he jocosely pretends to be porter at hell gate, the audience
feels (as Bodenstedt notes) that he is more nearly right than
he is aware. The contrast between his low comedy and the
tragic facts is dramatically forcible. Again, something is absolutely necessary to make an interval between the exit of
Macbeth and his reëntrance at l. 47.

2. **should:** certainly would.—**old:** a great deal of. *Old* was
in common colloquial use to express emphasis: as, 'old swearing' for 'hard swearing' (*Merchant of Venice*, iv, 2, 15); 'old
tumbling' (Fletcher, *The Pilgrim*, iii, 7); 'old utis' for 'a
high old time,' 'high jinks' (*2 Henry IV*, ii, 4, 21).

5. The farmer had held his wheat for a high price, regardless
of the needs of the poor. But the next crop seemed likely to be
heavy, and, desperate at the prospect of a drop in prices, he
committed suicide. Such speculating in foodstuffs has been a
favourite subject for denunciation ever since the Middle Ages.
See Introduction. Cf. Rowlands, *Looke to it: for Ile Stabbe
Ye*, 1604, p. 26:

> You that at plentie euermore repine,
> And hang your selues for griefe, to see the same.

Sordido, in Ben Jonson's *Every Man Out of His Humour*,
1599, hangs himself for the same reason.

5. **Come in time!** Your arrival is opportune (a mere phrase of welcome).—**napkins:** handkerchiefs.—**enow:** enough (usually plural).

7. **in th' other devil's name.** The porter cannot remember the name of any devil but Belzebub.—**equivocator.** A fling at the Jesuits, who were believed to justify deceptive ambiguity and 'mental reservations.' Many Catholics were executed for treason in Elizabeth's time and there was much excitement about plots against the government.

8. **swear . . . scale:** make an ambiguous statement and swear to it; swear to a form of words that has two meanings, so that, whichever way the oath is understood by the hearer, the swearer can say to himself that he meant the other thing. *Scale* has no reference to the 'scales of justice'; it suggests merely the exact balance between the two meanings of the ambiguous assertion.

8, 9. **committed treason enough for God's sake.** The Roman Catholic plots against the government were, of course, entered into conscientiously by the plotters. Queen Elizabeth had been excommunicated in 1570 by Pope Pius V, who had released her subjects from their oath of allegiance.

11, 12. **tailor . . . hose.** Tailors were proverbially said to steal cloth in the process of cutting out clothes for their customers. The kind of French hose (i.e., breeches) here intended was tight-fitting and required little cloth. It would take a skilful thief, therefore, to embezzle any.

18. **goose:** the tailor's pressing iron, so called from its shape and the shape of its handle.

20. **devil-porter it:** act the part of a demon porter at hell gate.

21. **professions:** occupations.—**the primrose way.** Cf. *All's Well*, iv, 5, 57: 'the flow'ry way that leads to the broad gate and the great fire'; *Hamlet*, i, 3, 50: 'the primrose path of dalliance'; *Matthew*, vii, 13: 'Wide is the gate, and broad is the way, that leadeth to destruction.'

22. **Anon, anon!** In a moment!—addressed to those who are knocking. Cf. i, 1, 9.

23. **remember the porter:** holding out his hand for a tip.

25. **so late.** It is early in the morning (l. 51); but it is late for the porter to be on duty.

26. **the second cock.** The times of cockcrow were conventionally fixed as follows: first cock, midnight; second cock, 3 A.M. (cf. *Romeo and Juliet*, iv, 4, 3, 4); third cock, an hour before day. The murder was committed shortly after two o'clock in the morning (v, 1, 39, 40). It is now about four or five o'clock (l. 51). Thus scene ii must take up at least two or three hours. This is mathematically impossible, but involves no dramatic inconsistency; for the long-continued emotional strain leaves on the audience the impression that time enough has elapsed to account for the interval required. Cf. note on iii, 4, 127.

41. **gave you the lie:** floored you and sent you sound asleep —with a pun on *lie*.

42. **i' the very throat on me.** To lie in one's throat was to tell a deep or deliberate lie, as opposed to a mere lip falsehood. The porter's pun is obvious. *On* in the sense of *of* is extremely common, and so is *of* in the sense of *on*.

45, 46. **took up my legs:** succeeded in getting my feet off the ground. The figure is from wrestling.—**made a shift:** contrived, managed.—**cast:** throw, with a pun on *cast* in the sense of 'vomit.'

51, 52. **timely:** early.—**bring:** conduct, escort.

53. **this:** the trouble of conducting me to the King's chamber.

55. **The labour,** etc.: when any kind of labour gives us pleasure, the pleasure relieves all the effort that the labour involves.

56. **the door:** not the door of the King's chamber, but a door that leads to the staircase. Macbeth has led Macduff to one of the exits at the rear of the stage.—**to:** as to.

57. **my limited service:** my specially appointed duty.

58. **to-day.** Cf. i, 5, 60, 61.—**appoint:** arrange, plan.

59. **Where we lay.** We have already noted (p. 133) that these nobles were lodged in a different part of the castle from that occupied by Macbeth, Duncan, and the Princes.

61 ff. Lamentings heard i' th' air. Such prodigies were regularly supposed to announce or accompany the death of princes or great men. Cf. *Julius Cæsar*, ii, 2, 17–24.

63. combustion: tumult and disorder in the state.

64. hatch'd to. As we say 'A son was born to him.' Cf. *2 Henry IV*, iii, 1, 86: 'Such things become the hatch and brood of time.'—**the óbscure bird:** the bird of darkness; the owl (cf. ii, 2, 3, 4). For the accent of *obscure* see i, 3, 84.

66. feverous. Malarial fever (fever and ague) was prevalent in Shakespeare's England, for there were immense undrained marshes, and the chills and shaking that accompany it are often used in metaphor. Cf. 'life's fitful fever' (iii, 2, 23); 'Then comes my fit again' (iii, 4, 21); 'the fits o' th' season' (iv, 2, 17).

71. Confusion: destruction.

73. The Lord's anointed temple: the sacred body of the King, which is not only God's temple, but God's *anointed* temple. Our bodies are God's temples according to the passage in *2 Corinthians*, vi, 16: 'Ye are the temple of the living God.' So Laertes refers to the body as 'this temple' in *Hamlet*, i, 3, 12. Duncan, as king, is in biblical phrase 'the Lord's anointed' (*1 Samuel*, xxiv, 10). Anointing was a part of the ceremony of coronation.

77. Gorgon. The horrible sight will, like the Gorgon Medusa, turn his eyes to stone. We still speak of 'a stony stare.'

79. alarum bell: literally, the bell that calls to arms (*all' arme*). Cf. ii, 1, 53; v, 5, 51.

81. counterfeit: imitation, likeness. Cf. *Midsummer Night's Dream*, iii, 2, 364: 'death-counterfeiting sleep.'

83. great doom's image: a sight as dreadful as the Day of Doom. Cf. *Lear*, v, 3, 263, 264:

> *Kent.* Is this the promis'd end?
> *Edgar.* Or image of that horror?

Image means 'exact likeness,' as when we say 'The girl is the image of her mother.'

84. **As from your graves.** Macduff dwells upon the thought of the Day of Doom, when the dead shall arise in their shrouds. —**like sprites:** in the guise of spirits (all in white). Cf. i, 3, 9; i, 7, 21; iii, 4, 100; iv, 1, 87.

85. **To countenance this horror:** to keep the horrid sight in countenance; that is, to accord with it, to give it a proper setting.

90. **repetition:** recital, report.

93. **What, in our house?** A natural expression for an innocent hostess, horrified at the thought that such a thing has happened to one of her own guests. So the Lord Mayor, in Heywood's *1 King Edward IV* (Pearson ed., I, 62), when the King pretends to be ill and hurries away, cries out:

> O God! here to be ill!
> My house to cause my soureigns discontent!

98. **nothing serious in mortality:** nothing worth while in human life.

99. **toys:** trifles.—**grace:** goodness, virtue.

100, 101. **The wine of life . . . brag of:** Everything that gave zest to existence is gone, now that Duncan is dead, and this world (like an empty wine vault) has nothing left of its vaunted pleasures—nothing but the nauseous dregs of life.

102. **You are.** How Malcolm is 'amiss' (i.e., out of order; in a bad condition of health and fortune) is explained in what follows. Such half-punning shifts in meaning from one speech to another are very common in Shakespeare. From the Elizabethan point of view there was nothing in Macbeth's language to suggest the artificial style of one who is acting a part. Compare, indeed, the style of Macduff in ll. 71–85.

103. **head:** well-head or source. Macbeth uses four synonyms. We have already noted how apt he is to dwell upon an idea and express it in different figures of speech (see i, 7, 4).

106. Cf. Holinshed's account of the murder of King Duff: 'In the morning when the noise was raised in the kings chamber how the king was slaine, his bodie conueied awaie, and the

bed all beraied [i.e., daubed] with bloud; he [Donwald] with the watch ran thither, as though he had knowne nothing of the matter, and breaking into the chamber, and finding cakes of bloud in the bed, and on the floore about the sides of it, he foorthwith slue the chamberleins, as guiltie of that heinous murther.'

107. **badg'd:** marked. The figure comes from the badges or cognizances which retainers of great houses were accustomed to wear. These consisted usually of the arms or crest of the head of the house. Cf. *Hamlet*, ii, 2, 474–480.

110. **They star'd and were distracted:** that is, when roused from their heavy, drugged sleep. Macbeth killed the chamberlains before they had a chance to say a word (see iii, 6, 15, 16).

112. **fury:** madness, frenzy (not, wrath). Cf. l. 114.

113. Macduff's question implies neither anger nor suspicion. He simply regrets that it is not possible to interrogate the grooms. Yet even here we find him instinctively uneasy with regard to Macbeth, and this feeling grows steadily (cf. ii, 4, 37, 38) until he becomes Macbeth's chief opponent.

114. **amaz'd:** utterly confused in mind, mentally paralyzed (*not*, as in modern English, surprised).—**temp'rate:** self-controlled, calm. Cf. iv, 3, 92.—**furious:** frenzied.

116. **expedition:** haste.

118–122. The vivid and eccentric figures in Macbeth's speech are in accord, psychologically, with his visualizing habit of mind, stimulated as that is by the horror he feels at his crime and by fear of detection. Eighteenth-century critics, however, found the whole speech in very bad taste. Warburton calls it 'an unnatural mixture of far-fetch'd and commonplace thoughts, that shews him to be acting a part'; and Dr. Johnson conjectures 'that Shakespeare put these forced and unnatural metaphors into the mouth of Macbeth as a mark of artifice and dissimulation, to show the difference between the studied language of hypocrisy, and the natural outcries of sudden passion.' Clearly, however, the other characters find nothing suspiciously artificial in Macbeth's language. His theory of the guilt of the chamberlains is accepted by Lennox and (as the next scene shows) by Macduff and Ross.

118. **silver skin.** The figure gives a vivid idea of bloodless pallour. Blood is called golden because it is red, and 'red gold' is a common expression. See ii, 2, 55, 56. Cf. Rowlands, *Doctor Merrie-man*, 1609, p. 6: 'His Rapier hilts embrew'd in Golden blood.'—**lac'd:** marked as if in the figures of lace.

119. **a breach.** The figure is of a city wall in which assailants have made a breach by which they can enter and lay waste the town. Cf. Yarington, *Two Tragedies in One*, 1601, C2 vº:

> Or with my sworde Ile open wide a gate,
> For wrath and bloudie death to enter in.

—**nature:** life, vitality.

120. **wasteful:** destructive.

122. **Unmannerly breech'd:** covered in an unseemly fashion.
—**refrain:** hold one's self back, check one's impulse.

124. **'s love:** his love.—**Help me hence, ho!** Here Rowe inserts '*Seeming to faint.*' Lady Macbeth's swoon is manifestly genuine, though the contrary has sometimes been maintained. It is one of several indications of the strain to which she is subjected and under which she finally gives way. Others are 'So, it will make us mad' (ii, 2, 34); 'Nought's had, all's spent,' etc. (iii, 2, 4–7). Her strength is rather nervous than physical, and it has been taxed to the utmost—not only by what she has thought and seen and done herself, but by the necessity of first inspiring her husband and afterwards calming his agitation and preparing him for the present ordeal. Now that all is done—the murder discovered, and the guilt fixed upon the chamberlains—her strength gives out as the hideous details are brought before her mind's eye by Macbeth's description.

125. **Look to the lady.** Macduff, who is standing at some distance from Lady Macbeth, calls out instinctively to those who are near her. There is some confusion as she is supported and helped toward the door, and Malcolm and Donalbain take advantage of it to exchange a few hasty words.

126. That . . . ours: who have the best right to talk on this subject. *Argument* is common in the sense of 'topic,' 'plot of a play,' 'subject matter.'

127. here: emphatic. This castle—fatal to our family—is no place for our laments. We are in danger ourselves, and must first provide for our own safety.

128. Hid in an auger hole: lurking in some unsuspected hiding place.

130. tears . . . brew'd: the time has not come for us to weep for our father.

130, 131. Nor . . . motion: nor has our grief, strong as it is, yet begun to act—it is felt, not shown.—**Look to the lady.** Banquo's parting injunction to the servants who conduct Lady Macbeth to her chamber.

132. our . . . hid: clothed our poor shivering bodies.

135. scruples: vague suspicions.

136. thence: making God's strength my fortress.

137. undivulg'd pretence: the as yet undiscovered purpose of the traitor (whoever he is) who has contrived this foul deed. Banquo has, as yet, no distinct suspicion of Macbeth.

139. briefly: quickly, hurriedly.—**put on manly readiness:** clothe ourselves properly (not, put on our armour). *Ready* and *unready* were the ordinary adjectives for 'dressed' and 'undressed.' *Manly readiness* suggests also 'self-possession'—that frame of mind that shall make us ready for action.

140–142. Well contented: well and good.—**office:** function.

143. the false man: i.e., any false man. The young Princes suspect everybody. Macbeth, as their near kinsman and a probable candidate for the throne, seems to them likely to have contrived the murder (ll. 146, 147), but they are by no means certain that Banquo and Macduff are not his accomplices. Malcolm's suspicion of Macduff comes out clearly in their interview in iv, 3.—**I'll to England.** Cf. Holinshed: 'Malcolm Cammore and Donald Bane the sons of king Duncane, for feare of their liues (which they might well know that Mackbeth would seeke to bring to end for his more sure confirmation in the estate) fled into Cumberland, where Malcolme remained, till time that saint Edward the sonne of Ethelred recouered the dominion of England from the Danish power, the which Edward receiued Malcolme by way of most friendlie enterteinment: but Donald passed ouer into Ireland.'

144. **Our . . . fortune:** this separation for our fortune; the fact that we try our luck separately.

146, 147. **There's daggers.** A singular verb for a plural is common, especially in the contraction *there's* when the subject follows. Cf. v, 3, 13.—**the near . . . bloody.** *Near* is a comparative: The nearer one of these nobles is to us in kindred, the more likely he is to wish to murder us. Cf. *Richard III*, ii, 1, 92: 'Nearer in bloody thoughts, but not in blood.' The remark, though specially applicable to the present circumstances, is proverbial in tone, and suggests the prophesy in *Matthew*, x, 36: 'A man's foes shall be they of his own household.' Cf. *Hamlet*, i, 2, 65: 'A little more than kin, and less than kind!' and Webster, *The Duchess of Malfi*, iv, 2, 288–290 (ed. Lucas, II, 101):

> You have bloodely approv'd the auncient truth,
> That kindred commonly do worse agree
> Then remote strangers.

147, 148. **This . . . lighted:** This arrow of murder is still in the air; this murderous plot has not yet attained its full object (our death as well as our father's).

150. **dainty of:** punctilious about.

151, 152. **shift away:** steal away unperceived.—**warrant:** justification. A man has a right to steal when what he takes away is merely—*himself* from a place of deadly peril.

Scene IV.

This scene takes place on the same day as scene iii, but much has occurred in the interval. The young Princes have made their escape; the electors have met and chosen Macbeth king, and he and his wife have set out for Scone for the coronation. The place of the scene is still Inverness, either just outside the walls of Macbeth's castle or in one of the courtyards.

1. The old man is a person of some rank, as well as of long and varied experience. His age gives him the wisdom of a seer, as we may infer from ll. 40, 41. His benign and dignified figure serves as a kind of chorus to the tragedy, and his prophetic speech at the end brings the stormy Second Act to a calm and impressive close.

1–4. The omens and prodigies are continued from ii, 3, 61–66. They are taken from Holinshed's account of the murder of King Duff, and such things are often recorded in similar cases. Cf. *Julius Cæsar*, i, 3, 1–32; ii, 2, 1–31.—**sore:** dreadful. —**trifled former knowings:** made all my previous experiences seem trivial.—**father.** Used in addressing any venerable man.

6. **his bloody stage:** this earth, on which man performs his bloody deeds. The idea that 'all the world's a stage And all the men and women merely players' (*As You Like It*, ii, 7, 139ff.) occurs often in Shakespeare. It was, indeed, the motto of his theatre, the Globe (*Totus mundus agit histrionem*, 'All the world plays the actor'). Cf. *Winter's Tale*, v, 1, 58.

7. **dark night.** Cf. Holinshed: 'For the space of six moneths togither, after this heinous murther thus committed [the murder of King Duff], there appeered no sunne by day, nor moone by night in anie part of the realme, but still was the skie couered with continuall clouds.'—**the travelling lamp:** the travelling torch (of Phœbus). Cf. Spenser, *The Faerie Queene*, i, 1, Proem, st. 4: 'Phœbus lampe'; Peele, *A Farewell*, 28, 29 (ed. Bullen, II, 238):

> Phœbus' eye,
> Th' eternal lamp of heaven.

Travelling recalls *Psalm* xix, 6: 'His going forth is from the end of the heaven, and his circuit unto the ends of it.'

8–10. **Is't . . . kiss it?** Is the darkness due to Night's having become more powerful in the world than Day, or to Day's hiding his face in shame?

12. **tow'ring ... place:** soaring proudly, and at the very summit (or highest pitch) of her flight.

13. **mousing owl:** an owl, whose natural prey is mice, not falcons. Cf. Holinshed: 'There was a sparhawke also strangled by an owle.'

15. **minions of their race:** the darlings of the horse tribe; the finest of all horses. Cf. i, 2, 19.

16, 17. **flung out:** kicked and plunged wildly. Cf. *Captain Underwit*, ii, 2 (ed. Bullen, *Old Plays*, II, 352): 'She kicks and flings out like a Colt.'—**as:** as if.

18. **they eat each other.** Cf. Holinshed: 'Horsses in Louthian, being of singular beautie and swiftnesse, did eate their owne flesh, and would in no wise taste anie other meate.'

19. **amazement:** stupefaction. Cf. ii, 3, 114.

20. Macduff comes out of the castle (or out of the hall into the courtyard) from the meeting of the electors.

23–27. Macduff has accepted the official theory of the murder. Yet he has a vague feeling of uneasiness, and shows it in his somewhat dry and short answers.—**pretend:** intend to gain for themselves by such an act. Cf. *pretence* for 'intention,' 'purpose,' in ii, 3, 137.—**suborn'd:** secretly bribed or induced —used of 'procuring' any crime, not, as in the modern idiom, limited to perjury and treason.—**'Gainst nature still:** continuing the Old Man's thought in ll. 10, 11.

28. **Thriftless:** improvident.—**raven up:** devour ravenously. In their mad ambition to reign, they have destroyed all their own prospects of succeeding to the throne.

30. **upon Macbeth:** who stands next in succession.

31. **nam'd:** elected (by the council of nobles).—**Scone:** where the Scottish kings were regularly crowned. The Stone of Scone, on which the Scottish kings sat during the ceremony, was taken to England by Edward I and is preserved in Westminster Abbey.

32. **invested:** clothed with sovereignty (at the coronation). Cf. Holinshed: 'Then hauing a companie about him of such as he had made priuie to his enterprise, he caused himself to be

proclaimed king, and foorthwith went vnto Scone, where (by common consent) he receiued the inuesture of the kingdome according to the accustomed maner.'

33. Colmekill: Columba's cell—the island now usually called Iona, where St. Columba had a monastery and where he and the ancient Scottish kings were buried. Cf. Holinshed: 'The bodie of Duncane was first conueied vnto Elgine, & there buried in kinglie wise; but afterwards it was remoued and conueied vnto Colmekill, and there laid in a sepulture among his predecessors.'

36. Fife: Macduff's own home.

37. well done: May the coronation of Macbeth really be a good thing for Scotland. Macduff fears (as the next line shows) that Macbeth's reign may be less agreeable to the nobility than the mild sway of Duncan. His words have no suggestion that he suspects Macbeth's guilt. Holinshed remarks that Duncan was 'soft and gentle of nature' and 'negligent in punishing offendors,' so that, during his reign, 'manie misruled persons tooke occasion thereof to trouble the peace and quiet state of the common-wealth.' Shakespeare represents him as gentle, but not as remiss in government.

40, 41. God's benison . . . foes: God's blessing go with you both—and with all other well-meaning and unsuspicious persons who, like you, insist on regarding bad men as good and your foes as your friends. The old man, being something of a seer, does harbour suspicion of Macbeth's guilt; but he dare not express it, except to himself. 'And with those,' etc., is spoken after Macduff and Ross have turned to depart, and is not heard by them. It applies to them both and is not intended to mark Ross as a facile courtier or mere time-server. Such an idea (though it has found some favour among critics) is justified neither by his conduct in attending the coronation at Scone nor by anything else in the play. He may be less keen-sighted and energetic than Macduff and Banquo, but, like them, he accepts Macbeth as his legally elected sovereign. When Macbeth proves a tyrant, he joins the other nobles in their patriotic rebellion.

ACT III. Scene I.

Some months have elapsed since the coronation. The young princes have reached places of safety—Malcolm in England and Donalbain in Ireland—and reports have come back to Scotland that they accuse Macbeth of the murder (ll. 30–33). Banquo, who has had time to think and has heard these reports, fears they are true; but the time for action has not yet come. Macduff has grown more and more hostile to Macbeth and keeps away from court. The King himself, now well established in power, has begun to suffer both from remorse and from fear—fear of Banquo especially. We get the impression of a much longer interval than can be reckoned by strict computation. See Introduction, p. xvi.

3. **Thou play'dst most foully.** Cf. Lady Macbeth's words (i, 5, 22, 23):

> Wouldst not play false,
> And yet wouldst wrongly win.

In no other play of Shakespeare's, perhaps, are there so many echoes as in *Macbeth*. This may be an indication of the continuous burst of inspiration in which most of the drama was composed.—**most foully for't.** Holinshed says that Macbeth, 'communicating his purposed intent [to seize the crown] with his trustie friends, amongst whome Banquho was the chiefest, vpon confidence of their promised aid, slue the king.' Shakespeare's departure from the record is significant. As King James's supposed ancestor, Banquo must be a loyal man.

6. **truth.** Compare Banquo's half-jesting exclamation: 'What, can the devil speak true?' (i, 3, 107).

7. **As ... shine:** as [well may be the case, for] upon thee their speeches are not only fulfilled, but *brilliantly* fulfilled. —**shine** (emphatic): shine with the lustre of splendid reality.

10. **Sennet:** a series of notes on a trumpet announcing the entrance of a person of high degree or of a stately procession.

13. **all-thing:** altogether.

14. **solemn supper:** a supper of ceremony, a state supper.

15. **I'll.** Macbeth's use of *I* instead of the royal *we* gives the invitation a personal quality that makes it especially gracious. Banquo's reply is very formal (in contrast), not because he is hiding his feelings, but because such is the proper way to address the King.

16. **Command:** in emphatic contrast with Macbeth's word *request*. Royal invitations are still called commands.—**the which:** i.e., your royal commands. The antecedent noun (as often) is implied in the verb.

19. **Ride you this afternoon?** In the dialogue that follows, three questions stand out with sinister emphasis among the gracious words of the King: 'Ride you this afternoon?' 'Is't far you ride?' 'Goes Fleance with you?' Macbeth has already planned the murder of Banquo and Fleance, and Banquo's replies give him what information he needs to carry out the plot that very night. All his compliments are mere wrappings for these three questions.

22. **still:** always.—**grave and prosperous:** weighty and good in its results. Note the implication that there have been previous councils: Macbeth has now reigned for some time.

26–28. **Go ... twain:** Unless my horse goes too fast to make that necessary, I shall have to continue my ride an hour or two after dark. *The better* means 'better than *that*,' i.e., 'too well for *that*' (too well to keep me out so late). The idiom was in common use from the thirteenth[1] to the late seventeenth century; but since it has usually been misunderstood in this passage, examples are added:—*Gammer Gurton's Needle*, v, 2, 205 (ed. Manly, *The Pre-Shaksperean Drama*, II, 150): 'And chad [i.e., If I had] not had the better wit, chad bene made a doult' (cf. ii, 4, 27; v, 2, 43–45, 234–235); *Hycke Scorner*, ll. 286, 287 (ed. Manly, I, 396): 'And I had not scused me the better, I

[1]For Middle English see *The Seven Sages*, ed. Campbell, 547–550 (ed. Weber, 483–488); *Piers Plowman*, B, v, 198, 199 (ed. Skeat, I, 146); Chaucer, *Troilus*, i, 743–746; cf. *The Boy and the Mantle*, st. 5 (ed. Child, I, 271).

knowe well I sholde have daunsed in a fetter)'; Nashe, *Have with You to Saffron-Walden*, 1596 (ed. McKerrow, III, 39): 'A fire that the sea will coole, or Haruey find water inough to quench, if you looke not too it the better'; John Day, *Humour out of Breath,* 1608, iv, 3 (ed. Bullen, I, 61): '*Hort*[*ensio*]. Haue you deceiu'd me, madam? *Flo*[*rimell*]. Not yet, but I will and you look not the better too't'; Middleton, *Your Five Gallants*, iv, 4 (ed. Bullen, III, 203): 'The sight of these jewels is able to cloy me, did I not preserve my stomach the better for the wedding-dinner'; Fletcher, *The Woman's Prize*, i, 3 (ed. Dyce, VII, 118): '*Petru*[*chio*]. I come not to use violence. *Maria.* I think You cannot, sir; I am better fortified'; Gabriel Harvey, *Pierces Supererogation*, 1593 (ed. Grosart, II, 238): 'If thou entreate me not the fayrer, . . . I will batter thy carrion to dirt'; *Arden of Feversham*, ii, 2 (ed. Tucker Brooke, *The Shakespeare Apocrypha*, p. 13): 'If you get you not away all the sooner, you shall be well beaten'; Fletcher, *The Maid in the Mill*, v, 2 (ed. Dyce, IX, 291): 'You'll pull your destiny upon you, If you cease not the sooner'; Dryden, *The Wild Gallant*, i, 2 (ed. 1669, sig. B 2 lf. 3 r°): 'If you pay me not the sooner, I must provide you another Lodging'; *A Larum for London*, 1602 (sig. A 2 v°): 'Not one . . . dare approach so neere, The Castle shot keepes them in greater awe'; Middleton, *The Mayor of Queenborough*, v, 1, 145 (ed. Bullen, II, 94): 'For your finding fault, our hopes are greater.'

30. **cousins:** Malcolm and Donalbain.—**are bestow'd:** have taken refuge.

33. **strange invention.** They have been accusing Macbeth of the murder, and the report has reached Scotland.

34. **therewithal:** therewith, besides that.—**cause of state:** public business.

35. **Craving us jointly:** requiring both your attention and mine. Thus Macbeth associates himself with Banquo in a very particular manner, as if they had common interests which the others did not share. Banquo may well think that the business meant is the prophecy made by the Weird Sisters to him.

37. **Our time . . . upon's:** time summons us to depart.

39. **commend you:** entrust you—with my best wishes.

42-44. **To make . . . alone:** In order that company (your society) may be all the more agreeable to me, I will deprive myself of it for a time.—**The sweeter welcome:** the more sweetly
welcome to me.—**ourself:** the regular emphatic and reflexive
form of the royal *we*.—**While then, God be with you:** Until
then, good-bye. *Good-bye* is simply a clipped form of *God be
wi' ye*. It was written in all sorts of ways: *God b'ye, God boy
ye, God b' w' ye*, etc.

45. **Sirrah.** Often used in addressing a servant, an inferior,
or a child (iv, 2, 30).

48. **To be thus:** to be King.

49 ff. **But to be safely thus:** without being (unless I am to
be) safe on my throne. Macbeth finds that the assassination has
not 'trammelled up the consequence' (i, 7, 3). The general
fear that he expressed in his soliloquy—that in killing Duncan
he might be 'teaching bloody instructions'—has now become
specific: he thinks that Banquo may plot his murder. Macbeth has definitely 'jumped the life to come.' He no longer
concerns himself about the next world, but attends solely to
establishing safety in this life. His vacillating temper has given
place to resolution.

51. **that:** that quality (i.e., ambition).—**would be:** requires
to be.

52. **to:** in addition to, besides.—**temper:** quality, disposition.

53. **wisdom.** 'The better part of valour,' says Falstaff, 'is
discretion' (*1 Henry IV*, v, 4, 120, 121).

56, 57. An Egyptian soothsayer, according to Plutarch's *Life
of Antony*, 'tolde Antonius plainely, that his fortune (which of
it selfe was excellent good, and very great) was altogether
bleamished and obscured by Cæsar's fortune: and therefore
he counselled him vtterly to leaue his company, and to get him
as farre from him as he could. "For thy Demon," said he,
"(that is to say, the good angell and spirit that keepeth thee)
is affraide of his: and being coragious and high when he is

alone, becometh fearfull and timerous when he commeth neere
vnto the other"' (North's translation, used by Shakespeare).[1]
This story took strong hold on Shakespeare's imagination:
see *Antony and Cleopatra*, ii, 3, 10–38.—**Genius:** guardian
spirit.—**rebuk'd:** put to shame, abashed, cowed.

60–65. **line.** Empathic.—**with:** by.—**fil'd:** defiled.

67. **Put rancours … peace.** Before the murder, Macbeth was
at peace with God and man and with his own conscience: now
he feels at enmity with all three. *Rancour* is the strongest possible word for 'malignant enmity.' The figure is of a vessel
full of some wholesome liquid (like milk) into which poison
has been poured. Cf. the 'poison'd chalice' (i, 7, 11) and 'the
milk of human kindness' (i, 5, 18). The figure of a vessel is
similarly used in *2 Henry IV*, iv, 4, 41–48:

> Learn this, Thomas,
> And thou shalt prove a shelter to thy friends;
> A hoop of gold to bind thy brothers in,
> That the united vessel of their blood,
> Mingled with venom of suggestion
> (As, force perforce, the age will pour it in),
> Shall never leak, though it do work as strong
> As aconitum or rash gunpowder.

[1]It is interesting to compare Robert Greene's version of this impressive
anecdote: 'For that (quoth *Aretino*) you haue brought *Augustus* that
worthie Monarche to memorie, giue me leaue to say thus much of him,
that great familiaritie and acquaintance growing betwixt him and *Anthonie*,
his companion in the empire, they often passed away the time together
with sundry sortes of playes and pastimes, wherein *Anthonie* alwaies went
away vanquished. Whereupon one of his familier friends, well seene in
the art of diuination, tooke occasion many times to vtter his mind vnto
him in these or the like speeches. Sir, what doe you so neare this young
man? Be not so familiar and conuersant with him: your fame is greater
then his, you are elder then he, you command more then he, you are better
exercised in feats of armes, you haue greater experience, and euery way
are his superiour: But this let me say which I haue found out by the secrets
of my science, that your familiar spirite feareth his, and your fortune which
of it selfe is great, flattereth his: so that if you sequester not your selfe farre
from him, like a deceitful goddesse, she will take the garland of honour
from your head, and set it vpon his' (*The Second Part of the Tritameron
of Love*, 1587, ed. Grosart, III, 131, 132).

68. **mine eternal jewel:** my immortal treasure (my soul). Another echo of the soliloquy before the murder (i, 7, 7).

71, 72. **list:** the lists.—**champion me:** meet me face to face in combat as a champion meets his opponent.—**to th' utterance:** *à outrance*, in a duel to the death. Macbeth, though a strong fatalist, determines to attempt the overthrow of Fate in one particular point.—**Who's there?** A summons to the servant who attends in the lobby. We should expect the interview with the murderers to take place in a private room; but, since there was no moveable scenery in the Elizabethan theatre, the stage was simply cleared of the courtiers, and the murderers were brought into the hall in which the King has just appeared in state.

74. The murderers are not mere hired assassins. They are Scottish gentlemen of desperate fortunes, and have hitherto been Macbeth's enemies, for to him they have ascribed their troubles. In a previous interview, however, he has convinced them that it was Banquo who had wronged them; and he now spurs them to revenge. Thus they are sharply distinguished from the brutal hirelings who butcher Lady Macduff and her son (iv, 2, 79-85). It has been objected to the splendid dialogue that follows that it is too long and that 'two hired cutthroats would have done the deed better and asked no questions' (Grierson). In Holinshed, Macbeth does, in fact, entrust the business to 'certeine murderers, whom he hired to execute that deed'; but Shakespeare's Macbeth wishes to make it appear, when the murder is discovered (as of course it must be), that Banquo has been killed as a result of a private feud (see l. 133). This plan was balked by the appearance of the ghost at the banquet (iii, 4).

75. **your Highness:** your Majesty.

77-79. **it was he:** i.e., Banquo. As, in the great soliloquy (i, 7), *his* is used in l. 4, and *he* in l. 12, and the name *Duncan* is not mentioned until l. 16—so here Banquo's name occurs first in l. 84.—**held you . . . So under fortune:** kept you down in your fortunes; thwarted your careers.—**made good:** proved.

80. **pass'd in probation with you:** I reviewed the facts with you and gave you the proofs. The object of *pass'd* is what follows, 'How you were borne in hand,' etc.

81. **borne in hand:** deluded (by Banquo). To bear a man in hand is not merely to deceive him, but to do so by means of a regular course of treachery; to play the hypocrite with him; to nourish false hopes, etc. Chaucer uses *hold in hand* in the same sense.—**cross'd:** thwarted in all your efforts.—**the instruments:** the tools. Macbeth says that he named the very agents by means of whom Banquo had worked against them.

83. **half a soul:** even to one who had only half a man's wits. —**notion:** mind, intellect.

84. **Banquo.** With this word, we learn for the first time whom Macbeth has been accusing.—**You made it known to us.** Grimly concise, as if spoken through the man's teeth. They have no doubt that Macbeth has told them the truth.

86. **Our point of second meeting:** the point or purpose of this second meeting.

87. **patience:** passive endurance.—**so predominant:** so much more powerful than all other qualities. *Predominant* is an astrological term applied to that planet which is powerful above all others at a given time.

88. **so gospell'd:** so tamely submissive to the gospel precept to 'love your enemies, bless them that curse you, do good to them that hate you, and pray for them which despitefully use you and persecute you' (*Matthew*, v, 44).

89. **To:** as to.—**for his issue.** An intensely significant addition. Cf. ll. 133–138.

91. **yours:** your families and descendants.—**liege:** liege lord, sovereign.

92. **in the catalogue:** in a mere list; as we might say 'in the census.'—**go for:** pass for, count for.

94. **Shoughs:** a kind of shaggy Iceland dog, in favour as a lady's pet in Shakespeare's time. Pronounced *shocks*.—**water-rugs:** some kind of shaggy water-dog.—**demi-wolves:** a cross between wolf and dog.—**clipt:** yclept, called.

95. **The valued file:** the list which (as opposed to an indiscriminate *catalogue*) notes the *valuable quality* which distinguishes each breed. *Valued* here is not a past participle, but an adjective made by adding *-ed* to the noun *value*; it means 'furnished with *value*' (i.e., with a note of it). Cf. such adjectives as *web-footed, red-haired, blue-eyed, bearded.*

97. **housekeeper:** the keeper, or guard, of the house; the watchdog.

99. **Hath in him clos'd:** has put into him; endowed him with.—**whereby:** by virtue of which.

100, 101. **Particular ... alike:** a special name or title, in distinction from the list (*bill*) that writes them all down indiscriminately as *dogs*. *Bill* was applied to almost any kind of document.—**from:** away from—and so, 'in opposition to,' 'in distinction from.' In this use it must have had a special emphasis.

102. **file:** the same word used in l. 95 for 'list'; but it immediately suggests to Macbeth the military sense, and hence he goes on to speak of *rank* in the next verse.

103. **worst:** dissyllabic, the *r* being dwelt on.

105, 106. **takes your enemy off.** Two motives are suggested for killing Banquo—revenge and the hope of winning the King's favour. *Takes off* is the same phrase used by Macbeth in i, 7, 20—another echo.—**Grapples you.** Cf. *Hamlet,* i, 3, 62, 63:

> Those friends thou hast, and their adoption tried,
> Grapple them unto thy soul with hoops of steel.

107. **wear ... life:** have but feeble health so long as he is alive (since his life endangers mine).

112. **tugg'd:** pulled about, roughly handled.—**with:** by, as in l. 63.

113. **set:** stake, venture.—**chance:** cast of the dice, hazard. Cf. *Richard III,* v, 4, 9, 10:

> Slave, I have set my life upon a cast
> And I will stand the hazard of the die.

116. **bloody distance:** mortal enmity.

117. **being:** existence (as in l. 55).

118. **my near'st of life:** my most vital spot. Banquo's mere existence is a dagger, set at Macbeth's breast over his heart and pressed in steadily and inexorably minute by minute.

119. **With barefac'd power:** with frank and undisguised exercise of my royal authority.

120. **avouch it:** authorize the deed; justify it—on the tyrant's principle of 'Hoc volo, sic iubeo: sit pro ratione voluntas' (Juvenal, vi, 223).

121. **For:** because of.

122, 123. **loves.** Abstract nouns are often pluralized when more persons than one are in question. Cf. v, 8, 61.—**may not:** must not.—**but wail...down:** but [I must] seem to lament the death of him whom I myself slew. *Who* for *whom* is common. Cf. iii, 4, 42; iv, 3, 171.

127. **Though our lives—.** Macbeth, now sure of his men, cuts short their protestations.

128. **Your spirits,** etc.: Your courage and resolution appear in your sparkling eyes and eager faces.

129. **advise you:** send you information.

130. **with ... time:** with absolutely full and exact indication of the time when the deed should be done. This information is to be given by the Third Murderer (scene iii).—**spy:** literally, espial, observation.

132. **something from:** at some distance from. Cf. note on l. 100.—**always thought:** it being always understood.

133. **I:** emphatic.—**clearness:** complete freedom from risk of being suspected. Holinshed tells us that Macbeth wished to have the murder so carried out that his own 'house' should not be 'slandered' and that he might 'cleare himselfe, if anie thing were laid to his charge.'—We may assume that the nobles do not suspect Macbeth's enmity toward Banquo.

134. **rubs nor botches:** flaws or defects (due to bungling). Macbeth wishes the murderers 'to make a clean job of it.' A rub in bowling is any impediment that deflects or hinders the

course of the bowl; hence, also, the course thus impeded or thwarted. The word was common in the figurative use. Cf. *Richard II*, iii, 4, 3, 4:

> *Lady.* Madam, we'll play at bowls.
> *Queen.* 'Twill make me think the world is full of rubs.

138. Resolve yourselves apart: Make up your minds, by conferring in private, whether you will undertake the business or not.

140. straight: straightway, immediately.

141, 142. Cf. ii, 1, 63, 64:

> Hear it not, Duncan, for it is a knell
> That summons thee to heaven, or to hell.

Scene II.

This scene is practically continuous with scene i. It begins— as that scene ends—with 'Banquo.' He is the burden of Lady Macbeth's thoughts as of her husband's. Macbeth has acted in this case without his wife's direct instigation, but he appeals to her for such instigation (ll. 36, 37), precisely as if the murder of Banquo and Fleance had not been already planned; and she replies with the same sinister indirectness ('But in them Nature's copy's not eterne') with which she had prompted him to murder Duncan (i, 5, 60)—'And when goes hence?' His response (ll. 39 ff.) gives her (in effect) assurance that Banquo and his son are to die that night. Thus, throughout scene iv, the audience knows that Lady Macbeth is aware of her husband's crime, though she does not overhear his talk with the Murderers.

4–7. These lines and the question in line 1 show that Lady Macbeth shares her husband's fear of Banquo. They echo his words in iii, 1, 48, 49:

> To be thus is nothing,
> But to be safely thus.

Yet, as soon as Macbeth enters, she throws off her mood of anxiety and is as ready as ever to inspire him with her native energy. It is this necessity of carrying a double load that breaks her down at last. The soliloquy is a premonition of v, 1.— **content:** happiness.

9. **sorriest:** most paltry, despicable.

10. **Using:** associating with. The word carries out the figure of the preceding verse.

11, 12. **them.** Duncan alone is meant, but the plural is used in the common generalizing sense.—**Things . . . regard.** Cf. *Richard II*, ii, 3, 171: 'Things past redress are now with me past care.'—**without all:** beyond all.

12. The tragic element consists in the fact that it is *not* 'done.' Cf. Macbeth's scruple before the murder (i, 7, 1): 'If it were done when 'tis done'; and the Lady's own words (v, 1, 74): 'What's done cannot be undone.'

13. **scotch'd:** slashed, gashed. The Folios and Davenant have 'scorch'd'—a variant spelling. Theobald restored what was doubtless Shakespeare's form. Cf. *Coriolanus*, iv, 5, 197, 198 ('he scotch'd him and notch'd him'); *Antony and Cleopatra*, iv, 7, 10 ('six scotches more'). The form *scorch*, however, occurs in *Comedy of Errors*, v, 1, 183.

14. **close:** come together again; join and be as strong as ever. It was a common notion (not yet obsolete) that a snake, when cut in two, will reunite unless the head is crushed. Cf. Greene, *Alphonsus*, i, 2, 287 ff. (ed. Collins, I, 87):

> The sillie serpent, found by Country swaine,
> And cut in pieces by his furious blowes,
> Yet if her head do scape away vntoucht,
> As many write, it very stranglye goes
> To fetch an herbe, with which in litle time
> Her battered corpes againe she doth conioyne:
> But if by chance the ploughmans sturdie staffe
> Do happe to hit vpon the Serpents head,
> And bruse the same, though all the rest be sound,
> Yet doth the Sillie Serpent lie for dead,
> Nor can the rest of all her body serue
> To finde a salue which may her life preserue.

Macbeth now counts the murdered Duncan among his enemies. The snake is a figure for all those who stand or have stood in the way of his getting, holding, and enjoying the crown, and of these Banquo (so he feels) is one.

14, 15. **our poor malice . . . tooth:** our feeble enmity has proved of no avail and leaves us exposed to the same danger (from the serpent) as when it was uninjured.

16–19. **let...disjoint:** let the whole fabric (or structure) of the universe go to pieces; let chaos come again. Cf. *Hamlet*, ii, 2, 310: 'this goodly frame, the earth.'—**both the worlds:** this world and the next.—**suffer:** die, perish. *Suffer* in the sense of 'suffer death' is common. The magnificent and desperate egoism of this outburst—'Heaven and earth shall be destroyed before I will consent to lead my life in fear'—is matched by that of Macbeth's address to the Weird Sisters in iv, 1, 50–61.

20. **Whom . . . peace:** We killed Duncan not merely to win the crown (without which we could not rest) but also to enjoy it in secure and peaceful possession: the result of our crime is—peace for Duncan, but torment for ourselves. The thought is developed in the following lines. The repetition of the same or a similar word within the line or sentence is a common feature of Shakespeare's style. For other examples see i, 5, 64, 65; ii, 2, 56, 57; v, 3, 44; v, 8, 60, 72; cf. iv, 3, 178, 179. For *our peace*, the reading of the First Folio, the other three Folios substitute the prosaic reading *our place*, which some editors adopt. Davenant's version has 'to gain the Crown.'

21. **on . . . lie:** to find that our bed is a rack on which we are stretched in torment.

22. **In restless ecstasy:** in a frenzy of sleeplessness and unrest.

23. **life's fitful fever.** Life seems to Macbeth a tormenting malarial fever (see note on ii, 3, 66)—now hot, now cold, never at rest: only in death is there peace (cf. iv, 3, 179). Cf. *Measure for Measure*, iii, 1, 75: 'a feverous life.'

24. **his:** the usual genitive of *it*.

25. **Malice domestic, foreign levy.** Macbeth fears both—
malice domestic from Banquo and Macduff, foreign levy from
the friends of Malcolm in England and of Donalbain in Ireland (iii, 1, 30–33).

27. **Gentle my lord.** Since *my lord* is practically a single word,
it is often preceded by an adjective.—**sleek o'er:** smooth over.
—**rugged:** agitated; literally, rough, shaggy (iii, 4, 100). Macbeth, being of an emotional temperament, has far less control
over his features than his wife habitually exercises over hers.
Cf. i, 5, 63–67, 72.

30. **Let . . . Banquo:** Remember to show particular attention
to Banquo. *Apply to* means 'to adapt one's self to a person,'
and hence 'to be subservient or attentive to him,' 'to court his
favour,' or the like. *Remembrance* has four syllables (*remem-
berance*): cf. *entrance* in i, 5, 40.

31. **Present him eminence:** do him special honour.

32. **Unsafe the while.** Macbeth interrupts himself with the
bitter reflection that, while they are thus attentive to Banquo,
they are themselves unsafe: the very necessity of flattering
Banquo shows their fear of him. *Unsafe* refers to the persons
mentioned in the preceding lines—you and me. The break in
the metre is very expressive. There is no reason to suspect an
omission in the text.—**that:** in that, because.

33. **Must lave . . . streams:** must wash the honours that we
have in streams of flattery to keep them clean. A grotesque and
violent figure which shows the impatient self-contempt of the
speaker. The thought is that, to retain their position, they
must court the favour of Banquo and the rest.

34. **vizards:** masks.

35. **You must leave this:** such wild remarks and the mood
that prompts them. Cf. ii, 2, 33, 34:

> These deeds must not be thought
> After these ways. So, it will make us mad.

37. **Banquo . . . lives.** Macbeth had not meant to inform his
wife of his murderous purpose; but his feelings are too strong

for him, and, besides, he has long been in the habit of telling her everything.

37. **lives.** A singular verb with two subjects is common.

38. **But ... eterne:** Nature has granted them, not a perpetual lease of life but a mere copyhold tenure, easy to revoke or to terminate. Cf. Middleton, *Women Beware Women*, iii, 1, 59: 'By that copy this land still I hold.' Copyhold tenure was originally tenure at the will of the lord of the manor. The tenant had no deed or lease; his sole evidence was a copy of an entry or entries in the roll of the manorial court. This interpretation of the passage is confirmed by frequent reference to copyhold (literal and figurative) in the Elizabethan dramatists (including Greene, Jonson, Chapman, Fletcher, Middleton, and Dekker), as well as by the figure of a cancelled bond in ll. 48–50, and by 'live the lease of nature' in iv, 1, 99. A less probable explanation regards Banquo and Fleance as Nature's copies (or specimens) of mankind, formed by Nature according to model—'particular casts from Nature's mould' (Knight). Such copies are, of course, not indestructible. A passage in Massinger (*The Fatal Dowry*, iv, 1) suggests that he took the words in this sense:

> Put it [the mirror] by,
> Lest thou, dear lord, Narcissus-like shouldst dote
> Upon thyself, and die; and rob the world
> Of Nature's copy that she works form by.

39. **There's comfort yet!** There's still comfort *in that*! *There* is emphatic. Macbeth is quick to catch his wife's meaning, for it matches his purpose.

41–43. **cloister'd.** The bat's flight is not, like a bird's, in the open air, but in belfries and cloisters—in darkness and solitude.—**ere ... peal:** ere the droning beetle, in obedience to Hecate's summons, has announced the coming of drowsy night. Hecate, the goddess of darkness and of the deeds that befit it, issues the call for night to come, and the beetle rings the peal that publishes the summons to sleep. Here again (as in ii, 1,

52) Hecate is a goddess, not (as in the interpolated passages: iii, 5, and iv, 1, 39–43) a mere mistress witch.—**shard-borne:** borne upon wings that are like potsherds (fragments of pottery). The wing-cases of the beetle, which are elevated in flying, are commonly thought to be its wings. Cf. *Antony and Cleopatra*, iii, 2, 19: 'They are his shards, and he their beetle.'

44. **of dreadful note:** dreadful to be known.—**What's to be done?** The directness and concrete simplicity of Lady Macbeth's speeches are noteworthy; they accord with her strength of purpose and her habit of looking facts in the face. She finds that her husband no longer waits for her instigation, though he still requires comfort and encouragement from her.

45. In form, Macbeth still carries out his original intent to conceal his purpose; but in effect he leaves no doubt in his wife's mind. The homely term of endearment (*chuck*, i.e., 'chick') sounds grim in the savage context. The word was not grotesque, but merely familiar and affectionate. Cf. Marston, *Antonio's Revenge*, ii, 2, 119: 'Go sup, sweet chuck; drink and securely sleep.' Incidentally, its use by Macbeth is evidence that his wife is no creature of heroic frame. We cannot imagine Goneril's husband addressing her thus. Cf. v, 1, 57: 'this little hand.'

46. **seeling night.** What follows is a soliloquy, though Lady Macbeth is listening. To *seel* is to sew up the eyelids (of a falcon) with silk—to keep it in the dark and tame it.

47. **Scarf up:** muffle (as with a scarf), blindfold. See Lady Macbeth's appeal to darkness (i, 5, 51–55) and cf. ii, 1, 49–56.

49. **bond:** the prophecy by which Fate has bound itself to give the throne to Banquo's descendants.

50. **thickens:** grows dim with the shades of night. Cf. *Antony and Cleopatra*, ii, 3, 27: 'Thy lustre thickens.'

51. **th' rooky wood.** There were ravens about Macbeth's castle (cf. i, 5, 39), and doubtless also rooks. A less probable interpretation makes *rooky* equivalent to the old adjective *roky*, 'misty,' 'gloomy' (from *roke*, 'smoke'; cf. *reek*). Davenant's version reads: 'The Crow makes wing to the thick shady Grove.'

52, 53. **droop:** hang the head in sleep.—**agents:** all evil beings that act by night—beasts of prey, murderers, and the 'spirits that tend on mortal thoughts' (i, 5, 41, 42).

54, 55. A superfluous rhyme-tag. See Introduction, p. vii.

56. **go with me.** He gives her his hand to lead her off the stage. Cf. i, 6, 31. Some editors take the words as figurative: 'agree with me,' 'consent to my design'; but this is both forced and feeble. Why should Macbeth ask his wife to consent to his design when he has hitherto been led by her and (especially) when he has just told her to be innocent of the knowledge until she applauds the deed?

Scene III.

1. We hear only the end of the dialogue. The Third Murderer has given the other two the information which Macbeth had promised to send them (iii, 1, 128–131) and has proved that he is in the King's confidence by repeating such directions as they had already received. Some critics imagine that this Third Murderer was Macbeth himself. If this were so, the interview between Macbeth and the First Murderer (iii, 4, 12 ff.) would lose all its force and become not only useless but absurd. Note particularly iii, 4, 15–25.

2–4. **delivers:** reports.—**offices:** duties.—**to the direction:** according to our instructions.

5. The time is carefully indicated. The sun has set, but there is a faint light in the west. When Banquo enters, however, it is dark enough for a torch.

6. **lated:** belated.

7. **To gain the timely inn:** to reach the inn in good season (before it is quite dark).—**near approaches.** This does not mean that he hears Banquo, but that the time is at hand when he is expected (cf. iii, 1, 131).

8. **subject:** object.

9. **Give ... ho!** a call from Banquo to a servant of the palace

who takes charge of the horses and gives the guests torches to light them as they walk up the avenue to the palace gate. Fleance takes the torch. Before Banquo and Fleance enter, they have entrusted their horses to the servant, and he has taken them out of sight. Thus the murderers are left alone with their victims.

10. **within . . . expectation:** in the list of expected guests.

11. **His horses go about.** The speaker hears the servant galloping off with the horses. To attack and kill two active riders is not easy unless there are a large number of assailants. Hence Macbeth has arranged that the murder shall take place after Banquo and Fleance have dismounted. Incidentally, this avoids the necessity of bringing horses upon the stage. See W. J. Lawrence, *Times Literary Supplement,* June 6, 1919.

16. **It will be rain to-night.** This casual remark about the weather is a master-stroke. It shows that Banquo is off his guard, and informs the audience that the night is cloudy and therefore fit for the murder. The savage jest of the murderer ('Let the storm come down, then!') fits the mood in which he commits the crime. He strikes Banquo with all the zest of revenge (cf. iii, 1, 86–91).

Scene IV.

For mediæval tales illustrating the scene see Beatrice Brown, *Publications of the Modern Language Association*, L (1935), 709 ff.

1, 2. **degrees:** your ranks, and hence the seat which each should take.—**At first And last:** at the beginning and the end of the supper; once for all. Cf. Heywood, *The Late Lancashire Witches* (Pearson ed., IV, 189):

> At meeting, and at parting, Gentlemen,
> I onely make use of that generall word,
> So frequent at all feasts, and that but once;
> Y'are welcome.

3–6. There is a dais in the hall, on which stand two chairs of state under a canopy. The Queen takes her seat in one of these, but Macbeth means to sit at the head of the table, like the host at the old-fashioned *table d' hôte*.—**keeps her state:** remains enthroned in her chair of state.—**in best time:** when the proper moment comes.—**require:** request, call for.

8. The first three speeches of the King and Queen each end with the word *welcome,* which is thus intentionally dwelt on. The Queen's word *heart* repeats her husband's *hearty* (l. 2).

9. encounter thee: meet thee, respond to thee.

10. Both sides are even. The table is full except for the seat at the head, reserved for Macbeth. Since Banquo has not arrived, his seat has been removed in order to avoid the awkwardness and (perhaps) the ill omen of an empty chair at a feast. Cf. l. 46.

11. large: lavish, abundant.—**mirth:** enjoyment.—**a measure:** a large goblet, a bumper.

12 ff. The simple arrangements of the Elizabethan stage account for this interview with the murderer at the door while the feast is going on in the hall. Such an arrangement may well have been thought realistic enough for the remote times in which Macbeth lived. There is a savage jocularity in the first few speeches of this dialogue which expresses, on Macbeth's part, a nervous revulsion of feeling from the horror of the deed, and, on the murderer's, a frank exultation in successful revenge.

14. 'Tis ... within: It's better that the blood should be outside of thee than inside of Banquo. *He* for *him* is good seventeenth-century grammar. Cf. Hall, *Satires,* vi, 1, 37: 'Patrons are honest now, o'er they of old.' See Abbott, *Shakespearian Grammar,* 1874, p. 140.

21. my fit: my ague fit; my fit of feverous anxiety. Cf. iii, 2, 23.

22. founded: firmly established.

23. broad and general: free and unconfined.—**casing:** all-embracing.

24, 25. **cabin'd, cribb'd:** shut up in a cabin—nay, in a mere hut. Cf. *2 Henry IV*, iii, 1, 9: 'in smoky cribs.'—**bound ... fears:** shut in, with no companions but importunate doubts and fears (that force themselves upon me and will not let me alone).—**safe:** safely out of the way; disposed of.

26. **Safe ... bides.** It is impossible not to be affected by the grim satisfaction that the murderer feels in having revenged himself on his supposed enemy.

27. **trenched:** deep-cut.

29. **worm:** serpent. Cf. iii, 2, 13.

32. **hear ourselves:** talk with each other; confer. At the conference thus appointed the murderers may expect some reward, as promised in iii, 1, 106.—**My royal lord.** Macbeth's interview with the murderer takes place at the back of the stage. The table is spread near the front, and the guests—who are applying themselves to the banquet (l. 11)—are not supposed to witness the interview or even to catch sight of the murderer. Lady Macbeth, however, must have known what was going on. While she speaks (ll. 32–37) Macbeth is advancing toward her chair of state. As her speech ends, the Ghost enters at the back of the stage. Stalking slowly forward, it takes Macbeth's seat while he is expressing his regret at Banquo's absence (ll. 40–43). Many editors shift the entrance of the Ghost to l. 39 (after 'sit'): see Textual Notes, p. 234, below.

33–35. **give the cheer:** make your guests feel cordially welcome.—**The feast ... welcome:** Unless the host's words and demeanour assure his guests that they are welcome, he might as well be an innkeeper.—**vouch'd:** certified.—**To feed:** to eat merely to satisfy hunger.

36. **From thence:** when away from home. Another case of the emphatic *from*. See note on iii, 1, 132.—**meat:** food.

37. Banquo's ghost has been much discussed, some holding that it was an actual ghost, others that it was a figment of Macbeth's guilty conscience, like the air-drawn dagger to which Lady Macbeth compares it. She, of course, had no belief in its actuality, because she could not see it, and she remained incredu-

lous to the end (v, 1, 70, 71). She even persuaded her husband
that he had been under a delusion (ll. 142–144). But the fact
that she and the guests saw nothing does not at all indicate that Shakespeare meant the ghost to be imaginary, for a
departed spirit (it was thought) might appear to one person in
a company and remain invisible to the rest (cf. *Hamlet*, iii, 4,
101 ff.). In Shakespeare's theatre (as the stage direction shows)
Banquo's ghost entered, stalked across the stage, and sat down
in Macbeth's chair. This is proof positive that Shakespeare
meant the audience to regard the ghost as actual; for how else
could they regard it (in an age when belief in ghosts was universal) when they saw it with their own eyes? Two passages
from old plays, often regarded as early allusions to this scene,
illustrate the point (see Introduction, p. ix). Dr. Forman saw
the ghost on the stage in 1610 or 1611 at the Globe (see p. 239,
below). Whether it is well to make Banquo's ghost appear on
the modern stage is a very different question, and, even if
decided in the negative, cannot affect our opinion as to Shakespeare's plain intent.—**remembrancer:** one who reminds me
of my duty.

38. **wait on:** attend. Cf. *Henry VIII*, i, 4, 62: 'A good digestion to you all!'

40. **had we ... roof'd:** we should now have all the noblest
men of Scotland under one roof.

41. **grac'd:** honoured, noble.

42, 43. **Who may I ... mischance!** whom I hope I should
rather blame for unkindness (in staying away on purpose)
than pity for some accident (that has prevented his coming).
For *who* cf. iii, 1, 123; iv, 3, 171.

45. **grace:** honour.

48. **moves:** disturbs.—**your Highness.** Cf. iii, 1, 75.

49. **Which of you have done this?** Two interpretations are
manifestly possible: (1) 'Which of you has killed Banquo?'
(2) 'Which of you has set this corpse in my chair?' That the
first is correct is shown by Macbeth's words in l. 50: 'Thou
canst not say I did it.' Thus Otway understood the passage,

which he imitates in *The Souldier's Fortune*, v (ed. 1681, p. 62): 'Hah! whatsoe're thou art, thou canst not eat me, speak to me, who has done this? thou canst not say I did it.' To the astonished guests Macbeth's question is inexplicable.

51. gory locks. The long hair of the apparition is matted with blood from the 'twenty trenched gashes.' Cf. iv, 1, 113, 123. This speech makes it clear to Lady Macbeth that her husband has received the report of Banquo's murder.

53. often thus. Macbeth was subject to fits of abstraction, and even to hallucinations. Lady Macbeth's excuse, then, accords, in plausible measure, with the facts. Cf. i, 3, 127 ff.; ii, 1, 33 ff.; ii, 2, 35 ff.

55. upon a thought: in a moment.

57. shall: will surely; will be sure to.—**offend him:** make him worse.—**passion:** attack.

58-60. Feed. The guests apply themselves once more to the banquet, and what follows between Macbeth and his wife is neither seen nor heard by them. She has descended hastily from the dais to attend to her husband.—**Are you a man?** Cf. i, 7, 46–51.—**O proper stuff!** A fine thing this!

62. you said: i.e., in the interval between scenes ii and iii of Act ii.—**air-drawn:** unsheathed and floating in the air — with a contemptuous implication of unreality, as if drawn (delineated) by the air.

63. Led. Cf. ii, 1, 42: 'Thou marshall'st me the way that I was going.'—**flaws:** outbursts—from the sense of 'a sudden gust of wind.'—**starts:** nervous movements.

64. to: in comparison with. These are mere tricks of the nerves, unworthy to be called genuine fear. They are like the shudders with which children listen to a ghost story, safely gathered round the cottage fire. Cf. *Winter's Tale*, ii, 1, 25 ff.:

> *Mamillius.* A sad tale's best for winter. I have one
> Of sprites and goblins.
> *Hermione.*   Let's have that, good sir.
> Come on, sit down; come on, and do your best
> To fright me with your sprites; you're pow'rful at it.

66. **Authóriz'd:** vouched for. The woman who tells the old wife's tale can cite only her grandmother as authority.

67. **Why . . . faces?** Here again Lady Macbeth chides her husband for not being able to control his countenance. Cf. i, 5, 63 ff., 72, 73; iii, 2, 27, 28.

69–73. During the utterance of these lines, the ghost rises, glares fixedly at Macbeth, nods its head, and moves slowly toward the back of the stage. Macbeth follows it with his eyes until it passes through the door. Cf. *Hamlet*, iii, 4, 134–136:

> Why, look you there! Look how it steals away!
> My father, in his habit as he liv'd!
> Look where he goes even now out at the portal!

71. **charnel houses.** A charnel house was a vault or small building attached to a church and used as a storehouse for such skulls and bones as came to light in digging new graves. Cf. *Hamlet*, v, 1, 83 ff.

72, 73. **our monuments . . . kites:** the dead shall be thrown out in the open fields to be devoured by birds of prey, and thus the only monuments we allow them shall be the bellies of kites. Then, perhaps, they will not come back to haunt us. So, in Nashe's *Summer's Last Will and Testament*, 1600 (G 4 v°; ed. McKerrow, III, 281), the son of Nebuchadnezzar, when his father died,

> Fearing lest he should come from death againe,
> . . . .
> Wil'd that his body spoylde of couerture,
> Should be cast foorth into the open fieldes,
> For Birds and Rauens, to deuoure at will,
> Thinking if they bare euery one of them,
> A bill full of his flesh into their nests,
> He would not rise, to trouble him in haste.

Cf. Kyd, *Cornelia*, v (ed. Boas, pp. 148–149):

> The earth, the sea, the vultures and the Crowes,
> Lyons and Beares, are theyr best Sepulchers;

Yarington, *Two Tragedies in One*, 1600, H3 1 r⁰:

> As for our bodies, they shall be inter'd
> In rauening mawes, of Ravens, Puttockes [i.e.,
>   kites], Crowes,
> Of tatlin[g] Magpies, and deathes harbingers.

76. **Ere . . . weal:** before civilizing law cleansed society (of primeval savagery) and made it gentle (i.e., in the old times of lawless barbarism). *Humane* is accented on the first syllable. For the proleptic use of *gentle* cf. i, 6, 3.

77. **since too:** even under the reign of law and order (as opposed to primeval anarchy).

81. **twenty . . . crowns.** An echo of the murderer's words in ll. 27, 28. Cf. Heywood, *The English Traveller*, ii (Pearson ed., IV, 39, 40):

> This murdered Ghost appeared,
> His body gasht, and all ore-stucke with wounds.

—**mortal murthers:** murderous wounds.

83, 84. **My worthy lord,** etc. Spoken with gentle ceremony, since it is meant to be heard by the guests. Now that Macbeth is regaining self-control, it is his wife's cue to save appearances and get him back to the table.—**worthy:** noble.—**lack you:** miss your company.

85. **muse:** wonder, be astonished.

90, 91. Macbeth has persuaded himself that the ghost was an illusion, like the air-drawn dagger, 'proceeding from the heat-oppressed brain.' With superb hardihood, he repeats his wish that Banquo were present. Cf. ll. 40–43. Instantly the ghost accepts the challenge.—**To all . . . thirst:** I am eager to drink to you all, and to Banquo in particular.

92. **And all to all:** and let everybody drink to everybody. The toast is to be a general health. Cf. Middleton, *Michaelmas Term*, iii, 1, 211–214 (ed. Bullen, I, 274):

> *Lethe.* Then here comes Rhenish to confirm our amity.—
> Wagtail, salute them all; they are friends.
>   *Country Wench.* Then, saving my quarrel, to you all.
>   *Shortyard.* To's [i.e., us] all.   *They drink.*

Our duties, and the pledge: Our toast is—homage to your Majesty, and a health to the whole table and to Banquo.

95. **speculation:** intelligent sight. The ghost's eyes are like a dead man's—fixed in a glassy stare.

97. **no other:** nothing else.

99. **What man dare, I dare:** an echo of i, 7, 46: 'I dare do all that may become a man.'

100. **like:** in the shape of. Cf. i, 3, 9; i, 7, 21; ii, 3, 84; iv, 1, 87.—**rugged:** shaggy and fierce. Cf. iii, 2, 27.—**Russian:** bears were imported from Russia for the bear-baiting at Paris Garden. Cf. *Henry V,* iii, 7, 153–155.

101, 102. **arm'd:** arm-clad, armoured. Cf. Sidney, *Arcadia,* ii, 23, 7 (ed. 1590, fol. 207 r°): 'a monstrous beast, of most vgly shape, armed like a Rhinoceros.'—**Hyrcan tiger.** A classical reminiscence. See *Æneid,* iv, 367: 'Hyrcanae tigres'; *3 Henry VI,* i, 4, 155; *Hamlet,* ii, 2, 472. The Hyrcanians lived near the Caspian Sea.—**nerves:** sinews. Cf. *Hamlet,* i, 4, 83: 'As hardy as the Nemean lion's nerve.'

104. **to the desert:** to some solitary place, for a duel to the death without seconds or witnesses. Cf. *Richard II,* iv, 1, 74: 'I dare meet Surrey in a wilderness'; also i, 1, 62–66.

105. **If trembling I inhabit then:** If then, as now, I live in terror. *Trembling* is a participle and *inhabit* means 'live and move and have my being.' No exact parallel has ever been cited. The nearest (and it is very close) is *Paradise Lost,* vii, 162: 'Meanwhile inhabit lax, ye powers of heaven' (i.e., 'live at your ease'). Hunter explains *inhabit* as 'remain at home,' which is possible. Davenant substitutes 'If any Sinew shrinke.' Many emendations have been suggested (see p. 234, below), but no change is necessary. Some scholars take *trembling* as a verbal noun, the object of *inhabit,* and Grant White quotes *Psalm* xxii, 3: 'O thou that inhabitest the praises of Israel.'— **protest:** declare, pronounce.

106. **The baby of a girl:** the child of a very young mother— and so, 'a timid weakling.' This is far more likely than the alternative—'a girl's doll.'

107. **Unreal mock'ry.** Macbeth tries hard to believe that the ghost is a creature of his imagination, and the closing lines of the scene show that, with his wife's help, he succeeds. But he knows better in the long run, and later he refers to the spectre as indeed 'the spirit of Banquo' (iv, 1, 112).—**mock'ry:** illusion.—**so!** very well!—**Being gone:** now that it is gone.

108. **Pray you sit still.** Macbeth recovers himself more rapidly than on the occasion of the ghost's first appearance. The guests, however, can no longer ignore his agitation, and they are rising from their chairs in horrified amazement at the King's strange words. Dr. Simon Forman, who saw the play at the Globe in 1610 or 1611, remarks that Macbeth 'fell into a great passion of fear and fury [i.e., frenzy], uttering many words about his [Banquo's] murder, by which, when they heard that Banquo was murdered, they suspected Macbeth' (cf. iii, 6).

110. **With most admir'd disorder:** by an amazing fit of distraction. Davenant has 'with your wild disorder.' *Disorder* refers to Macbeth's wild speech and behaviour, not to the disturbance among the guests. Cf. *King John*, iii, 4, 102: 'such disorder in my wit.' In Macbeth's reply he excuses his 'disorder' as only natural under such terrifying circumstances.

111, 112. **overcome . . . wonder?** come over us as suddenly as a cloud in summer, and yet excite no more surprise than such a cloud?

112, 113. **You . . . owe:** You make me feel that I do not know my own nature, which I had supposed to be that of a brave man.—**disposition:** mental and moral make-up or constitution.—**owe:** own.

116. **mine:** the natural ruby of *my* cheeks.

118. **enrages:** drives into a frenzy.—**At once, good night:** I bid you all a hasty good-night in a body, without waiting to take ceremonious leave of each in turn. Cf. *Twelfth Night*, ii, 1, 40; *Richard II*, ii, 2, 147.

119. **Stand . . . going:** Do not be punctilious about precedence as you leave the hall. Under ordinary circumstances the

nobles would depart slowly and ceremoniously, in the order of their rank.

122. The proverb occurs in various forms: as, 'Blood will have blood, foul murder scape no scourge' (Peele, *The Battle of Alcazar*; ed. Bullen, I, 282); 'Blood axeth blood' (Whetstone, *1 Promos and Cassandra*, ii, 6); 'Blood asketh blood, and death must death requite' (Sackville and Norton, *Gorboduc*, iv, Chorus). There is always a reminiscence of *Genesis*, ix, 6: 'Whoso sheddeth man's blood, by man shall his blood be shed.'

123-126. **Stones . . . blood.** Macbeth recalls various instances in which murders have been miraculously brought to light. The theory was that murder is so atrocious in God's eyes that he will not suffer it to go undetected. So Chaucer, *Nun's Priest's Tale*, 230-237:

> O blisful God, that art so just and trewe,
> Lo, how that thou biwreyest mordre alway!
> *Mordre wol out*, that se we day by day.
> Mordre is so wlatsom and abhomynable
> To God, that is so just and resonable,
> That he ne wol nat suffre it heled [i.e., concealed] be.
> Though it abyde a yeer, or two, or thre,
> *Mordre wol out*, this my conclusioun.

This principle is illustrated with many ghastly examples in a famous book of the seventeenth century, *Triumphs of God's Revenge against the Crying and Execrable Sin of Murther*, by John Reynolds.

123. **Stones have been known to move:** so as to reveal the body that the murderer had hidden.—**trees to speak:** as in the case of the murdered Polydorus in the Æneid, iii, 19-68.

124. **Augures:** auguries, signs from the flight of birds.— **understood relations:** reports properly comprehended. The appearance and flight of the birds give the *relation* or *report*, but this must be interpreted by a person skilled in augury before it can be understood. *Relation* almost always means 'report or recital' in Shakespeare (cf. iv, 3, 173). Otherwise one might be tempted to explain *understood relations* as 'a right

understanding of the relation or connection between the *sign* (from the birds) and the *thing signified* (the murder).'

125. **By:** by means of.—**maggot-pies:** magpies.—**choughs:** a kind of crow.—**rooks.** Cf. iii, 2, 51.—**brought forth:** revealed, brought to light.

126. **What is the night?** What time of night is it? By this sudden question Macbeth shows that he has recovered his self-control.

127. **at odds:** at variance, disputing. It is, then, about midnight. Thus this scene accounts for several hours of dramatic time. See note on ii, 3, 26. For the rest of the scene Lady Macbeth's speeches are very brief. The crisis is past, but she is worn out by the terrific strain. Her lassitude is another sign that she is breaking down.

128. **How say'st thou that . . .?** What do you say to the fact that . . .? From her reply it appears that Lady Macbeth has not heard of Macduff's refusal to come to court.

130. **by the way:** incidentally; in the ordinary course of affairs. Macbeth explains that the report has come from one of Macduff's household who is the King's spy. Macduff had avoided attending the coronation (ii, 4, 36) and has remained on his estates at Fife ever since. He has never positively refused a royal summons, but the spy has heard him declare that he means to stay away from court. His absence from the 'solemn supper' confirms Macbeth's suspicions of his hostility.

131, 132. **There's not . . . fee'd.** Macbeth's statement that he keeps a paid spy in the house of every one of the Scottish nobles is an indication that some time has elapsed since he came to the throne. Holinshed records that 'Makbeth had, in euerie noble mans house, one slie fellow or other in fee with him, to reueale all that was said or doone within the same.'

133. **betimes:** soon, without delay.

134. **More shall they speak.** An echo of what Macbeth says on the first appearance of the Sisters: 'Stay, you imperfect speakers, tell me more!' (i, 3, 70).—**bent:** determined.

135. **By the worst means:** i.e., *even* by the worst means. Macbeth no longer doubts that the Weird Sisters are powers of evil (cf. i, 3, 130–137).

136. **All causes:** all considerations. These include the scruples he would ordinarily have felt about seeking the help of the infernal powers.

139. **will to hand:** are bound to be executed.

140. **ere . . . scann'd:** before I pause to consider them.

141. **the season:** the preservative; that without which no living creature can remain sound and normal. The emphasis on sleep in iii, 2, 16 ff., and in the present scene is deeply significant. It looks back to the prophecy of the voice that cried 'Sleep no more!' (ii, 2, 35–43) and forward to the sleepwalking scene (v, 1).

142. **My strange and self-abuse:** my strange self-deception. Macbeth is now persuaded that the ghost was an illusion, like the 'dagger of the mind' (ii, 1, 38); but the audience knows better, and he later returns to his first opinion (iv, 1, 112). A fragment of a subsequent conversation recurs to Lady Macbeth when she talks in her sleep (v, 1): 'I tell you *yet again* Banquo's buried. He cannot come out on's grave.'

143. **the initiate fear:** fear felt by a novice (one just initiated in crime).—**wants:** lacks.—**hard use:** practice that hardens one.

Scene V.

This scene is an interpolation. See Introduction, p. vii.

1, 2. **angerly:** angrily.—**beldams:** hags.

7. **close:** secret.—**of all harms:** of all the evil deeds you do.

9. **the glory of our art.** The author of this scene regards the Sisters as mere witches, devotees of the art of sorcery.

11. **a wayward son.** It is quite out of accord with the situation for Hecate to call Macbeth a 'son'—i.e., a disciple of the demon-worshipping sect, an initiate in their Satanic mysteries. Such an expression is enough to prove that this scene is spurious.

12. **Spiteful and wrathful.** This has no pertinence. Macbeth has had no relations of any kind with the Sisters since the adventure on the Blasted Heath (i, 3).

13. **Loves.** Again a false note. Macbeth has never professed to love the Sisters or to be a devotee of art magic. In Middleton (*The Witch*, i, 2, 180; ed. Bullen, V, 376), Hecate says of Sebastian, who has applied to her for help: 'I know he loves me not, nor there's no hope on't.' This helps to confirm the hypothesis that our text of *Macbeth* is a revisal by Middleton.

15. **the pit of Acheron.** Certainly it is not to Acheron (a river of the infernal regions) that Macbeth comes to seek the witches, but to a Scottish cavern (iv, 1).

21. **dismal:** disastrous. Cf. i, 2, 53.

24. **a vap'rous drop profound:** a drop of condensed vapour, deep-hanging, pear-shaped, and so about to fall. Steevens notes that 'lunar venom' is meant—a foamy substance, powerful in magic, supposed by the ancients to be exuded by the moon (Lucan, *Pharsalia*, vi, 669; Statius, *Thebaid*, ii, 284, 285; Valerius Flaccus, *Argonautica*, vi, 447, 448). The allusion is, like Acheron, rather out of place in Scottish wizardry. When we come to the scene in the cavern (iv, 1), this moon-vapour is nowhere mentioned among the ingredients of the cauldron, though Hecate here regards it as of prime importance.

26. **sleights:** secret arts.

27. **artificial sprites:** spirits produced by art magic.

29. **confusion:** destruction, ruin. Cf. ii, 3, 71: 'Confusion now hath made his masterpiece!'

31. **grace:** goodness, virtue.

32. **security:** overweening confidence.

33. **song.** The song (from Middleton's tragicomedy of *The Witch*) is in the 1673 Quarto of *Macbeth* and in Davenant's adaptation. See p. 237, below. Perhaps only the first two lines are to be sung here.

> Come away! come away!
> Hecate, Hecate, come away!

Scene VI.

In the interval, short as it is, between scene iv and scene vi Macbeth has carried out his purpose of summoning Macduff (iii, 4, 130), and the messenger has returned with a curt refusal. Macduff has fled and is on his way to England. The other nobles, already more or less suspicious (cf. iii, 1, 1–3, 30–33), have learned that Banquo was murdered, and are now convinced that both his death and Duncan's were Macbeth's work.[1] These things all come out in a conversation between Lennox and a Lord. Contrast Lennox's state of mind immediately after the murder of Duncan (ii, 3, 106–111).

1. **My former speeches.** Lennox has been telling what happened at the banquet.—**hit your thoughts:** agreed with what you had been thinking.

2. **Which...farther:** Your mind can easily draw its own conclusions from the hints I have given.—**Only:** All I have to say is——.

3. **strangely borne:** oddly managed by Macbeth. Cf. l. 17. What follows in ll. 3–20 is in a strain of studied irony.

4. **of:** by.—**Marry:** an oath, 'by the Virgin Mary'; but often used lightly, as here, where it means simply 'to be sure.' —**was dead:** Macbeth pitied Duncan after he was dead, but not before!

6, 7. **Whom...fled.** The ironic argument may be stated thus: Macbeth's theory is that Malcolm and Donalbain procured their father's murder. His sole proof is their flight. The same argument will hold equally well against Fleance, who also fled. Yet nobody accuses Fleance of killing Banquo; for it is clear that he fled to escape Macbeth.—**Men must not walk too late.** Profoundly ironical. In Scotland, as things are now, it is not safe for anybody whom Macbeth dislikes to be out

---

[1] It may not be mathematically feasible to crowd all these events into the interval between midnight on the day of the 'solemn supper' and the visit of Macbeth to the Weird Sisters 'betimes' on the next day (iii, 4, 132, 133); but such difficulties are not felt by the audience.

after dark! In Kyd's *Spanish Tragedy*, when Pedringano has murdered Serberine, and been caught in the act, the Watchman asks, 'Why hast thou thus vnkindely kild the man?' and the cynical ruffian replies with a jest: 'Why? because he walkt abroad so late!' (iii, 3, 28–40; ed. Boas, pp. 44, 45).

8. Who cannot want the thought? Who can help thinking? This is simply an instance of the double negative: *cannot want* for *can want*. Cf. *Winter's Tale*, iii, 2, 55–58:

> 　　　　　　　　　I ne'er heard yet
> That any of these bolder vices wanted
> Less impudence to gainsay what they did
> Than to perform it first.

That is, 'I never heard yet that any person who was guilty of so shameless a fault as this, had less impudence in denying it than in committing it in the first place.'—**monstrous:** a trisyllable (as if *monsterous*). Cf. i, 5, 40 (*entrance*) and iii, 2, 30 (*remembrance*).

10. fact: evil deed, crime.

11. Did he not straight, etc. Macbeth's hasty act is ironically ascribed to indignation at the enormity of the crime, but his real motive is plainly hinted in l. 16—to get the chamberlains out of the way before they could protest their innocence.—**straight:** straightway, immediately.

12. pious rage: a frenzy of loyalty. *Pious* often describes the filial affection of children or the loyal devotion of subjects.—**delinquents:** offenders.

13. the slaves of drink. Lennox insinuates that the chamberlains could not have killed Duncan, for they had slept the sleep of drunkenness all night long.

16, 17. So that ... well: The upshot of the whole matter is—Macbeth has managed everything wisely.

19. an: if. The Folio, as usual, gives the full form, *and.*—**should find:** would certainly find; would be sure to find.

20. So should Fleance. This repeats, with condensed ironic power, the argument of ll. 6, 7. The implication is that Mal-

colm and Donalbain are just as innocent as Fleance, whom
nobody suspects; and, furthermore, that Macbeth would be as
glad to kill the young Princes as he has already shown himself
eager to murder Fleance.

21. **from broad words:** because of too free or unguarded expressions. These have been reported to Macbeth by a spy (see
iii, 4, 128–132). Cf. *Leicester's Commonwealth*, 1641, p. 14:
'Have you not heard of the *proviso* made in the last Parliament
for punishment of those who speake so broad of such men as
my L. of *Leycester* is?'

22. **tyrant's:** usurper's.

24. **bestows himself:** has taken refuge. Cf. iii, 1, 30, 31.

25. **holds:** withholds.—**due of birth:** birthright.

27. **Of:** by.—**Edward:** Edward the Confessor, who reigned
from 1042 to 1066 (see iv, 3, 140–159).—**grace:** favour.

29. **his high respect:** the high regard in which he is held.

30. **upon his aid:** for his assistance.

31. **wake:** call to arms.—**Northumberland:** i.e., the people
of that region.—**Siward:** Earl of Northumberland.

34. **meat:** food.

36. **faithful:** sincere.—**free:** unconstrained; i.e., granted
with good will on the King's part. At present their homage to
Macbeth is insincere, and the honour that he shows them in
return is not voluntary (free), because it is the result of fear.
Cf. what Macbeth says in iii, 2, 32–35.

37. **this report:** the report of the favour with which Malcolm
is treated. Macbeth fears an invasion. Cf. iii, 1, 30–33.

38. **exasperate:** exasperated. Participles in *-ate* (from the
Latin *-atus*) are common in the more elevated Elizabethan
style, both in prose and verse.

40. **He did.** This refers, not to an invitation to the supper,
but to a summons sent since (see iii, 4, 130).

41. **cloudy:** frowning, gloomy. Cf. *Antony and Cleopatra*,
iii, 2, 51: 'He has a cloud in's face.' The messenger looks
gloomy because he is reluctant to carry such unwelcome tidings
to a man of Macbeth's temper. Compare Macbeth's treatment

of the person who reports the approach of Birnam Wood (v, 5, 35–40), and the violence shown by Cleopatra to the messenger who brings word of Antony's marriage (*Antony and Cleopatra*, ii, 5, 25–73. Cf. the same play, i, 2, 99: 'The nature of bad news infects the teller'), and *Richard III*, iv, 4, 506–514.—
me. The so-called ethical dative. It adds nothing to the sense, but merely gives a colloquial turn to the phraseology—something like the use of 'don't you know?' and similar tags in modern speech.

42. **hums.** This indicates a surly murmuring sound.—**as who should say:** as if he were saying; as if to say.

43. **clogs me:** makes me return with reluctant feet.

46. **unfold:** disclose, reveal.

48, 49. **our … accurs'd:** our country, suffering under, etc. A common order. Cf. 'A long-parted mother with her child' (*Richard II*, iii, 2, 8) for 'A mother, long parted from her child.'

Act IV. Scene I.

There is no indication of place in the Folios except 'Open locks, Whoever knocks' (ll. 46, 47). Most editors lay the scene in a cavern. An old ruin in a desolate region would do as well. The time appears to be early in the morning on the day after the supper (iii, 4, 132, 133). The somewhat similar scene in *2 Henry VI*, i, 4, is laid in the open air, probably in the Duke of Gloucester's garden. For an immense quantity of pertinent lore, with learned notes, see Jonson's *Masque of Queens*.

1–3. **brinded:** brindled, striped. The cat, the hedgehog, and Harpier are familiar (i.e., attendant) spirits, like Graymalkin and Paddock in i, 1. *Harpier* is a proper name formed, apparently, from *harpy*.—**'tis time.** Some editors make Harpier say this.

5 ff. Compare the ingredients of Medea's cauldron in Ovid's *Metamorphoses*, vii, 262–278.

6. **cold.** The *o* is prolonged, with a change of pitch, though no cessation of vocal tone, and thus the effect of two syllables is produced. Cf. *sight* (l. 122); *hail* (i, 2, 5); *our* (i, 6, 30).

8. **Swelt'red:** coming out in drops, like sweat. Cf. Dekker, *The Dead Tearme*, 1608 (ed. Grosart, IV, 67): 'The Iawes of a Toade (sweating & foaming out poyson).' See Kittredge, *The Old Farmer and his Almanack*, pp. 104 ff.

10. **Double.** This may be either a verb or an adjective. The sense is the same in either case. The verb would afford an easier grammatical construction, but rigid syntax is hardly requisite in the idiom of incantations.

12. **Fillet:** slice.

16. The blindworm (or slowworm) is a small snake-like lizard erroneously supposed to be sightless. Though not in fact venomous, it is still popularly regarded as dangerous. An old rhyme makes the deaf adder say to the blindworm,

> If I could hear, and thou couldst see,
> There would none live but you and me:

Hazlitt, *English Proverbs*, ed. 1869, p. 219 (ed. 1907, p. 245). See also Burne and Jackson, *Shropshire Folk-Lore*, p. 239; Northall, *English Folk-Rhymes*, p. 281.

17. **howlet:** owlet.

23. **Witch's mummy:** mummified fragment of a witch. Human flesh was thought to be powerful in magic—especially the flesh of criminals, of non-Christians, or of persons who had met with a violent death or had not had Christian burial. See Kittredge, *Witchcraft*, pp. 141 ff. Cf. ll. 26, 29–31.—**maw and gulf:** stomach and gullet.

24. **ravin'd:** ravenous. Formed from the noun *ravin* or *raven* (Lat. *rapina*), 'voracity,' by means of the suffix *-ed* (meaning 'provided with,' or 'characterized by'). Beasts of prey were often called 'beasts of ravin.' Cf. *All's Well*, iii, 2, 120: 'the ravin lion.'

25. **i' th' dark.** The time when an herb was gathered was supposed to affect its potency in medicine (cf. l. 28).

27. **yew**: a graveyard tree thought to be poisonous.

28. **eclipse**: a particularly ill-omened time. Cf. Milton, *Lycidas*, ll. 100–102:

> It was that fatal and perfidious bark,
> Built i' the eclipse, and rigg'd with curses dark,
> That sunk so low that sacred head of thine.

30. **birth-strangled**: strangled as soon as born, and hence not baptized. Infants who die unchristened were the object of many superstitions. Sometimes they were thought to haunt the earth as a kind of demon. In any case, their flesh was regarded as powerful in evil spells. 'It is observable,' writes Dr. Johnson, 'that Shakespeare, on this great occasion, which involves the fate of a king, multiplies all the circumstances of horror. The babe, whose finger is used, must be strangled in its birth; the grease must not only be human, but must have dropped from a gibbet, the gibbet of a murderer; and even the sow, whose blood is used, must have offended nature by devouring her own farrow.'

31. **Ditch-deliver'd**: born in a ditch.—**drab**: harlot, trull.

32. **gruel.** A bit of savage grotesqueness, like 'hell-broth.'—**slab**: thick, viscous.

33. **chaudron**: liver and lights.

34. **ingredience**: composition. Cf. i, 7, 11. *Cauldron* rhymes with *chaudron*. It is spelled *Cawdron* in the First and Second Folios.

39–43. Hecate's speech is in an iambic metre (the same that she uses in iii, 5), very different in its effect from the trochaic metre that precedes, and is obviously by the same hand as iii, 5. She does not bring the lunar venom which she mentioned as to be used in 'raising artificial sprites.' There are other contradictions. The mention of 'gains' is one, for there are no gains: the Sisters expect nothing from Macbeth; they disappear without waiting for a reward. The comparison with elves and fairies is quite out of tune. L. 43 makes no sense, for all the ingredients have already been 'put in,' the charm is already 'firm and good,' and the incantation has been finished in l. 38 (cf. i, 3, 37). In the stage direction the Folios read 'and the other.' The correction was made by Clark and Wright; but possibly the interpolator meant to have six witches (besides Hecate) on the stage for a final dance round the cauldron.

43. **Black spirits.** See p. 238, below. This song, of which the Folios give only the first two words, is doubtless by Middleton, in whose tragicomedy of *The Witch* it occurs. It is inserted (obviously from *The Witch*) in Davenant's version of *Macbeth*.

44. **pricking:** an old sign of the approach of some evil person or some strange event.

46. **Open locks.** This does not imply that the Sisters are in a locked room rather than a cave. It is a formula of admission, releasing any spells that prevent the entrance of intruders.

50. **cónjure:** in the sense of *conjúre*—call upon solemnly.— **by ... profess:** i.e., the prophetic power which, as their words to him and Banquo had implied, they profess to have (i, 3, 48 ff.).

51. **Howe'er ... it:** no matter if your knowledge comes from infernal sources. He is determined to know 'by the worst means the worst' (iii, 4, 135). See i, 3, 131, note.

52-61. **Though you untie,** etc.: Though the evil spells which you must use are so powerful as to bring utter ruin upon the whole earth, yet I will have you reveal the future to me. Cf. iii, 2, 16-19.—**untie the winds:** an allusion to the power which witches (especially those of the North) were believed to exercise over wind and weather (cf. i, 3, 11 ff.). See Kittredge, *Witchcraft in Old and New England*, Chap. viii.

53. **yesty:** yeasty, foaming.

54. **Confound:** destroy.

55. **bladed corn.** If wheat in the blade is lodged (beaten down flat by wind and rain), the crop fails and famine ensues. Cf. *Richard II*, iii, 3, 161-163:

> We'll make foul weather with despised tears;
> Our sighs and they shall lodge the summer corn
> And make a dearth in this revolting land.

56. **topple:** fall in ruins.

57. **slope:** let fall.

58, 59. **the treasure . . . germens:** the accumulated store of those elemental seeds or germs from which everything in the future is to spring. This is equivalent to saying, 'though the orderly universe be destroyed and chaos come again.' For the metaphor cf. 'the seeds of time' in i, 3, 58. On the history of the idea see a learned paper by W. C. Curry, *Studies in Philology*, XXIX, 15–28 (Chapel Hill, N.C., 1932).

60. **sicken:** is satiated, and sickens at its own work.

61. **Demand:** ask.

62, 63. **Say . . . masters.** The Weird Sisters give Macbeth his choice between visions and mere prophecy. This proves that they are managing their own affairs, as ministers of fate, without the interference of Hecate.—**our masters:** the great powers of fate whom we serve. These are not to be confused with the imps or familiars—Paddock, Graymalkin, and Harpier.—**Call 'em! Let me see 'em.** The bare colloquial simplicity of these words, as contrasted with the solemn adjuration of Macbeth's preceding speech, produces an effect of fierce intensity of purpose. He wishes to know the truth and is determined to get it at first hand.

65. **farrow:** young pigs. For the mystic *nine*, cf. i, 3, 36.—**grease.** The flame is made to flare up by adding the fat of a murderer.—**sweaten:** sweated.

67. **high or low:** wherever thou art, whether in the upper or lower air, under the earth, or in hell. This is much better than to interpret *high or low* as 'spirits of high or low degree'; for no 'weak masters' are now invoked (cf. *Tempest*, v, 1, 41), and, besides, the summons is to one spirit only, as 'thyself' shows. What follows in this scene may be profitably compared with *2 Henry VI*, i, 4, 19–43.

68. **office:** function.—**deftly:** skilfully.—**an Armed Head.** This typifies Macduff as he is known to Macbeth—i.e., as a warrior who may return to fight against the tyrant (cf. l. 97 and note). The speech of the apparition tells nothing that

Macbeth does not already know: it merely expresses the fear that haunts his mind. The first apparition, then, is parallel to the greeting of the First Sister, 'Hail to thee, Thane of Glamis!' (i, 3, 48), and corresponds to the function of the First Norn, who may be said to represent the Past. Some think that the Armed Head prefigures Macbeth's head, which is cut off and exhibited by Macduff at the end of the play; but nothing indicates that the Armed Head is severed and bleeding. Besides, as in the other two cases, the apparition should typify the person from whom danger is to be feared. Finally, the First Apparition should not represent something that comes to pass later than the events foretold by the Second and Third.

70. **Hear . . . naught.** The powers which the Sisters have evoked are so tremendous that they themselves stand in awe of them (cf. l. 89). When Faustus conjured up spirits in the likeness of Alexander the Great and his paramour, he cautioned the Emperor to 'demaund no question of them, nor speake vnto them' (*The Damnable Life, and Deserued Death of Dr. Iohn Faustus*, 1592, chap. 29, sig. G 2 v⁰).

72. **Dismiss me. Enough.** Cf. *2 Henry VI*, i, 4, 31, 41, where the spirits are eager for dismissal.

74. **harp'd my fear aright:** sounded it forth on the right string (expressed it truly).—**But one word more.** Cf. i, 3, 70.

76. The Second Apparition represents Macduff, but Macduff in a character in which he is unknown to Macbeth until the end of the play—i.e., as not born of woman. Thus this apparition and his prophecy accord with the greeting of the Second Witch, 'Hail to thee, Thane of Cawdor!' (i, 3, 49). They stand for something which is true at the moment but unknown to Macbeth.—**More potent.** Macduff, as the man not born of woman, and therefore the fated agent of Macbeth's destruction, is more potent than Macduff as a mere human enemy.

80. **none of woman born.** Cf. Holinshed: 'A certeine witch, whome hee had in great trust, had told that he should neuer be slaine with man borne of anie woman, nor vanquished till the wood of Bernane came to the castell of Dunsinane.'

84. **take a bond of fate.** Fate has given its word that none born of woman shall harm Macbeth, but he is not satisfied with Fate's *word*—he requires a *bond*. Rushton suggests that Shakespeare here alludes to a bond with 'double forfeiture'— one by virtue of which, if the sum borrowed was not repaid when due, the creditor could recover double the principal. This is very probable. By killing Macduff, Macbeth will put it out of Fate's power to harm him unless Fate is ready to break two of her fixed laws: the law of birth and the law of death; she must bring forward a man who was never born, and must bring back a man (not a mere ghost) from the dead.

86. **a Child Crowned,** etc. The Third Apparition typifies Malcolm as king and the advance of his soldiers with branches of Birnam Wood in their hands.

87. **like:** in the shape of. Cf. i, 3, 9; i, 7, 21; ii, 3, 84; iii, 4, 100.

88. **round.** Cf. i, 5, 29: 'the golden round.'

89. **top:** diadem.—**speak not.** Cf. l. 70.

91. **chafes:** is resentful or discontented.

93. **Dunsínane.** Elsewhere in the play, *Dúnsinane*. The Moving Wood is a widespread incident in folklore and saga.

94. **That will never be.** Macbeth, in eager acceptance of the oracle, continues it in the same rhymed form. In effect, he makes himself his own prophet: he identifies himself, as it were, with the lying spirits whom he has consulted, and whom he trusts to the end. Thus *our* in l. 98 is in perfect keeping (as if the speaker were still the apparition, not Macbeth himself).

95. **impress:** enlist forcibly; press into service.

96. **bodements:** prophecies.

97. **Rebellion's head.** Theobald's correction of the Folios, which read 'rebellious dead.' Rebellion seems to be conceived as a monstrous serpent or dragon. The Folio reading might refer to Banquo, or else to Macduff, whom Macbeth intends to kill; but it is doubtless a misprint. In any case, *head* recalls the First Apparition and shows that the armed head does not represent the head of Macbeth.

99. **live the lease of nature:** live the allotted term of his natural life and die a natural death. Cf. iii, 2, 38: 'Nature's copy.'

100. **mortal custom:** the custom of dying, which is common to all men.—**Yet:** the emphatic *yet*, which is often used with great effect in Shakespeare. 'Though I have learned so much, yet, after all is said and done, there is one thing more that I long to know.' Cf. iv, 3, 46, 69; v, 1, 35.

103. **Seek to know no more.** The Weird Sisters seem to be almost exhausted by the terrific nature of their spells, and shrink from further revelations. Such, at least, is the effect of this impressive warning, uttered by all three with one voice. Macbeth is made only the more eager by their reluctance.

104. **I will be satisfied:** I am determined to have full information.

106. **noise:** common in the sense of 'music.'

111. **A show:** i.e., a dumb show; an exhibition of actors that do not speak. Cf. *Hamlet*, iii, 2, 145, where the dumb show is also heralded by the music of hautboys.

112. **Thou . . . Banquo.** Said to the first of the Eight Kings. Banquo himself is not seen until the last king has passed.

113. **thy hair.** The hair (worn as Banquo doubtless wore it, straight and hanging to the shoulders) is a striking feature and an obvious point of family likeness. Nothing dwelt more fixedly in Macbeth's memory than Banquo's hair; for it had held his gaze at the banquet, matted with blood from the 'twenty trenched gashes' (iii, 4, 27). These phantom kings are surely Banquo's descendants—they have *Banquo's hair*! And then, when they have passed by, comes Banquo himself, 'blood-bolter'd,' as at the feast (iii, 4, 81), 'and points at them for his.' Cf. *Richard III*, i, 4, 52–54:

> Then came wand'ring by
> A shadow like an angel, with bright hair
> Dabbled in blood.

116. **Start, eyes!** Cf. *Hamlet*, i, 5, 17: 'Make thy two eyes, like stars, start from their spheres.'

117. **crack of doom.** Cf. i, 2, 37.

119. **a glass:** a mirror. For mirror magic see Kittredge, *Witchcraft*, Chap. xi.

121. **balls.** The 'ball,' 'apple,' 'globe,' or 'orb' was one of the insignia of sovereignty. *Twofold* refers to England and Scotland. *Treble* refers either to England, Scotland, and Ireland, or, more probably, to the title 'King of Great Britain, France, and Ireland,' assumed by James I in 1604. Banquo was the mythical ancestor of the Stuarts, of whom James was the first to rule in England. Cf. Matthew Gwinne's Latin poem (p. viii, above).

122. **sight.** The vowel of *sight* is prolonged with a shudder and a change of pitch, and thus the effect of two syllables is produced. Cf. *hail* (i, 2, 5), *our* (i, 6, 30), *cold* (iv, 1, 6).

123. **blood-bolter'd:** having his hair matted with blood.

124-132. As Macbeth is staring at the blood-boltered Banquo, the apparitions vanish, and with a question—'What? Is this *so*?' 'Is this the *truth*?'—he turns to the Sisters, only to find that they too have vanished—'Where are they? Gone?' The speech of the First Witch, with the dance, is a manifest interpolation. The idea of cheering up Macbeth by an antic round is worthy of comic opera. The iambic metre is like that of the Hecate speeches and quite different from the trochaic verse which the witches always use except in the interpolated scene (iii, 5).

126-130. **amazedly:** like a man in a trance. Cf. ii, 4, 19.— **sprites:** spirits.—**antic:** fantastic.—**round:** dance in a circle.

132. Macbeth has not 'welcomed' the Sisters, unless 'How now, you secret, black, and midnight hags?' (l. 48) can be called a welcome. Nor do they owe him any 'duty' (i.e., loyal service). The whole speech is absurdly out of tune.

135. Lennox has been on guard at the mouth of the cave. He is one of Macbeth's most trusted advisers, but (as we have seen in iii, 6) he is a ringleader in the conspiracy now forming against him.

139. **damn'd.** Thus Macbeth, by implication, curses himself, for he trusts the Weird Sisters to the very end (v, 8).

140. **horse:** plural or collective—horses or horsemen.

142. **Macduff is fled to England.** Here (as in i, 3, 104) the predictions begin to fulfil themselves instantly, and thus their trustworthiness is established in Macbeth's mind (i, 3, 133). Lennox already knew of Macduff's escape (iii, 6), but he has concealed it from the King.

144. **anticipat'st:** forestallest.

145. **The flighty purpose:** Every purpose is fleeting and will never be fulfilled unless it is accompanied by the act proposed, i.e., unless it is fulfilled as soon as formed. *The* is the 'generic article.' Cf. *Hamlet,* iii, 2, 204, 205:

> What to ourselves in passion we propose,
> The passion ending, doth the purpose lose.

147. **firstlings:** first-born. The firstlings of his heart are the first purposes that he may form.

150. **surprise:** seize upon suddenly.

152. **unfortunate.** A touch of pity, a remnant of 'human kindness' (i, 5, 18).

153. **trace:** follow. Macduff is the head of his family, and his relatives are therefore said to follow, or come after, him in his line.

153, 154. **No ... cool.** This may well be classed with other spurious rhyme-tags (ii, 1, 60, 61; iii, 2, 54, 55). See Introduction, p. vii.

155. **these gentlemen:** those who bring the news of Macduff's escape.

Scene II.

Between scene i and scene ii the interval is only long enough to enable Macbeth to send the murderers to Macduff's castle. For the present scene Holinshed furnishes merely the following passage: 'He [Macbeth] came hastily with a great power [i.e., troop] into Fife, and foorthwith besieged the castell where

Makduffe dwelled, trusting to haue found him therein. They that kept the house, without anie resistance opened the gates, and suffered him to enter, mistrusting none euill. But neuerthelesse Makbeth most cruellie caused the wife and children of Makduffe, with all other whom he found in that castell, to be slaine.'

2. **patience:** self-control.

3, 4. **When ... traitors.** Macduff had done nothing treasonable. Yet fear had made him flee to the English court, and this action had made him a traitor in fact.

7. **his titles:** his title deeds, and so—all his hereditary possessions and honours.

9. **the natural touch:** the natural trait which prompts all creatures to fight in defence of their young.

10. **diminitive:** a variant form of *diminutive*.

11. **in her nest:** still being in her nest, and therefore in her charge.

14. **coz:** an affectionate abbreviation of *cousin*.

15. **school yourself:** control yourself.—**for:** as for.

17. **The fits o' th' season:** the fits and starts, the spasmodic and irregular happenings, the strange accidents, that mark this time in Scotland. The metaphor is from a fever fit. Cf. *Coriolanus*, iii, 2, 33: 'the violent fit o' th' time.'

18, 19. **when we ... ourselves:** when we are, in the King's eyes, traitors; yet do not know ourselves to be such, are not conscious of having committed treason.

19–22. **when we hold rumour ... none:** when every rumour of danger is credited by us because of our fears, and yet we do not really know what there is to be afraid of, since we are not conscious of having committed any offence. Thus we are like a drifting hulk at sea, that is tossed about in every direction by shifting winds but makes no progress in any direction. Cf. *Soliman and Perseda*, i, 2, 1–3 (Kyd, ed. Boas, p. 165):

> Why, when, Perseda? wilt thou not assure me?
> But shall I, like a mastlesse ship at sea,
> Goe euery way, and not the way I would?

Cf. *3 Henry VI*, ii, 5, 5–13; *Antony and Cleopatra*, i, 4, 44–47. The Folio reading, *and moue*, was conjecturally emended to *and none* by Aldis Wright but is retained by most editors. The alternative interpretation ('when we have the reputation [of being traitors] on account of actions prompted by our fears') is harder and less in accord with Shakespeare's use of *hold* and *rumour* elsewhere; but it accords with Lady Macduff's words—'When ... traitors' (ll. 3, 4).

23. **Shall:** it shall.

24. **climb upward:** improve, take a turn for the better. Cf. such proverbs as 'The darkest hour is just before the dawn'; 'When bale is highest, boot (i.e., amendment) is nighest.'

29. **It ... discomfort:** I should shed tears, which would disgrace me as a man and would distress you to see. The conventional idea that tears are unmanly recurs often in Shakespeare. See, for example, iv, 3, 230; *King John*, iv, 1, 35, 36; v, 2, 56, 57; *3 Henry VI*, v, 4, 6–12; *Hamlet*, iv, 7, 186–191; *Lear*, i, 4, 318–326; ii, 4, 280, 281.

30. **Sirrah.** Used in familiar address, sometimes to express anger, contempt, or superiority; often (to boys) as a playful and affectionate term.

32. **As birds do.** The stage child always seems a little artificial when we read his speeches; less so, however, when we hear them in the theatre. The effect of unnatural cleverness is due in the main to dramatic condensation. The stage child simply says as many clever things in five minutes as a real child might say in a fortnight; just as, in the drama, negotiations that would take months in real life are settled in a day or two.

34. **lime:** birdlime, a sticky substance daubed on twigs to catch birds.

35. **pitfall:** a kind of trap.—**gin:** short for *engine*; used for any kind of contrivance or device, mental or physical; here, for a snare or the like.

36. **Poor** (emphatic): Nobody would care to trap a poor little bird like me!—**they:** the net, trap, etc.

42, 43. **Thou speak'st ... thee:** What you say is childish, for you have but a child's wisdom, even when you use all of it—and yet, for a child, your wit is well enough. *Wit*, as usual, means 'intelligence,' 'sense.' Cf. *The Two Angry Women of Abington*, sc. 3, l. 430 (Gayley, I, 569): 'Alas, poore foole, he uses all his wit!'

47. one...lies: one that takes an oath (of allegiance) and then breaks it. Lady Macduff alludes to her husband's marriage vow to protect his wife, which he has broken by his flight. The boy takes her to mean 'uses profane language and tells lies.' Cf. Lyly, *Love's Metamorphosis*, v, 2, 18 (ed. Bond, III, 326): 'If men sweare and lie, how will you trie their loues?'—be. An old form of the plural.

57. enow: enough (often, but not exclusively, plural).

59. monkey: used tenderly, in the fantasticality of affection. So *sirrah, wretch, rogue, fool,* and the like.

65. The messenger comes from Lennox or some other friend of the Macduffs who has learned of Macbeth's purpose. He arrives in time to warn Lady Macduff but not in time to enable her to escape; for in this case Macbeth acts with the promptitude which he has promised at the end of iv, 1: 'Be it thought and done!'—Bless you: God bless you.

66. in your state ... perfect: I am fully informed as to your honourable condition; I know you well, honoured lady.

67. doubt: fear.

68. homely: i.e., of no exalted rank—a plain man, a mere gentleman (not a noble).

70. To fright you thus: in frightening you as I do by this warning.

71. To do worse to you: i.e., to harm you, as Macbeth intends to do.—fell: fierce.

73. I dare, etc.: It would be death to myself to be discovered giving you this information.

76. sometime: sometimes.

78. womanly: womanish.

79. faces. As Macbeth sees particularly the *hair* of the apparitions that resemble Banquo (iv, 1, 113), so here the savage *faces*

of the murderers so impress themselves on Lady Macduff's imagination that she uses that word for the men themselves. Cf. v, 3, 19: 'Take thy face hence.' These murderers are easily distinguished from those who killed Banquo. They are professional ruffians.

80. **Where is your husband?** The murderers must know that Macduff has fled to England; but they have to say something, and to call for the lord of the castle is the most natural way to begin.

83. **shag-ear'd.** The long shaggy hair falling over the ruffian's ears reminds the boy of a dog's ears. Cf. *The Wit of a Woman* (ed. Farmer, E 3, 2): 'with hayre like a Water-dogge'; Ford, *The Lady's Trial*, iii, 1: 'He has chang'd hair with a shag-dog'; *Arden of Feversham*, ii, 1, 51–56 (ed. Tucker Brooke, *Shakespeare Apocrypha*, p. 12):

> A leane faced writhen knaue,
> Hauke nosde and verye hollow eied,
> With mightye furrowes in his stormye browes;
> Long haire down his shoulders curled;
> His Chinne was bare, but on his vpper lippe
> A mutchado, which he wound about his eare.

The Elizabethan ruffian let his hair grow and prided himself on his unkempt locks. *Shag-hair'd* is the usual adjective, and may be what Shakespeare wrote; as Steevens conjectured, comparing *2 Henry VI*, iii, 1, 367: 'a shag-hair'd crafty kern'; but no change seems necessary. In *Sir Thomas More*, iii, 2, 116–118 (*Shakespeare Apocrypha*, p. 400), Sir Thomas says to one Fawkner, a ruffian:

> Sirra, tell me now,
> When were you last at barbars? how longe time
> Have you vppon your head woorne this shagg haire?

Shag-rag is used for 'ruffian' in Chapman, *May Day*, ii, 2: 'Nay if I thought twould euer come to that, I'de hire some shag-ragge or other for halfe a chickeene [i.e., sequin] to cut's throat.'—**egg:** unhatched chick, youngster.

84. **fry:** spawn.

Scene III.

Between this scene and iii, 6, time enough has elapsed to enable Macduff to reach the court of the English king, Edward the
Confessor. Macduff has described to Malcolm the oppressive
rule of Macbeth and has offered his services, and those of other
Scottish nobles, if Malcolm will take command; but Malcolm is
offish, suspecting a trick to get him into Macbeth's power.

3. **mortal:** deadly.

4. **Bestride ... birthdom:** fight in defence of our prostrate
native land. The figure is from the old hand-to-hand combats,
where it was common for a man to bestride a fallen comrade
to protect him in a mêlée. Cf. Falstaff's request of Prince Hal
(*1 Henry IV*, v, 1, 121, 122): 'If thou see me down in the battle
and bestride me, so! [i.e., well and good!] 'Tis a point of
friendship.' Cf. also *Comedy of Errors*, v, 1, 190–193:

> Justice, most gracious Duke! O, grant me justice!
> Even for the service that long since I did thee
> When I bestrid thee in the wars and took
> Deep scars to save thy life.

So in Heywood, *The Royal King and the Loyal Subject* (Pearson ed., VI, 6):

> Twice that perillous day
> Did he bestride me, and beneath his Targe
> Methought that instant did I lie as safe
> As in my best and strongest Cittadell;
> The whilst his bright Sword like the Bolt of Ioue,
> Pierc't the steele-crests of barbarous Infidels.

—**Each new morn,** etc. Nothing that occurs in the play jus-
tifies this description of Macbeth's reign in ll. 4–8, but it accords
with Holinshed's account.

6. **that:** so that.

8–10. **Like syllable of dolour:** words of sorrow that reëcho
those which all Scotland is uttering.—**What I believe ... will.**
An expression of caution, almost of incredulity.—**As ... friend:**

whenever I find opportunity favourable. *To friend* means 'as
a friend,' and so 'friendly.'

12. **sole:** mere.

13. **honest:** honourable; good and noble.

14-17. **I am young ... god:** Though I am young and inexperienced, I cannot help seeing that you may be trying to en-
trap me in order to maintain yourself in Macbeth's favour. We
learn later that Macbeth has often tried to entice Malcolm back
to Scotland (ll. 117-119; cf. iii, 6, 17-20). Perhaps, however,
I am young means 'I am young and helpless, and possibly
Macbeth does not worry much about any danger from me.'—
deserve: win, earn. The Folio reads *discerne* (corrected by
Theobald).—**through me:** by betraying me into Macbeth's
power.—**and wisdom:** and [it is] wisdom.

19, 20. **may recoil ... charge:** may give way under pressure
from a monarch. The figure is either that of retiring before the
onslaught (*charge*) of a superior force, or that of a cannon
which recoils when the charge (or load) is too great; cf.
2 Henry VI, iii, 2, 331: 'like an overcharged gun, recoil.' In
the latter case, *charge* suggests also 'orders,' 'duty imposed.'
The first interpretation is simpler, and *recoil* often means
merely 'retire,' 'go back,' 'give way' (as in v, 2, 23), without
suggesting gunnery.—**In:** causal.—**I ... pardon:** I must beg
your pardon. Malcolm sees indignant grief in Macduff's face.

21. **transpose:** transform. If Macduff is innocent of treachery, Malcolm's suspicions cannot make him guilty.

22. **the brightest:** Lucifer. Cf. *Isaiah*, xiv, 12: 'How art
thou fallen from heaven, O Lucifer, son of the morning!'

23. **would wear:** should strive to wear.—**the brows of grace:**
the face or appearance of virtue.

24. **so:** like herself, like virtue. The existence of many hypo-
crites does not make a good man any the less good, though it
may cause him to be mistrusted.—**my hopes:** i.e., my hope of
persuading Malcolm to take command in the revolt, and therefore all my hopes for Scotland.

25. **Perchance ... doubts:** Perhaps what has made you

lose your hopes is the very circumstance that has made me suspicious of you, i.e., your leaving your family in Macbeth's power, as you would hardly have done if you were his enemy.

26. **in that rawness:** in so unprotected a condition. Cf. *Henry V*, iv, 1, 147: 'their children rawly left,' i.e., 'left helpless and unprovided for.'

27. **motives:** incentives to action.

29, 30. **Let not . . . safeties:** Do not regard my suspicions as meant to dishonour you, but rather as proceeding from a due regard for my own safety. All the abstract nouns are plural because the first one is plural.—**rightly just:** perfectly good and honourable.

32. **tyranny:** usurpation.—**basis:** foundation.

33. **check thee:** rebuke thee; call thee to account.—**Wear thou thy wrongs:** Continue to hold what thou hast wrongly obtained—thy ill-gotten titles and honours. The address is still to 'great tyranny' (as personified in Macbeth).

34. **affeer'd:** legally confirmed. Macbeth's title is established beyond dispute, since Malcolm refuses to contest it.

41. **withal:** also, besides.

43. **gracious England:** the good king of England.

44. **But, for all this.** Malcolm's reluctance to trust Macduff has been natural enough. It is not until this point that his curious device for further testing begins. The incident is taken from Holinshed, whom Shakespeare follows rather closely. Its improbability is evident, but in Shakespeare's time it was accepted as historical, and therefore (like the even more fantastic legend of King Lear's plan for dividing his kingdom) it was available for dramatic treatment. A long lapse of time since Macbeth's accession is strongly suggested, though not mathematically demonstrable; for, when Malcolm left Scotland, his true character must have been known to Macduff.

46. **yet:** after all that. The emphatic *yet*. See iv, 1, 100.

49. **What should he be?** An amazed and incredulous question: 'What worse king could there be than Macbeth?'

51. **particulars:** particular kinds, special varieties.—**grafted:**

engrafted, implanted. The figure implies that these faults are
so thoroughly incorporated in Malcolm that they have become a
part of his very being.

52. **open'd:** developed and brought to view. The figure is
from the opening of the bud, and is suggested by the use of
grafted.

55. **confineless harms:** the boundless injuries that I should do
to my people.

57. **top:** surpass.

58. **Luxurious:** lascivious. This adjective does not fit Macbeth's character. However, Malcolm is not asserting that it does.
He merely admits, for the sake of argument, that Macbeth has
every known vice, and then proceeds to describe himself as still
worse.

59. **Sudden:** violent.

63. **cistern:** tank, vat.

64. **continent:** restraining. *Continent* is common in the active
sense of 'holding in,' 'confining.' So, as a noun, it is used of
the bank of a river ('the opposed continent') in *1 Henry IV*, iii,
1, 110.—**o'erbear:** overpower, sweep away.

65. **will:** desire, lust.

66, 67. **Boundless . . . tyranny:** Boundless incontinence is a
tyranny in a man's nature, for it usurps absolute sway over all
his other qualities.

69. **fall of many kings.** Cf. Holinshed: 'This suerlie is a
verie euill fault, for manie noble princes and kings haue lost
both liues and kingdomes for the same.'—**fear not yet.** Macduff
is testing Malcolm in his turn, and what he says in this and his
next speech must be interpreted in accordance with the upshot
of the conversation, when he declares that such a man as Malcolm is not fit to live.—**yet:** in spite of all you have said. Cf.
l. 46; iv, 1, 100.

71. **Convey:** manage craftily or secretly. Cf. Holinshed:
'Make thy selfe king, and I shall conueie the matter so wiselie,
that thou shalt be so satisfied at thy pleasure in such secret wise,
that no man shall be aware thereof.'

72. **time**: the times, the people. Cf. i, 5, 64, 65.—**hoodwink**: blindfold, delude.

74-76. **vulture**: ravenous appetite.—**dedicate**: offer up, devote. —**Finding**: if they find.

77. **ill-compos'd affection**: character made up of evil elements.

78. **stanchless**: insatiable.—**that**: so that.

80. **his**: this man's.

81. **more-having**: increase in wealth. Cf. Tilley, *Elizabethan Proverb Lore*, No. 449.

82, 83. **forge**: devise falsely.—**Quarrels**: causes of complaint.

85. **Sticks deeper**: is less easily uprooted. If a man is prone to avarice, he is likely to grow worse as he grows older.

86. **summer-seeming**: befitting only the summertime of life, the warm and vigorous age, and therefore not lasting so long as avarice.

87. **The sword of our slain kings**: that which has caused their violent death. Cf. Holinshed: 'For that crime the most part of our kings haue beene slaine.'

88. **foisons**: abundant supplies, stores.—**will**: covetousness.

89, 90. **your mere own**: what is absolutely your own property. —**All . . . weigh'd**: All the vices you have mentioned are endurable, when counterbalanced by other qualities that are virtues. Cf. Webster, *The Devil's Law Case*, i, 1, 63-66 (ed. Lucas, II, 238, 239):

> Yet I have heard
> Of divers, that in passing of the Alpes,
> Have but exchang'd their vertues at deare rate
> For other vices.

91-94. **The king-becoming graces,** etc. Cf. Holinshed: 'There is nothing that more becommeth a prince than constancie, veritie, truth, and iustice, with the other laudable fellowship of those faire and noble vertues which are comprehended onelie in soothfastnesse.'—**graces**: virtues.—**temp'rance**: self-control, moderation. Cf. ii, 3, 114.—**persêverance.** Note the accent; as in the verb *perséver*.

95, 96. **no relish**: no trace, no taste. Cf. l. 59.—**abound . . .**

crime: in my actions I am abundantly guilty of every possible form of each sin.

98. **milk.** Cf. i, 5, 18, 49; iii, 1, 67.

99. **Uproar:** change to tumultuous strife.

103–113. Cf. Holinshed: 'Oh ye vnhappie and miserable Scotishmen, which are thus scourged with so manie and sundrie calamities, ech one aboue other! Ye haue one curssed and wicked tyrant that now reigneth over you, without anie right or title, oppressing you with his most bloudie crueltie. This other that hath the right to the crowne, is so replet with the inconstant behauiour and manifest vices of Englishmen, that he is nothing worthie to inioy it. . . . Adieu Scotland, for now I account my selfe a banished man for euer.'

104. **tyrant:** usurper. Cf. iii, 6, 22.

107. **interdiction:** the act of putting one 'under the ban' of the Church. Malcolm has virtually pronounced against himself a curse which excludes him from the throne.

108. **does . . . breed:** slanders his parents by implying that they could naturally produce such a monster.

111. **Died every day she liv'd:** referring to the penances and religious exercises by which she 'died to the world.' The phrase is a reminiscence of St. Paul's 'I die daily' (*1 Corinthians*, xv, 31). Cf. the religious sense of *mortification*.

112. **repeat'st upon:** recitest against.

113. **banish'd.** He cannot return to Scotland unless Malcolm becomes king, and Malcolm is not fit to reign.

114. **ends here!** i.e., here and now, as I listen to what you say of yourself.—**passion:** strong emotion.

115. **Child of integrity:** which can proceed only from integrity of character.

116, 117. **scruples:** the suspicions that made me hesitate.—**reconcil'd . . . honour:** brought my opinion of you into accord with your real character as a loyal and honourable man.

118. **trains:** plots, subtle devices (such as he has suspected in Macduff's case). This remark strengthens our impression that considerable time has elapsed since Malcolm took refuge at the

English court.—**win**: entice. Cf. Holinshed: 'Diuerse times heeretofore hath Makbeth sought by this manner of meanes to bring me into his hands.'

119. **modest wisdom**: wise moderation, i.e., prudent caution. —**plucks me**: pulls me back; restrains me.

121. **Deal . . . me!** Be judge between us in the matter. This amounts to a solemn oath that what he is about to say is true.

122, 123. **to thy direction**: under thy guidance.—**mine own detraction**: the slanderous charges I have brought against myself.—**abjure**: deny solemnly, as upon oath.

124. **taints**: stains, disgraceful accusations.

125. **For . . . nature**: as being quite foreign to my actual character.

131. **upon**: against. Cf. l. 112.

132. **Is . . . command**: is at your service and at that of my unfortunate country.

134. **Siward.** Cf. Holinshed: 'Malcolme purchased [i.e., obtained] such fauor at king Edwards hands, that old Siward earle of Northumberland was appointed with ten thousand men to go with him into Scotland, to support him in this enterprise, for recouerie of his right.'

135. **at a point**: fully prepared. Cf. *Hamlet*, i, 2, 200: 'armed at point exactly.'

136, 137. **we'll together**: we'll set out together.—**the chance . . . quarrel**: may our chance of success be as good as our cause is just! Cf. i, 2, 14.—**Why are you silent?** Malcolm is rather naïvely astonished that Macduff does not instantly adapt himself to this sudden change of base and accept the situation with prompt enthusiasm.

140–159. This passage provides the interval of time needed before the arrival of Ross with the news of the murder of Macduff's wife and children. It also serves as a satisfactory substitute for what might well be expected by the audience, but would encumber the action—the actual appearance of Edward the Confessor on the stage. To Shakespeare's contemporaries the most familiar fact about King Edward was the legend that he was the first English King to cure scrofula by touching. Incidentally, this episode reminded the audience that James I was descended from a native English ruler as well as (according to tradition) from Banquo. King James, as Scaramelli wrote to the Doge of Venice in 1603, shortly before the coronation, 'says that neither he nor any other king can have power to heal scrofula, for the age of miracles is past, and God alone can work them. However, he will have the full ceremony [*sc.* of coronation, anointing included], so as not to lose this prerogative [*sc.* of touching for the king's evil], which belongs to the Kings of England as kings of France.' 'He was a King in understanding,' says Arthur Wilson, a contemporary (1595–1652), 'and was content to have his Subjects ignorant in many things. As in curing the *Kings-Evil*, which he knew a *Device*, to aggrandize the *Virtue* of *Kings*, when Miracles were in fashion; but he let the World believe it, though he smiled at it, in his owne Reason, finding the strength of the Imagination a more powerful *Agent* in the *Cure*, then the *Plasters* his *Chirurgions* prescribed for the *Sore*' (*History of Great Britain*, 1653, p. 289). See Manly, *Macbeth*, 1900, pp. xvi–xviii; Kittredge, *Witchcraft in Old and New England*, p. 316; *Shakespeare's England*, 1916, I, 427. Cf. Holinshed: 'As hath beene thought he [Edward] was inspired with the gift of prophesie, and also to haue had the gift of healing infirmities and diseases. He vsed to helpe those that were vexed with the disease, commonlie called the kings euill, and left that vertue as it were a portion of inheritance vnto his successors the kings of this realme.'

142, 143. **stay:** await.—**convinces ... art:** baffles the utmost efforts of medical science. To *convince* is 'to conquer utterly' (Latin *convinco*).

145. **presently:** instantly.—**amend:** recover, are made well.

146. **the evil:** scrofula or 'the king's evil' (i.e., disease), so called because it was thought to be cured by the royal touch.

148. **my here-remain:** my sojourn here. Cf. l. 133.

149. **solicits heaven:** by prayer prevails upon heaven (to work this miracle).

150. **strangely-visited:** afflicted with hideous disease. Cf. 'a visitation of Providence.'

152. **The mere despair:** the utter despair; i.e., quite beyond all hope from surgical treatment.

153. **stamp:** a coin which the King gave to the scrofulous patient whom he touched.

155, 156. **the succeeding royalty:** the royal line that shall succeed him.—**virtue:** healing power.

159. **grace:** sanctity, holiness. The rest of this scene is original—not based on Holinshed.

160. **My countryman . . . not.** Malcolm knows that Ross is a Scot from his costume, but he fails to recognize him until he speaks. This indicates that Malcolm has been long absent from Scotland (cf. note on l. 118).

162. **betimes:** speedily.

163. **The means . . . strangers!** i.e., Macbeth, who is responsible for Malcolm's absence from Scotland.

165. **to know itself!** to look its own misfortunes in the face!

167–169. **who:** one who.—**rent:** rend.—**not mark'd:** because they are so common.

170. **A modern ecstasy:** an ordinary, commonplace fit of excitement. Cf. iii, 2, 22.

171. **who.** Cf. iii, 1, 123; iii, 4, 42.

172. **flowers.** It was an Elizabethan fashion to wear a flower in the cap.

173. **Dying or ere they sicken:** dying before they sicken—i.e., by violence, not a natural death.—**or:** not the conjunction *or* but a variant form of *ere* (A.-S. *ær*), so that *or-ere* is a reduplicated 'before.'—**relation:** recital. Cf. iii, 4, 124.

174. **too nice:** too minutely accurate, because the details are so distressing.

175. **That . . . speaker:** The report of any dreadful thing that happened but an hour ago causes the teller to be hissed for his stale news, so much has occurred in the interim.—**hour's:** dissyllabic. The word was often spelled *hower*.

176. **teems:** brings forth.

177. **well:** intentionally ambiguous, and often used in breaking bad news gently. It means not only 'in good health' but also 'well off,' i.e., 'in heaven.' Cf. Chettle, *Hoffman* (sig. H3, lf. l r°): 'Your son noe doubt is well, in blessed state'; *Antony and Cleopatra*, ii, 5, 32, 33: 'We use To say the dead are well'; Heywood, *Love's Mistress*, ii (Pearson ed., V, 111):

> So among mortalls it is often sed,
> Children and friends are well, when they are dead.

182. **heavily:** sadly, sorrowfully.

183. **out:** in the field, under arms.

185. **For that:** because.—**power:** forces, troops.—**afoot:** in motion, mobilized.

188. **doff their dire distresses.** Cf. the alliteration in i, 5, 71.

189. **England:** the King of England. Cf. i, 2, 50.

191, 192. **none:** there is none. For the ellipsis cf. l. 15.— **gives out:** publishes, proclaims. There is no one who in all Christendom has the reputation of being an older or a better soldier. Cf. *Julius Cæsar*, iv, 3, 56.

194. **would be:** require to be, should be. Cf. i, 7, 34.

195. **latch:** catch.

196, 197. **a fee-grief:** a grief that is one man's possession; a personal sorrow—one that belongs to him alone, as in fee simple.—**Due:** belonging.—**honest:** good and honourable.

202. **heaviest:** saddest. Cf. l. 182.

204. **surpris'd:** seized, captured. Cf. iv, 1, 150.

206. **quarry:** slaughtered bodies; literally, the whole amount of game killed in a single hunt. The pun on *deer* and *dear* was so common as not to shock the hearer. Cf. *Julius Cæsar*, iii, 1, 204–210:

> Here wast thou bay'd, brave hart;
> Here didst thou fall; and here thy hunters stand,
> Sign'd in thy spoil, and crimson'd in thy lethe.
> O world, thou wast the forest to this hart;
> And this indeed, O world, the heart of thee!
> How like a deer, stroken by many princes,
> Dost thou here lie!

210. Whispers . . . heart: whispers to the over-burdened heart. *Fraught* means 'freighted.' The proverb is common in various forms. Cf. Seneca, *Hippolytus*, 607: 'Curae leves lo-cuntur, ingentes stupent'; Webster, *The White Devil*, ii, 1, 278, 279 (ed. Lucas, I, 129):

> Unkindnesse do thy office, poore heart breake,
> Those are the killing greifes which dare not speake;

The Misfortunes of Arthur, iv, 2, 14: 'Small griefes can speake; the great, astonisht stand'; Herrick, *Hesperides* (Riverside ed., I, 44):

> Small griefs find tongues; full casques are ever found
> To give, if any, yet but little sound.

212. And I must be from thence? Spoken in bitter self-reproach. *Must* is here the preterite.

216. He has no children: Macbeth has none: if he had, he could not have killed mine. Cf. the words of Queen Margaret to the slayers of her son (*3 Henry VI*, v, 5, 63, 64):

> You have no children, butchers! If you had,
> The thought of them would have stirr'd up remorse.

Remorse means 'compassion.' This passage was at one time interpolated in the acting version of *Macbeth*. Chetwood (*A General History of the Stage*, 1749, p. 32), speaking of Robert Wilks, the famous actor, remarks: 'In the 4th Act of *Macbeth*, when he [Macduff] is told . . . of the Loss of his Wife and Children, his Mixture of Sorrow and manly Grief at

> *He has no Children! Butcher! If he had,*
> *The Thought of them would sure have stirr'd Remorse!*

drew *Tears* from almost every *Eye*.' Some editors take *He* in l. 216 to mean Malcolm, and this was apparently Davenant's understanding of the passage, for his adaptation reads:

> He has no Children, nor can he feel
> A fathers Grief.

But Macduff is paying no attention to Malcolm's well-meant commonplaces: he is listening to Ross and does not turn to Malcolm until l. 220. A peculiarly savage interpretation makes Macduff express regret at Macbeth's childless condition because that prevents him from killing Macbeth's children in retaliation. This explanation confutes itself. That Shakespeare's Macbeth is childless during the whole course of the drama is abundantly evident. The historical Macbeth had a stepson, Lulach Fatuus ('Lugtake surnamed the foole' in Holinshed), who was set up as king after Macbeth's death but soon fell in battle with Malcolm. Holinshed says that he was 'either the sonne or (as some write) the coosen of Macbeth.' These facts account well enough for Lady Macbeth's words in i, 7, 54–59. We are to suppose that the babe she mentions died in infancy.

217. **hell-kite**: hellish bird of prey.

220, 221. **Dispute it**: resist it; withstand your grief.—**I shall do so**, etc. Here for the first time Macduff attends to what Malcolm is saying. His dignity will not allow him to remain quiet under the imputation of unmanly grief.

225. **Naught that I am**: wicked man that I am. Macduff blames himself for fleeing from Scotland, thus justifying the language of Lady Macduff in calling his flight 'madness' (iv, 2, 3). We are expected, however, to excuse his error of judgment because he could not suspect even Macbeth of such cruelty to the innocent and helpless.

226, 227. **Not for their own demerits.** They were slain because of Macduff's offences against Macbeth; but that is not quite all that Macduff has in mind. He thinks of their murder as also a judgment sent from God upon his sins in general.

229. **Convert**: change, turn.

230. **play the woman.** See note on iv, 2, 29.

232. **intermission**: interval of time.—**Front to front**: face to face (literally, forehead to forehead).

235. **Heaven ... too!** *Heaven* is emphatic: 'If I let him escape, I will not only forgive him myself, but I pray God to forgive him also!' Full vengeance, according to an idea that

occurs again and again in Elizabethan writers, includes both the
death of the offender and his damnation (cf. *Hamlet*, iii, 3,
73–95). Complete forgiveness, on the other hand, involves obedience to the biblical precept—'Pray for them which despitefully
use you and persecute you' (*Matthew*, v, 44). See Macbeth's
words to the murderers in iii, 1, 88–91. Cf. Fletcher, *The
Chances*, ii, 4:

> He scap'd me yesternight; which if he dare
> Again adventure for, heaven pardon him!
> I shall, with all my heart.

—**tune.** The Folios read *time*; corrected by Rowe.

236. **power:** forces (as in l. 185).

237. **Our ... leave:** Nothing remains to do except to take our
leave of King Edward and receive his permission to depart.

238. **ripe for shaking.** The figure is from ripe fruit which is
ready to fall when the tree is shaken.

239. **Put on their instruments:** are urging us, their agents, to
action. The war upon which they are entering is, then, a 'holy
war.'—**cheer:** comfort.—**may:** can.

Act V. Scene I.

After the long scene that closes the fourth Act, we feel that
much time has elapsed since we have seen Lady Macbeth, and
are ready to believe that the nervous strain under which several
speeches of hers (especially iii, 2, 4–7) have shown that she was
gradually giving way, may have broken her down at last. Thus
we are prepared for the infinite horror and pathos of the scene
which follows. This scene is in prose for an obvious reason. The
disjointed, incoherent utterances of Lady Macbeth call for it.
Metre would deprive them, by its very regularity, of their inco-
herence and fragmentary character. This is also the reason why
King Lear, when his delirium is at its height, speaks in prose.

In the present case, there is the further reason that the simplicity of style and matter which the subject and the situation call for, is best expressed in prose. The speeches of the Doctor and the Waiting Gentlewoman are to sound as much like real conversation as possible. At the end, when the tension is relaxed, and the Doctor utters his reflections, verse appropriately brings the scene to a quiet and solemn close. For mediæval tales illustrating the bloodstain that will not be washed away, see Beatrice Brown, *Publications of the Modern Language Association*, L (1935), 703 ff.

3. **went into the field.** Macbeth had taken the field against his rebellious subjects (the 'many worthy fellows that were out') before Ross went to England (see iv, 3, 185).

6. **nightgown:** dressing gown (as in ii, 2, 70).

8. **this while:** this time. *While* is the noun, not the adverb.

10–15. The professional elevation of the Doctor's language is noteworthy. Physicians were, and still are, expected to speak of their patients' ailments in a dignified and rather technical fashion.—**effects of watching:** the acts proper to a waking condition. —**slumb'ry agitation:** disturbed action in sleep.—**actual performances:** performances in the way of acts. The emphatic words are *actual* and *say*.

19. **meet:** fitting, proper.

22. **her very guise:** the exact way in which I have described her appearance.

24. **close:** out of sight, in concealment. They draw back instinctively, for Lady Macbeth's eyes are open, though they know that she cannot see them. Thus the centre of the stage is left to her.

29. **their sense:** their faculty of sight.—**is:** the Folios read *are* (corrected by Rowe). Davenant has 'her Sense is.'

35. **Yet:** emphatic—after all this washing. Cf. iv, 1, 100; iv, 3, 46, 69.

37. **satisfy:** reinforce, confirm.

38, 39. **One; two.** The murder of Duncan, then, was committed soon after two o'clock in the morning.—**Hell is murky.**

Spoken with a shudder. Since what Lady Macbeth utters consists in large part of things that she has said before, we may infer that this too reproduces an impression she had formerly had—a moment of horror between the striking of the hour and the entrance of Macbeth after the deed was done (ii, 2, 14). Cf. i, 5, 51–55.

41–45. Fie ... in him? This repeats what she said to her husband in the interval between ii, 2, and ii, 3, after they had retired to their chamber to 'wash this filthy witness from their hands.' —**accompt:** account.

49–50. No more o' that ... starting. A reminiscence of the banquet scene (iii, 4, 63): 'O, these flaws and starts.'

51. Go to! Here an exclamation of reproof. It means literally 'Go away!' and, like our colloquial *Go way!* (which is an old idiom) may be used in expostulation, reproof, impatience, or incredulity. Sometimes it merely closes or shuts off discussion like 'Very well!' or 'Enough said!'

56. The spot, she thinks, has disappeared, and her hands are clean at last; but, as she raises the palms to her face with an instinctive gesture, she perceives the lingering smell of the blood. *Smell*, then, is the emphatic word, not *blood*. Verplanck remarks: 'The smell has never been successfully used as the means of impressing the imagination with terror, pity, or any of the deeper emotions, except in this dreadful sleep-walking of the guilty Queen, and in one parallel scene of the Greek drama, as wildly terrible as this. It is that passage of the *Agamemnon* of Æschylus [ll. 1306–1311], where the captive prophetess Cassandra, wrapt in visionary inspiration, scents the first smell of blood, and then the vapours of the tomb breathing from the palace of Atrides, as ominous of his approaching murder.'[1]

---

[1] ΧΟ. τί δ' ἐστὶ χρῆμα; τίς σ' ἀποστρέφει φόβος;
ΚΑ. φεῦ, φεῦ.
ΧΟ. τί τοῦτ' ἔφευξας; εἴ τι μὴ φρενῶν στύγος.
ΚΑ. φόνον δόμοι πνέουσιν αἱματοσταγῆ.
ΧΟ. καὶ πῶς; τόδ' ὄζει θυμάτων ἐφεστίων.
ΚΑ. ὅμοιος ἀτμὸς ὥσπερ ἐκ τάφου πρέπει.

58. **little.** A plain indication that Mrs. Siddons was right in regarding Lady Macbeth as a woman of delicate frame. This accords with her swooning in ii, 3, 124. Cf. iii, 2, 45, and note.

60. **charg'd:** burdened. Cf. v, 3, 43–45.

64. The Gentlewoman catches up the Doctor's vaguely pensive 'well' and gives it a definite meaning.

65. **beyond my practice:** beyond my ability to cure; not, outside of my experience. It is one of those cases in which 'the patient must minister to himself' (v, 3, 45, 46).

67. **holily.** The good and charitable Doctor assures the lady-in-waiting that sleepwalking is not necessarily a symptom of a guilty conscience, though it is clear that in this case he has his suspicions.

69–71. **Wash your hands.** Here, in her dream, she confuses the two murders, Duncan's and Banquo's. Thus dreams do, in fact, behave.—**yet again:** as she had told him in the interval between the scenes after the close of iii, 4. In this interval he had of course talked of Banquo's murder and of the ghost.—**on's:** of his.

75. **What's ... undone.** An echo of her words in iii, 2, 12: 'What's done is done.' Cf. i, 7, 1, 2.

79. **Foul whisp'rings.** The Doctor has heard rumours of Macbeth's guilt. Cf. iii, 1, 1–3, 30–33.

80. **Infected:** diseased because of guilt. Cf. v, 3, 40.

81. **discharge:** unload, reveal. Cf. l. 60.

84, 85. **annoyance:** injury. He fears suicide, and justly, as the sequel shows (v, 8, 70, 71).—**still:** always.

86. **mated:** paralyzed (so that I know not what to think). **To** *mate* is 'to take the life out of.' Cf. Sidney, *Arcadia*, iii, 7, 2 (ed. 1590, fol. 266 r⁰): 'his mated minde.'—**amaz'd:** reduced to utter confusion (so that I can hardly believe what I have seen). Cf. *Midsummer Night's Dream*, iii, 2, 344: 'I am amaz'd, and know not what to say.'

87. **Good night, good doctor.** This simple and natural speech, giving the impression which the Doctor, with his dignified mien and benignant disposition, has made on the Gentlewoman, is a most effective touch.

Scene II.

Many of the Scottish nobles had revolted before Ross went to England, and Macbeth had taken the field against them (iv, 3, 181–185); but he has been forced to retire to the strong castle of Dunsinane. The malcontents are now marching to join the army which they hear Malcolm is leading from England.

1. **pow'r:** forces, army.

2. **uncle.** In Holinshed, Malcolm's mother is Earl Siward's daughter.

3. **dear causes:** heartfelt causes, appealing to their deepest and strongest emotions. *Dear* is used of anything that comes near to one's heart or interests: the nearness may be pleasant or unpleasant, friendly or hostile. Thus Hamlet uses 'my dearest foe' for 'my most deadly enemy' (i, 2, 182), and the Countess in *All's Well* (iv, 5, 11) speaks of 'dearest groans.'

4, 5. **Would . . . man:** would rouse to action even a paralytic and make him join the rest in the fierce and bloody onset. —**bleeding:** bloody (adj. with *alarm*). Cf. *Richard II*, iii, 3, 94: 'bleeding war.'—**alarm:** call to arms—hence, rally, on-set, attack.—**mortified:** paralyzed (literally, deadened). Thus Roger North (*Lives*, ed. 1826, I, 376) speaks of a person 'maimed by an apoplexy' as living some years 'in this mortified state.' Cf. *Lear*, ii, 3, 15: 'their numb'd and mortified bare arms.'

6. **well:** probably; very likely.

8. **file:** list (as in iii, 1, 95).

10, 11. **unrough:** smooth-faced, beardless.—**Protest . . . man-hood:** declare (by going to war) that they are now first acting a man's part.—**tyrant:** usurper. Cf. iii, 6, 22; iv, 3, 32, 104.

14. **valiant fury:** the frenzy of desperate valour.

15, 16. **He cannot . . . rule:** The cause for which he fights is so bad that he cannot restrain himself within the bounds of self-control in supporting it. *Rule* means 'self-government.'—**distemper'd:** literally, diseased. The figure is of a dropsical person, swollen beyond the limits of a normal girdle. The same figure appears in a pun in *1 Henry IV*, where Falstaff says: 'I live out of all order, out of all compass' (i.e., all proper self-restraint and temperance); and Bardolph replies: 'Why, you are so fat, Sir John, that you must needs be out of all compass—out of all reasonable compass, Sir John' (iii, 3, 22–26). Many editors take *rule* in the sense of 'control over his followers'; but this is contrary to the general purport of the speech, which is to describe Macbeth's demeanour and state of mind. Menteith (in ll. 22–25) repeats the same thought in other words: 'He has a bad conscience, and it is not strange if his mind is giving way.' The purpose of ll. 11–24 is to prepare us for the almost maniacal excitement which Macbeth is to show in the next scene and which is quite different from his demeanour heretofore.

17. **sticking on his hands.** A graphic figure, suggesting the viscous quality of coagulated blood, and reminding us of Lady Macbeth's efforts to wash it from her hands.

18. **mínutely:** every minute.—**upbraid:** for every time a noble revolts, it reminds him of his own breach of faith—'th' ingredience of our poison'd chalice' again (i, 7, 11).

19. **in:** because of. Cf. iv, 3, 20.

20 **Nothing:** not at all. Cf. i, 3, 96; v, 4, 2.

21. **robe.** Cf. i, 3, 108–109, 145; ii, 4, 38.

23. **pester'd senses:** tormented mind.—**to recoil and start:** for giving way and becoming distracted.

24, 25. **When all . . . there:** for, when he looks into his mind, he sees nothing but consciousness of guilt.

27. **the med'cine of the sickly weal:** the physician who is to restore the commonweal to a healthy condition, i.e., Malcolm, whose army these nobles intend to join. Macbeth uses the same metaphor in v, 3, 50–56, dwelling on it with all the vivid detail of his poetical imagination.

28. **our country's purge:** the physic (cleansing draught) that is to purge our country of its present evils. 'Let us shed every drop of our blood to help Malcolm to deliver Scotland from Macbeth and his tyranny.'

29, 30. **Or . . . weeds:** a singularly infelicitous figure. Their blood is to 'bedew' or *water* the flower of legitimate sovereignty (Malcolm) and make it thrive, and at the same time is to *drown out* the weeds of usurpation and tyranny. If this line and a half is omitted, the metre does not suffer. Cf., however, *Richard II*, v, 6, 45, 46:

> Lords, I protest my soul is full of woe
> That blood should sprinkle me to make me grow;

and *3 Henry VI*, ii, 2, 167–169:

> Since we have begun to strike,
> We'll never leave till we have hewn thee down
> Or bath'd thy growing with our heated bloods.

And for *weeds* cf. *Richard II*, iii, 4, 37 ff.; *Hamlet*, i, 2, 133–137.

Scene III.

This scene doubtless takes place on the day after scene i, for in it Macbeth receives the Doctor's report of Lady Macbeth's condition. Scenes ii and iii, then, belong to the same day. Macbeth has had news of the revolt of the Scottish nobles and of their intention to join the English army of invasion. Scene ii has prepared us for his wild demeanour, which some call 'valiant fury.'

3. **taint:** become tainted.

5. **mortal consequences:** not, results; but simply, future events in human life. Cf. i, 7, 3: 'trammel up the consequence.'

8. **epicures.** The English were regarded by the Scots as living in luxurious plenty. Doubtless Shakespeare remembered a passage in Holinshed (cited by Steevens) where 'the riotous maners and superfluous gormandizing brought in among them [the Scots] by the Englishmen' are mentioned and 'the old customes and maners' of Scotland are contrasted with 'the English likerous delicats.'

9. **The mind I sway by:** the mind by which I move (literally, swing), i.e., the mind which governs my actions.

10. **sag,** etc.: in prose order—The mind I sway by shall never sag (give way, sink) with doubt, and the heart I bear shall never shake with fear. Cf. the order in i, 3, 55, 56, 60, 61.

11 ff. **The devil,** etc. Here the ungoverned demeanour of Macbeth, for which scene ii has prepared us, breaks out into a frenzy which may well have been called 'madness.'—**loon:** fool.

13. **There is.** Cf. ii, 3, 146.

15. **lily-liver'd:** white-livered, cowardly. Fear was supposed to be caused by lack of red blood in the liver. Cf. *2 Henry IV*, iv, 3, 113, 114; *Merchant of Venice*, iii, 2, 86; *Twelfth Night*, iii, 2, 65–67.—**patch:** fool.

16. **Death of thy soul!** A curse: Death upon thy soul.

17. **Are counsellors to fear:** prompt others to fear. Macbeth does not mean that the servant's white cheeks alarm *him*, but that they tend to infect his other followers with fear.—**whey-face:** pale-faced fellow.

19. **Take thy face hence.** A fine example of focussed impression. All that Macbeth sees of the servant is his white, panic-stricken face. So in the vision of the kings, what caught and held Macbeth's eye was the *hair*, so like Banquo's (iv, 1, 113, 114). Cf. also Lady Macduff's words when the murderers burst in (iv, 2, 79): 'What are these faces?'—**sick at heart.** His frenzy gives place, in an instant, to profound dejection.

20. **This push:** this final effort. Cf. *Hamlet*, v, 1, 318: 'We'll put the matter to the present push.'

21. **Will cheer . . . now:** will either give me peace and happiness for ever or dethrone me instantly and once for all. Cf. 'To be thus is nothing, But to be safely thus' (iii, 1, 48, 49), and 'Whom we, to gain our peace, have sent to peace' (iii, 2, 20); iii, 2, 4–7:

> Naught's had, all's spent,
> Where our desire is got without content.
> 'Tis safer to be that which we destroy
> Than by destruction dwell in doubtful joy.

It was not merely the crown that Macbeth desired, but peaceful enjoyment of the crown. The thought is continued in the lament that follows (ll. 22–28). After all, Macbeth says, even if he wins the fight, he must not look for happiness. There is no reason to change *cheer* to *chair* for the sake of a frigid antithesis to *disseat*. It is equally ill-judged to keep *cheer* and read *disease* (with the last three Folios) for *disseat*. The very word *now* shows that the verb required is one denoting instantaneous action, like *disseat*; not such an expression as *disease*. The First Folio reading is *dis-eate*, which may be read as *disseat* (Capell's and Jennens's conjecture) without calling the change an emendation. Cf. *The Two Noble Kinsmen*, v, 4, 72: 'to disseat his lord.'

22–28. **My way of life,** etc.: My life in its course has declined into the autumn (the season of dry and yellow leaves); and when old age comes, I must not look to have, etc. Here is another indication of a considerable lapse of time since the play began.—**honour . . . friends.** Macbeth contrasts the desolate old age to which he looks forward with the serene old age of the gracious Duncan, just as he has already contrasted with his own life of 'restless ecstasy' the peaceful sleep that Duncan enjoys in the grave (iii, 2, 16–26).—**mouth-honour.** The antithesis is between *mouth* and *heart*. All that Macbeth can expect is homage in words, which the heart of the liegeman does not prompt, but would refuse if it dared. Cf. iii, 6, 36: 'Do faithful homage and receive free honours.'

32. **I'll fight.** Macbeth's personal courage, the quality which is first emphasized in the tragedy (i, 2), remains with him to the last.

35. **moe:** more (not a clipped form of that word, but a different formation from the same root).—**skirr:** ride rapidly, scour (cf. *scurry*).

37. **Not so sick:** not so much afflicted with any bodily ailment.

39. **Cure her of that!** That is the very thing of which I wish you to cure her. I called you to the castle for that very purpose.

42. **Raze out:** erase, as from a waxed tablet. Cf. *Hamlet*, i, 5, 98, 99:

> Yea, from the table of my memory
> I'll wipe away all trivial fond records.

43. **oblivious:** causing oblivion or utter forgetfulness.

44. **the stuff'd bosom:** 'the o'erfraught heart' (iv, 3, 210). The breathless, asthmatic quality of this line is most effective. Utterance pants and labours as we pronounce the words. *Stuff'd* (i.e., 'clogged') and *stuff* express better than anything else could do the feeling of physical obstruction and oppression which Macbeth describes. For the repetition of the same word or sound, cf. i, 5, 64, 65; ii, 2, 56, 57; iii, 2, 20; iv, 3, 178, 179; v, 8, 60, 72. *Stuff* (noun and verb) is one of Shakespeare's favourite words.

45, 46. **Therein ... himself.** Cf. Greene, *James IV*, iv, 4 (ed. Collins, II, 136):

> The bodies woundes by medicines may be eased,
> But griefes of mindes, by salues are not appeased.

47. **I'll none of it:** I'll have nothing to do with it.

48. **staff:** his truncheon or baton, indicating his rank as commander-in-chief. The fits and starts in this speech are significant. Macbeth first expresses his disappointment at the Doctor's failure and his contempt for the whole art of medicine; then he repeats the order which he has just given to put on his armour and the order to 'send out' which he gave in l. 35; then he turns back to the Doctor with a familiar and confidential remark; then he reiterates his command to the squire who is arming him; and finally he addresses the Doctor once more and compares Scotland to a patient in need of medical treatment, interrupting himself with another impatient order to the squire.

49. **Doctor, the thanes fly from me.** A masterly touch. All physicians, by their very profession, invite confidences, and this is particularly true of the benignant Doctor whom Macbeth has

consulted about his wife (cf. v, 1, 87). That the King should turn to him in this familiar way suggests also the need he feels of a faithful friend.

50, 51. **Come, sir, dispatch:** make haste—addressed to the squire who is putting on Macbeth's armour.—**cast . . . land:** make a diagnosis of the disease from which Scotland is suffering. A medical figure from examination of a patient's urine.

52. **pristine:** such as she enjoyed in former times.

54. **Pull't off, I say:** i.e., some part of his armour, which Macbeth, in his restlessness, has got on wrong.

55. **senna.** The First Folio reads *Cyme*. In the Second and Third this is corrected to *Cæny*, an old pronunciation of *senna* (*seeny*), still current. The Fourth Folio reads *Senna*.

56. **scour:** purge, clear away (as by a violent purgative medicine).

58. **Bring it after me!** i.e., the piece of armour which has just been taken off.

59–62. **I will not . . . here.** The two rhyme-tags are significant of the action. Each marks an exit. Macbeth goes off the stage, uttering the first. This leaves the Doctor alone, and he shakes his head, looks grave, and follows, wishing himself well out of the dangerous situation in which he can do no good.—**bane:** destruction.

Scene IV.

The Scottish nobles who had taken the field against Macbeth have now joined forces with Malcolm at Birnam Wood according to their plan in scene ii.

2. **nothing:** not at all. Cf. i, 3, 96; v, 2, 20.

4. **Let every soldier,** etc. This stratagem is a very old piece of popular fiction and is widespread in folk-tales (see Introduction, p. xi). Holinshed records that Malcolm 'commanded euerie man to get a bough of some tree or other of

that wood in his hand, as big as he might beare, and to march foorth therewith in such wise, that on the next morrow they might come closelie and without sight in this manner within view of his enimies.' The same stratagem was used in very truth by the Indians of New England in 1675, as we learn from Major Daniel Gookin, an irreproachable witness: 'The enemy also used this stratagem, to apparel themselves from the waist upwards with green boughs, that our Englishmen could not readily discern them, or distinguish them from the natural bushes; this manner of fighting our men had little experience of, and hence were under great disadvantages' (*Historical Account*, 1677, American Antiquarian Society, *Collections*, II [1836], 441).

6. **discovery:** Macbeth's scouts.

8. **no other:** nothing else. Cf. iii, 4, 97.

10. **setting down:** encampment for laying siege.

11. **advantage ... given.** To *give advantage* is 'to offer or afford an opportunity.' The whole clause means, 'wherever the circumstances are such that an opportunity can be afforded them' or 'can offer itself.'

12. **more and less:** high and low; nobles and commoners.

13. **things:** used contemptuously for persons who, being constrained, have no will of their own and are therefore mere instruments rather than men.

14–16. **hearts:** emphatic.—**too:** as well as the *bodies* of those who have actually revolted. Cf. iv, 3, 235.—**Let...soldier- ship:** Let our opinions, in order that they may be accurate, wait for the outcome, which is sure to disclose the truth; and meantime let us use all our skill and energy in the campaign. Macduff, though confident enough of the issue, is older and less sanguine than Malcolm. He knows that Macbeth has not lost all his resources of defence. Siward (ll. 16–21) repeats the thought of Macduff in different language.—**put we on:** a metaphor from clothing (with armour). Cf. i, 3, 108, 145; v, 2, 21.—**industrious:** energetic.

18. **What . . . owe.** *Say* and *owe* are the emphatic words:

'What we shall merely *claim* as our own and what we shall actually *possess*.' At present there is a wide difference between what Malcolm and his party *say* belongs to them and what they really *have* in their possession. The battle will decide whether this distinction is to be permanent.

21. **Towards which:** towards which strokes; towards the fight.

Scene V.

---

1. **the outward walls.** Dunsinane is to be thought of as a large castle with various walls and fortifications, which must be taken one after another.

2. **still:** always.

3. **lie:** lie encamped.

4. **famine and the ague.** These were inseparable from a long siege in old times. *Ague* is used for 'pestilence' in general. It would have been almost impossible for the invaders to take Dunsinane if the garrison had remained faithful to Macbeth.

5. **forc'd:** reinforced.

6. **met them:** i.e., in the field.—**dareful:** boldly.

8. **It is the cry.** Seyton hurries out to learn the reason for the women's shrieks.

9. **forgot the taste of fears:** forgotten what dreadful things are like. *Fears* means 'objects or causes of fear.' Cf. i, 3, 137.

10. **cool'd:** felt the chill of terror.

11. **my fell of hair:** the hair upon my skin. Cf. *Job*, iv, 13–15 : 'In thoughts from the visions of the night, when deep sleep falleth on men, fear came upon me, and trembling, which made all my bones to shake. Then a spirit passed before my face: the hair of my flesh stood up.'

12. **treatise:** story. Cf. iii, 4, 63–66.

13. **As:** as if.

14. **Direness:** horror.

15. **start:** startle. Cf. iii, 4, 63; v, 2, 23.

17, 18. should: means (as very often) 'inevitably or certainly would.' *Word* is 'message.' L. 18 repeats and expands the sense of l. 17. Cf. Ford, *The Broken Heart*, v, 2:

> Those that are dead
> Are dead. Had they not now died, of necessity
> They must have paid the debt they ow'd to nature
> One time or other.

Macbeth receives the news of his wife's death with apathy, and does not even ask the manner or the cause. 'Ah, well! she would certainly have died *sometime*! some day this message must have come—on one of the many to-morrows by which time creeps slowly forward to eternity. And so, too, on every *yesterday* men and women have died. A little sooner or a little later—what difference can it make? For life is nothing and has no meaning.' In *Julius Cæsar*, iv, 3, 190–192, Brutus speaks of Portia's death in similar terms; but his reflections are those of philosophic calmness, Macbeth's show the apathy of despair:

> Why, farewell, Portia. We must die, Messala.
> With meditating that she must die once,
> I have the patience to endure it now.

21. recorded time: i.e., time, as opposed to eternity (in which there are no yesterdays and no to-morrows). *Syllable* is used because Macbeth is thinking of events as recorded as they happen, one after another, until the last syllable of human history has been registered and time is merged in eternity.

22. yesterdays: emphatic.—**fools:** used of men in general— us poor, weak, ignorant mortals.

23. brief: short-lived.

24. walking shadow. Cf. *Psalm* xxxix, 6 (Prayer-book version): 'Man walketh in a vain shadow.'—**a poor player.** The emphatic word is not *poor*, but *player*. The adjective is not meant to confine the comparison to *bad* actors but is of general application. It is the pathos of the actor's lot that his art perishes with him: he leaves nothing behind but a fading memory. *Poor*, then, expresses pity: 'Life is like an actor, who, poor fellow, struts and frets his hour,' etc. For the comparison of life to a play and the world to a stage, cf. *As You Like It*, ii, 7, 139–166.—**struts and frets** shows Macbeth's contempt, not for the actor, but for human life. The player does not act real life, he only imitates it; but after all, life itself is as poor a thing, as much of a mockery of reality, as the player's art is a mockery of life; and both life and the actor's art are pitifully transitory things.

30. **Gracious my lord.** Cf. iii, 2, 27.

35. **Liar and slave!** Macbeth's frenzy, alternating with his apathy, shows itself in passionate abuse, as in v, 3.

37. **mile:** a good old form of the plural.

38. **I say, a moving grove.** Shakespeare individualizes even so insignificant a character as this Messenger. He stands to his guns, reiterating his statement in the simplest and plainest language. Not every man could face Macbeth down in his present mood with a stout-hearted 'I say.'

40. **cling thee:** waste thee away till thy skin sticks to thy bones.—**sooth:** truth.

41. **I care not . . . much.** The sudden alternation between frenzy and apathy in this scene is well illustrated in the contrast between this sentence and the preceding. L. 41 is addressed as much to Macbeth himself as to the Messenger, and in what follows ('I pull in resolution . . . comes toward Dunsinane') he is not thinking of any hearers at all. Then, with 'Arm, arm, and out!' he addresses Seyton in a loud voice, only to fall again into soliloquy in the next line. But at the end of the speech his natural valour and energy reassert themselves.

42. **pull in:** rein in, check. 'I can no longer give free rein to confidence and determination.' Or the figure may be from a bird that pulls in its wings, as in Dekker, *Old Fortunatus*, Prologue:

A benumming feare,
(That your nice soules, cloy'd with dilicious sounds,
Will loath her lowly notes) makes her [our Muse] pull in
Her fainting pineons.

Cf. Fletcher, *The Sea Voyage*, iii, 1 (cited by Mason in defence of the Folio reading):

> All my spirits,
> As if they heard my passing bell go for me,
> Pull in their powers and give me up to destiny.

Johnson's conjecture, *pall* ('begin to fail,' 'weaken'), though tempting, is quite unnecessary.

43. **To doubt . . . fiend:** to suspect that Satan has been cheating me by his regular device of ambiguous prophecies. Compare the notorious ambiguity of oracles, as in 'Aio te, Aeacida, Romanos vincere posse.' See *2 Henry VI*, i, 4, 60–74; iv, 1, 31–37.

47. **avouches:** protests is true, vouches for, asserts.

49. **gin:** begin.

50. **th' estate o' th' world:** the orderly universe.—**undone:** returned to chaos.

51. **alarum bell.** Cf. ii, 3, 79.—**wrack:** ruin, destruction.

52. **harness:** armour.

Scene VI.

This short scene is rather formal in style, as befits a scene intended merely to convey information and advance the plot, not to depict character or express passion.

1. **leavy:** leafy.

2. **show:** appear.—**worthy:** noble.—**uncle:** Siward. Cf. v, 2, 2.

4. **battle:** battalion, division, troop.—**we.** Malcolm makes significant use of the royal *we*.

5. **upon's:** upon us.—**what:** whatever.

6. **our order:** the arrangements we have already made.

7. **Do we:** if we do.—**power:** forces.

Scene VII.

The encounter with young Siward is necessary to the suspense. Its result encourages Macbeth to trust 'the fiend' still, though so often deceived by 'equivocation.' The incident is suggested by Holinshed, who, however, does not say that Macbeth was the person with whom Siward fought.

1. tied me to a stake. A figure from bear-baiting, in which the bear was tied to a post and attacked by dogs. Macbeth's castle is surrounded, so that he cannot escape. He has made a sally (v, 5, 46), but has failed to break through the besiegers and has retired to his defences. Cf. *Julius Cæsar*, iv, 1, 48, 49:

> We are at the stake
> And bay'd about with many enemies;

King Edward III, v, 143–145 (ed. Tucker Brooke, *Shakespeare Apocrypha*, p. 100):

> As a beare fast chaind vnto a stake,
> Stood famous Edward, still expecting when
> Those doggs of Fraunce would fasten on his flesh.

2. the course. A course was one 'running' at the bear by the dogs, a 'bout.' Cf. Middleton, *The Roaring Girl*, iii, 3, 210, 211 (ed. Bullen, IV, 88):

> *Trapdoor.* A course, captain; a bear comes to the stake.
> *Moll.* It should be so, for the dogs struggle to be let loose.

16. still: forever. The word does not imply (as it would in modern English) that they had already haunted him.

17. kerns. See i, 2, 13. Here used in the general sense of 'mercenary soldiers.'

18. staves: spears.

20. undeeded: not honoured by any feat of arms.—**shouldst be:** ought to be, to judge by the din.

22. bruited: reported, proclaimed.

24. **gently rend'red:** surrendered without active defence.

26. **bravely:** finely, splendidly.

27. **professes:** declares itself.

29. **strike beside us:** let their blows fall by our sides without trying to hit us—a natural hyperbole to express the half-heartedness of Macbeth's followers. Some think the passage means: 'come over to our side and fight as our comrades,' but the language will not bear this interpretation. Cf. Beaumont and Fletcher, *The Maid's Tragedy*, v, 4:

> Thou canst not fight! The blows thou mak'st at me
> Are quite besides.

Scene VIII.

1. **the Roman fool:** like Brutus in *Julius Cæsar* (v, 5, 47–51) or Cato Uticensis or Mark Antony (who is mentioned by Macbeth in iii, 1, 57).

2. **Whiles . . . lives:** so long as I see any of the enemy alive.

4. **avoided thee.** Macbeth has avoided Macduff because of the warning of the apparition in iv, 1, 71: 'Beware Macduff.' But there is another reason, given in what follows: he feels sure that Macduff will fall if they fight. There is still a drop of the milk of human kindness in his veins.

5. **charg'd:** loaded, burdened. Cf. v, 1, 60.

8. **Than . . . out:** than words can declare thee. Cf. iv, 3, 192.

9. **mayst:** canst.—**intrenchant:** that cannot be gashed or wounded. See iii, 4, 27. Cf. *Hamlet*, iv, 1, 44: 'And hit the woundless air'; *All's Well*, iii, 2, 113: 'the still-piecing air.'

10. **impress:** make an impression on.

12, 13. **I bear . . . born.** This warning is meant to induce Macduff to cease fighting, for Macbeth does not wish to kill him.—**must not:** according to the decree of fate.—**Despair thy charm!** Let thy charm despair! i.e., Let whatever spell it is that makes thee believe thou bear'st a charmed life, cease to be a ground of confidence and become a cause for despair (as it must, when its true meaning is understood). This is preferable to the alternative explanation—'Despair of thy charm.'

14. **angel**: evil angel, demon.—**still**: always.

18. **my better part of man**: my courage, which is a man's better part; the quality which, more than anything else, makes me a man. Cf. i, 7, 46–51; iii, 4, 58–60, 73, 99, 108.

20. **palter**: deal deceitfully, play fast and loose, equivocate.

21, 22. **keep ... hope!** fulfil their promise in words but not in the sense we expect.—**I'll not fight with thee!** Here, for a moment, and for the first and last time, Macbeth feels actual fear of a human being. Yet, after all, it is not so much fear of Macduff as a feeling of helplessness at being thus abandoned by the Fates.

24. **gaze**: sight, spectacle, show.—**time**: the times, age.

25. **monsters.** The Elizabethans were particularly fond of what we call 'side shows.' Cf. *Tempest*, ii, 2, 29 ff: 'Were I in England now, ... and had but this fish painted, not a holiday fool there but would give a piece of silver. There would this monster make a man. Any strange beast there makes a man. When they will not give a doit to relieve a lame beggar, they will lay out ten to see a dead Indian.' Cf. also *The Birth of Merlin*, v, 2, 55–58 (ed. Tucker Brooke, *Shakespeare Apocrypha*, p. 381):

> Stuff the pelt with straw
> To be shown up and down at Fairs and Markets:
> Two pence a piece to see so foul a Monster
> Will be a fair Monopoly, and worth the begging.

26. **Painted upon a pole**: i.e., your picture painted on canvas and set up on a pole in front of a showman's booth.

29. **baited**: assailed on all sides, beset—an echo of the bear-baiting figure which Macbeth used in v, 7, 1, 2. To *bait* is the causative of *bite*.

32, 33. **the last**: i.e., strength and valour, which may yet prove stronger than fate. Cf. iii, 1, 71, 72.—**Before ... shield.** To omit these words improves the speech and does not injure the metre.—**Lay on**: strike hard.

34. **damn'd be him.** Good Elizabethan grammar.

35. Here a new scene might well be marked. *Retreat* in the stage direction calls for a trumpet signal indicating the defeat of the enemy and checking further pursuit.

36. **go off:** be lost, die.—**by:** to judge by.

39. **paid a soldier's debt:** since every soldier pledges his life to the cause for which he fights.

41. **The which:** i.e., the fact that he had become a man.— **confirm'd:** proved.

42. **the unshrinking station.** The adjective belongs logically to *man*, not to *station*; but such 'transference of epithet' is common in the poetry of all periods.

47. **God's soldier be he!** God has taken him in the performance of his duty, and so I leave him in God's hands.

50. **knoll'd:** knelled, tolled.

52. **parted well:** departed well, made a good end. The figure is of one who leaves an inn with his bill honestly paid.—**score:** account as scored up.

53. **God be with him!** Good-bye to him! See note on iii, 1, 44.—**newer comfort:** later news, and good news.

55. **The time:** the world; the people of our time, now delivered from Macbeth's tyranny. Cf. i, 5, 64, 65.

56. **compass'd:** surrounded.—**pearl:** pearls—a common plural.

60–75. The method of Elizabethan tragedy required that the closing speech should be uttered by the person of highest rank who survived, and this was seldom one of the characters in whom we have taken most interest. Such speeches, therefore, are always rather formal and serve as a kind of epilogue. The lack of a large curtain made the modern fashion of closing a play with a tableau impossible, for the stage had to be cleared.

60. For the repetition cf. l. 72; i, 5, 64, 65; ii, 2, 56, 57; iii, 2, 20; iv, 3, 178, 179; v, 3, 44.

61. **reckon . . . loves:** reward the devotion that each of you has shown in my cause.—**loves.** For the plural cf. iii, 1, 122.

63. **Earls.** Holinshed records that soon after Malcolm's cor-

onation in 1057 'manie of them that before were thanes, were made earles. . . . These were the first earles that haue beene heard of amongst the Scotishmen.'

64. **What's more to do:** whatever else remains to be done.

65. **Which would . . . time:** which the better times that have begun require to be established anew. In plain prose, 'any other improvements or reforms that the new order of things requires.' For the figure cf. i, 4, 28.

66. **our exil'd friends abroad:** our friends who are in exile abroad (like Donalbain in Ireland).

68. **Producing forth:** bringing to light, dragging out of concealment.—**ministers:** agents, instruments.

69. **Butcher** and **fiendlike** are crude terms to apply to Macbeth and his wife, but they correctly express Malcolm's sentiments. Of course he has not the same sympathetic interest in these characters that we have come to feel.

70. **self and violent:** her own violent. Thus we learn that the Doctor's fear that Lady Macbeth would commit suicide was well-founded (v, 1, 83–85).

71. **Took off.** Cf. i, 7, 20.—**what needful else:** whatever else that is necessary.

72. **calls upon us:** demands my attention as King.—**of Grace:** of gracious God.

73. **in measure:** with propriety and decorum, as opposed to the frantic rule of Macbeth.

74, 75. **one . . . Scone.** A good rhyme in Elizabethan English. Cf. iv, 1, 6, 7. For Scone see note on ii, 4, 31.

TEXTUAL NOTES

[Ff indicates the agreement of all four Folios—F₁ (1623), F₂ (1632), F₃ (1664), F₄ (1685). Q 1673: the Quarto edition of 1673. The figures 1 and 2 (as in 'Pope₁' and 'Pope₂') indicate respectively first and second edition. Conjectures are marked 'conj.'; omissions are marked 'om.']

Act i, Scene 1, 1 again (Hanmer)] againe? (F₁ F₂); again? (F₃ F₄ Q 1673); again, (Davenant).
2 or (Ff Q 1673)] and (Davenant; Hanmer).
9, 10, 2. *Witch.* Paddock calls. *3. Witch.* Anon! | *All.* Fair is] *All. Padock* calls anon: faire is (F₁) ; *All. Padocke* calls anon : faire is (F₂) ; *All. Padocke* calls anon: fair is (F₃) ; *All. Padocke* calls anon: Fair is (F₄); *2 Witch. Padocke* calls—anon! *All.* Fair is (Pope). The arrangement in the text, suggested by Joseph Hunter, *New Illustrations* (1845), II, 165, was adopted by Singer₂ and Grant White₁ and has been generally accepted.

Scene 2 (*stage direction*) *Sergeant* (Clark and Wright)] *Captaine* (F₁ F₂); *Captain* (F₃); Captain (F₄ Q 1673).
7, 25, 34 *Serg.*] *Cap.* (Ff Q 1673).
13 gallowglasses] Gallowgrosses (F₁ Q 1673); Gallow glasses (F₂ F₃ F₄).
14 quarrel (Hanmer)] Quarry (Ff Q 1673).
21 ne'er (Rowe₂)] neu'r (F₁ F₂); nev'r (F₃); never (F₄); n'ere (Q 1673).
26 break (Pope)] om. F₁ Q 1673; breaking (F₂ F₃ F₄).
32 furbish'd] furbusht (Ff Q 1673); furbisht (Rowe).
44 (*stage direction*). Ff Q 1673 make Angus enter with Ross. Corrected by Steevens.
56 point, rebellious arm] Point, rebellious Arme (F₁ F₂); Point, rebellious arm (F₃) ; Point, rebellious Arm (F₄); point, rebellious Arm (Q 1673); point rebellious, arm (Theobald).

Scene 3, 18 I will (Davenant; Pope)] Ile (F₁); I'le (F₂ F₃ Q 1673); I'll (F₄).
32 Weird] weyward (F₁ F₃ F₄); wey ward (F₂); wey-ward (Q 1673); Weïrd (Theobald from Holinshed's 'weird').
39 Forres] Soris (F₁ F₂); *Soris* (F₃ F₄ Q 1673; Davenant); *Foris* (Pope).
57 rapt (Pope)] wrapt (Ff Q 1673).
97 death. As (Pope)] death, as (Ff); Death, as (Q 1673); Death; as (Rowe).
97 tale (F₃ F₄)] Tale (F₁ F₂ Q 1673); Hail (Rowe).
98 Came (Rowe)] Can (Ff Q 1673).

Scene 4, 1 Are (F₂ F₃ F₄)] Or (F₁ Q 1673).
25 throne and state children and servants,] Throne, and State, | Children, and Seruants [Servants F₂] ; (F₁ F₂) ; Throne and State. | Children, and Servants; (F₃) ; Throne and State. | Children and Servants; (F₄).

Scene 5, 9 Weird] weyward (Ff Q 1673; Davenant); weird (Theobald).

231

24. No quotation marks in Ff. Some editors make 'Thus . . . undone' the quoted passage (so Pope and Theobald); others quote 'Thus . . . it' (so Capell).

48 it (F₃ F₄)] hit (F₁ F₂ Q 1673)—an old form of *it*.

Scene 6, 4 martlet] Barlet (Ff Q 1673); *Martin* (Davenant); Martlet (Rowe); Marlet (Collier MS.); marlet (Liddell)—an old name for the martin.

5 mansionry] Mansonry (Ff); Mansory (Q 1673); Mansionry (Theobald). Davenant has: 'by his choice | Of this place for his Mansion.'

9 most (Rowe)] must (Ff Q 1673).

13 God 'ield us] God-eyld vs (F₁); god-eyld us (F₂ F₃ F₄); God-eyld us (Q 1673); god-yeld us (Warburton); Godild us (Hanmer); god-ild us (Capell).

26, 27 theirs, in compt, | To (Hanmer)] theirs in compt, | To (Ff); theirs, in compt | To (Pope₁); theirs in compt | To (Pope₂); theirs, in compt; | To (Capell).

Scene 7, 5, 6 Might be the be-all and the end-all here, | But here, (Capell)] Might be the be all, and the end all. Heere, | But heere, (F₁ F₂); Might be the be all, and the end all. Here, | But here, (F₃ F₄ Q 1673); Might be the be all, and the end all—Here, | But here, (Rowe₁); Might be the all, and be the end of all—Here, | But here, (Rowe₂); Might be the Be-all, and the End-all—*Here,* | *Here* only (Pope).

6 shoal] Schoole (F₁ F₂); School (F₃ F₄ Q 1673); Shoal (Theobald).

6 time, (F₁ F₂ F₃ Q 1673)] time. (F₄) ; time—(Rowe).

11 ingredience (F₃ F₄)] Ingredience (F₁ F₂ Q 1673); ingredients (Pope).

18 angels, trumpet-tongu'd, against (Capell)] Angels, Trumpet-tongu'd against (F₁ F₂ F₃); Angels, Trumpet tongu'd against (F₄).

28 other side. (Hanmer)] other. (Ff Q 1673); other—(Rowe). Davenant has: 'Vaulting Ambition! thou o're-leap'st thy self | To fall upon another: now, what news?'

47 do (Rowe)] no (Ff Q 1673). Davenant has: 'he who dares more, is none.'

59 We fail? (F₃ F₄)] We faile? (F₁ F₂ Q 1673); We fail! (Rowe); We fail. (Capell); How fail! (Davenant).

68 lie (F₃ F₄)] lyes (F₁ Q 1673); lye (F₂).

Act ii, Scene 1, 20 Weird] weyward (Ff Q 1673; Davenant); weïrd (Theobald).

30 *Exeunt Banquo and Fleance*] *Exit Banquo* (F₁ F₂ F₃); *Exit* Banquo (F₄); corrected by Theobald.

51 Now] om. (Ff Q 1673); now (Davenant; Rowe).

55 strides (Pope)] sides (Ff Q 1673).

56 sure (Pope conj.; Capell)] sowre (F₁ F₂); sowr (F₃ Q 1673); sour (F₄); sound (Pope).

57 which way they (Rowe)] which they may (Ff Q 1673).

Scene 2, 9 Before 'Who's' Ff and Q 1673 mark the entrance of Macbeth. Steevens inserts *Within* and shifts the entrance to l. 14 (after 'husband'); Clark and Wright mark Macbeth's entrance after 'don't' (l. 14).

11 The comma after 'attempt' and that after 'deed' are in Ff and Q 1673.

28 hands,] hands: (Ff); hands; (Q 1673); Hands, (Rowe); hands. (Pope).

29 fear. I (Capell)] feare, I (F₁ F₂); fear, I (F₃ F₄ Q 1673); Fear; I (Rowe).

57 *Knocking within*] *Knocke* [*Knock* F₃ F₄] *within* (Ff).

63 the green one red] the Greene one, Red (F₁ F₂); the Green one, Red (F₃); the Green one Red (F₄ Q 1673); the green,—one red (Murphy conj.); the green, One red—(Johnson).

Scene 4, 4 Ah (Rowe)] Ha (Ff Q 1673).

6 Threaten (Rowe)] Threatens (Ff Q 1673).

7 travelling (F₃ F₄ Q 1673)] trauailing (F₁); travailing (F₂).

28 wilt (Warburton)] will (Ff Q 1673).

29 live's] liues (F₁); lives (F₂ F₃ F₄); Lives (Q 1673); life's (Pope).

Act iii, Scene 1, 2 Weird] weyard (F₁ Q 1673); weyward (F₂ F₃ F₄); weïrd (Theobald).

42 at night. To] at Night, to (Ff Q 1673); at night; to (Theobald).

43 welcome, we (Theobald)] welcome: | We (Ff); welcom: | We (Q 1673).

70 seed (Pope)] Seedes (F₁ F₂ Q 1673); Seeds (F₃ F₄).

71 come, Fate, into] come Fate into (Ff); come, fate, into (Capell).

74, 115, 139 *Murtherers.*] *Murth.* (Ff Q 1673).

94 clipt (Ff Q 1673)] cleped (Theobald); clep'd (Hanmer); clept (Capell).

106 heart and (Pope)] heart; and (Ff Q 1673); Heart, and (Rowe).

110 Have (Rowe)] Hath (Ff Q 1673; Davenant).

130 you with the perfect spy] you with the perfect Spy (Ff); you with a perfect spy (Johnson conj.); you, with a perfect spy, (Collier 1853 [MS]; White).

140 *Exeunt Murtherers* (Theobald)] om. Ff.

142 *Exit* (Theobald)] *Exeunt* (Ff).

Scene 2, 13 scotch'd (Theobald)] scorch'd (Ff Q 1673; Davenant)—merely an old spelling of *scotch'd*.

20 our peace (F₁ Q 1673)] our place (F₂ F₃ F₄); the Crown (Davenant).

42 shard-borne (F₁ F₂ Q 1673)] shard-born (F₃ F₄) ; sharp brow'd (Davenant).

51 rooky] Rookie (F₁ F₂ F₃ Q 1673); Rooky (F₄).

Scene 4, 34 a-making,] a making: (F₁ Q 1673); making: (F₂ F₃ F₄); making, (Pope).

37 For the first entrance of the Ghost the text follows the stage direction in Ff Q 1673. The first exit is after 'kites' (l. 73) in F₂ F₃ F₄; it is not marked in F₁ and Q 1673. For the second entrance (after l. 88) the text follows Ff Q 1673. The second exit is not marked in F₁ Q 1673; F₂ F₃ F₄ put *Exit* after 'shadow' (l. 106).

45 company?] Company? (Ff); Company. (Q 1673); company. (Dyce₁).

78 time has (Grant White)] times has (F₁ Q 1673); times have (F₂ F₃ F₄).

105 I inhabit then, (F₁ Q 1673)] I inhabit, then (F₂ F₃ F₄); I inhibit, then (Pope); I inhibit then, (Capell); me inhibit, then (Theobald conj.[1]); I inhibit thee, (Steevens conj.; Malone).

122 blood, they say; blood] blood they say: Blood (F₁ F₂); blould they say: Bloud (F₃ F₄); blood, they say: Blood (Q 1673); Blood they say. Blood (Davenant); blood.—They say, blood (Johnson).

124 Augures (Ff Q 1673)] Augurs (Theobald).

124 and understood (Ff)] that understood (Rowe).

133 Weird] weyard (F₁ Q 1673); wizard (F₂ F₃ F₄); Weyward (Davenant); weïrd (Theobald).

135, 136 the worst. For . . . good | All . . . way. I] the worst, for . . . good, | All . . . way. I (F₁); the worst, for . . . good, | All . . . way, I (F₂ F₃ F₄ Q 1673); the worst, for . . . good; | All . . . way, I (Rowe); the worst, for . . . good. | All . . . way; I (Theobald); the worst: for . . . good, All . . . way; I (Capell); the worst. For . . . good | All . . . way; I (Johnson).

144 in deed] indeed (Ff Q 1673); in Deed (Theobald).

Scene 5, 2, 3 reason, beldams as you are, | Saucy and overbold? How] reason (Beldams) as you are? | Sawcy, and ouer-bold, how (F₁); reason (Beldams) as you are? | Sawcy, and over-bold, how (F₂ F₄ Q 1673); reason (Beldames) as you are? | Sawcy, and over-bold, how (F₃); reason, beldams, as you are, | Saucy, and over-bold? How (Capell); reason, beldams as you are, | Saucy, and over-bold? How (Knight).

33 Ff have two stage directions: (1) after l. 33—*Musicke*, [*Musick*, (F₃ F₄)] *and a Song.* (2) after l. 35—*Sing within. Come away, come away, &c.* Corrected by Capell.

---

[1] *Shakespeare restor'd*, 1726, p. 186. In both his editions, however, Theobald reads: 'I inhibit, then' etc.

Scene 6, 24 son] sons (Q 1673); Sonnes (F_1 F_2 F_3); Sons (F_4); Son (Theobald).

38 the (Hanmer)] their (Ff Q 1673).

Act iv, Scene 1, 2 Thrice and once (Jennens)] Thrice, and once (Ff); Thrice; and once (Steevens 1778); Twice, and once (Theobald; Warburton).

7 has (F_3 F_4 Q 1673)] ha's (F_1 F_2); hast (Hanmer).

23 Witch's (Singer$_1$)] Witches (Ff); Witches' (Theobald$_2$).

34 ingredience] Ingredience (Ff); ingredients (Q 1673; Davenant).

34 cauldron] Cawdron (F_1 F_2 Q 1673; Davenant); Cauldron (F_3 F_4).

38 (*stage direction*) *to the other* (Globe ed.)] *and the other* (Ff Q 1673); *and other* (Rowe).

59 germens (Globe ed.)] Germaine, (F_1 F_2); Germain, (F_3 F_4 Q 1673); germains (Pope); Germins (Theobald).

59 all together (Pope)] altogether (Ff Q 1673).

83 assurance double sure (Pope)] assurance: double sure (F_1); assurance, double sure (F_2 F_3 F_4).

97 Rebellion's head rise] Rebellious dead, rise (Ff Q 1673); Rebellious Head rise (Theobald); Rebellion's Head rise (Theobald conj.[1]); Rebellion's head, rise (Hanmer).

111 The stage direction in Ff runs: *A shew of eight Kings, and Banquo last, with a glasse* [glass (F_3 F_4)] *in his hand.* Q 1673 reads: *A shadow of eight Kings, and Banquo last, with a Glass in his hand.* Davenant has: *A shadow of eight Kings, and* Banquo's *Ghost after them pass by.* Rowe reads: *Eight Kings appear and pass over in order, and* Banquo *last, with a Glass in his Hand.* This Theobald adjusted as follows: *Eight Kings appear and pass over in order, and* Banquo; *the last, with a glass in his hand.*

116–118 The notes of interrogation are in Ff and Q 1673.

119 eighth (F_3 F_4 Q 1673)] eight (F_1 F_2) —an old form of the ordinal.

136 Weird] Weyard (F_1); weyard (Q 1673); Wizard (F_2 F_3); Wizards (F_4); Wayward (Davenant); weïrd (Theobald).

Scene 2, 10 diminitive (F_3)] diminitiue (F_1); diminiuive (F_2); diminutive (F_4 Q 1673; Davenant).

22 none (Aldis Wright conj.)] moue (F_1); move (F_2 F_3 F_4 Q 1673); more (Davenant).

42 with all (F_2 F_3 F_4 Q 1673)] withall (F_1).

69, 70 ones! | To ... thus methinks I] ones | To ... thus. Me thinkes I (F_1); ones: | To ... thus, Me thinkes I (F_2); ones: | To ... thus, Me thinks I (F_3); ones: | thus, methinks I (F_4); ones:| To ... thus, Methinks I (Q 1673).

83 shag-ear'd (F_3 Q 1673)] shagge-ear'd (F_1 F_2); shag-eard (F_4); shag-hair'd (Steevens conj.; Singer$_2$; Hudson$_1$).

[1] *Shakespeare restored*, 1726, p. 187.

Scene 3, 4 downfall'n] downfall (F₁ F₂ F₃); downfal (F₄ Q 1673); downfaln (Warburton).

15 deserve (Theobald)] discerne (F₁ F₂); discern (F₃ F₄ Q 1673).

34 affeer'd (Hanmer)] affear'd (F₁ F₂ Q 1673); afear'd (F₃); afeard (F₄).

72 cold—the] cold. The (Ff Q 1673); cold: the (Pope); cold, the (Theobald).

107 accurs'd] accust (F₁); accurst (F₂ F₃ F₄ Q 1673).

113 Have (Rowe)] Hath (Ff Q 1673).

133 thy (F₂ F₃ F₄)] they (F₁ Q 1673).

235 tune (Rowe₂)] time (Ff Q 1673).

Act v, Scene 1, 29 their sense is (Q 1673; Rowe₂)] their sense are (Ff; Rowe₁); her Sense is (Davenant).

42 fear who knows it, when] feare? who knowes it, when (F₁); feare? who knows it, when (F₂); fear? who knows it, when (F₃ F₄).

45 him? (Rowe)] him. (Ff Q 1673).

Scene 2, 4 the bleeding and (Pope)] the bleeding, and (F₁ Q 1673). F₂ F₃ F₄ omit the line.

Scene 3, 21 cheer (F₃ F₄)] cheere (F₁ F₂); chear (Q 1673); chair (Percy conj.; Singer₂; Dyce₁).

21 disseat (Capell [dis-seate] and Jennens conj.; Steevens)] dis-eate (F₁); dis-eat (Q 1673); disease (F₂ F₃ F₄); dis-ease (Furness).

39 Cure her of (F₂)] Cure of (F₁ Q 1673); Cure her from (F₃ F₄).

55 senna] Cyme (F₁ Q 1673); Cæny (F₂ F₃); Senna (F₄).

Scene 5, 39 shalt (F₂ F₃ F₄ Q 1673)] shall (F₁).

Scene 8, 34 (*stage direction*) After *Alarums*, and before *Retreat*, Ff insert: *Enter Fighting*, [*fighting*, (F₃ F₄)] *and Macbeth* [Macbeth (F₄)] *slaine* [*slain* (F₃ F₄)]. Q 1673 agrees with Ff.

The text of the Quarto of 1673 is derived from the First Folio.

Davenant's acting version of Macbeth (Quarto of 1674) shows many omissions and insertions as well as countless changes in phraseology. There is a scene in which Macduff and Lady Macduff meet upon the heath and see the Witches, who utter three prophecies to Macduff; and another scene in which Macduff shows an inclination to seize the crown but is dissuaded by his wife. See Furness's *New Variorum* and cf. H. Spencer, *Shakespeare Improved*, 1927, pp. 78–81, 152 ff.

APPENDIX

THE SONGS

The two songs mentioned in the stage directions (iii, 5, 33; iv, 1, 43) are here given exactly as they stand in the manuscript of Middleton's tragicomedy *The Witch* (MS. Malone 12 in the Bodleian Library). The title of the play is 'A Tragi-Coemodie, Called the Witch, long since Acted by his Maties Seruants at the Black-Friers. Written by Tho. Middleton.' The first of these songs is in the 1673 Quarto of *Macbeth*, after iii, 5, 33; for the second, that Quarto has only '*Musick and a Song, Black spirits, &c.*' after iv, 1, 43. Both songs occur in full in Davenant's version (Quarto of 1674).[1]

I

[*The Witch*, iii, 3. MS., pp. 57–59.]

Song: Come away: Come away: ⎫
Heccat: Heccat: Come away. ⎭ in y̆ aire.

Hec. I come, I come, I come, I come,
    with all the speed I may,
    with all the speed I may.
Wher's Stadlin?
    Heere⎬in y̆ aire.
Wher's Puckle
    heere
And Hoppo too, and Hellwaine too ⎫
we lack but you; we lack but you, ⎬ in y̆ aire
Come away, make up the count ⎭

[1] Two other songs occur in the Quarto of 1673. One (beginning 'Speak, Sister, is the Deed done?') comes between ii, 2, and ii, 3, with the stage direction *Enter Witches, and Sing*. The other (beginning 'Let's have a Dance upon the Heath') comes between ii, 3, and ii, 4, with the stage direction *Enter Witches, Dance and Sing*. Davenant inserts both in a new scene (the fifth in Act ii) in which Macduff and his wife meet upon a heath and are surprised by the sudden entrance of the witches.

Hec. I will but noynt, and then I mount.
    Ther's one comes downe to fetch his dues ⎞
A Spirit like   { a kisse, a Coll,[1] a Sip of Blood ⎬ aboue
a Cat descends { and why thou staist so long ⎠
                      I muse, I muse.
    Since the Air's so sweet, and good.
Hec. oh art thou come
            what newes? what newes?
    All goes still to our delight,
      Either come, or els
                Refuse: Refuse:
Hec. Now I am furnishd for the Flight.
Fire. hark, hark, the Catt sings a brave Treble in
    her owne Language.[2]
Hec. going vp Now I goe, now I flie,
          Malkin my sweete Spirit, and I.
      oh what a daintie pleasure 'tis
        to ride in the Aire,
          when the Moone shines faire,
    and sing, and daunce, and toy, and kiss:
    Ouer Woods, high Rocks, and Mountaines,
    Ouer Seas, our Mistris Fountaines,
    Ouer Steepe[3] Towres, and Turretts,
    we fly by night, 'mongst troopes of Spiritts,
    No Ring of Bells, to our Eares sounds
    No howles of Woolues, no yelps of Hounds,
    No, not the noyse of waters-breache
    or Cannons throat, our height can reache.
        No Ring of Bells &c. } aboue.

II

[*The Witch*, v, 3 (error for 2). MS., pp. 87, 88.]

A Charme Song: about a Vessell.

Black Spiritts, and white: Red Spiritts, and Gray
Mingle, Mingle, Mingle, you that mingle may.

[1] I. e., a hug.
[2] This speech is prose. 'Fire.' is for Firestone, a character in the play,
who is described in the list of *dramatis personae* as 'ŷ Clowne & Heccats
Son.' Davenant omits the speech.
[3] The Quarto of 1673 and Davenant have 'Steeples.'

Titty, Tiffin: keepe it stiff in
Fire-Drake, Puckey, make it Luckey.
Liand,[1] Robin, you must bob in.
Round, a-round, a-round, about, about
All ill come runing-in, all Good keepe-out.
1. Witch. heeres the Blood of a Bat.
Hec. Put in that: oh put in that.
2. heer's Libbards Bane[2]
Hec. Put-in againe[3]
1. the Juice of Toad: the Oile of Adder
2. those will make the yonker madder.
Hec. Put in: ther's all, and rid the Stench.
Fire.[4] nay heeres three ounces of the red-hair'd wench.
all Round: around: around &c.

FORMAN'S RECORD OF *MACBETH*

Simon Forman (1552-1611), a famous astrologer, conjurer, and empiric physician of Lambeth, recorded his visits to the Globe on four occasions under the title 'The Bocke of Plaies and Notes thereof *per*[5] formans, for Common Pollicie,' that is, for general instruction in the conduct of life. These autograph notes are preserved in Ashmole MS. 208 in the Bodleian Library. The plays are: *Richard II* (not Shakespeare's *Richard II*), seen on Tuesday, April 30, 1611; *The Winter's Tale*, seen on Wednesday, May 15, 1611; *Cymbeline* (no date or name of theatre, but doubtless seen at the Globe in 1611); MACBETH, seen on Saturday, April 20, 1610. This last date is erroneous, for (as Halliwell notes) April 20 fell on a Friday in 1610. Perhaps Forman got the day of the month wrong, as one often does, and we should read '1610 the 21 of aprill.' But the two other dates which he gives are 1611, and in both instances the days of month and week agree. Probably, then, the MACBETH entry should be dated April 20, 1611. The inaccuracies in Forman's

[1] So the MS. Reed, Dyce, and Bullen read 'Liard,' without a note. The MS. calls this spirit 'Liard' in i, 2, 2. Davenant has 'Liar *Robin*.'
[2] Leopard's bane: arnica. Davenant has 'Lizards brain.'
[3] Davenant has 'a grain.'
[4] See p. 238, above, note. Davenant gives the line to Hecate.
[5] Italics indicate expansion of MS. abbreviations.

sketch of the plot are curious. Doubtless he consulted Holinshed's *Chronicle* before or after seeing the play. This would
account for his calling the Weird Sisters '3 women feiries or
Nimphes.' His testimony, at all events, indicates that they
did not appear to be ordinary witches.

[Ashmole MS. 208, fol. 207, in the Bodleian Library.]

In Mackbeth at the glod[1] 1610 the 20
of aprill ♄.[2] ther was to be obserued firste
howe Mackbeth and Bancko 2 noble me*n*
of Scotland Ridinge thorowe a wod the[r] stode
befor them 3 women feiries or Nimphes
And Saluted Mackbeth sayinge: 3 tyms
vnto him. Haille mackbeth. king of Codon[3]
for thou shalt be a kinge but shalt beget
No kinges. &c. then said Bancko What all
to mackbeth And nothing to me. Yes
said the nimphes Haille to thee Banko
thou shalt beget king*es*. yet be no kinge
And so they dep*a*rted & cam to the Courte
of Scotland to Dunkin king of Scot*es*
and yt was in the dais of Edward the
Confessor. And Dunkin bad them both kind
ly wellcom. And made Mackbeth forth
with Prince of Northumberland. and
sent him hom to his own castell and ap
pointed mackbeth to prouid for him for
he wold Sup wth him the next dai at
night. & did soe. And mackebeth contri·
ved to kill Dunkin. & thorowe the *p*ersuasi·
on of his wife did that night Murder
the kinge in his own Castell beinge his guest
And ther were many prodigies seen that
night & the dai before. And when Mack
Beth had murdred the kinge the blod on

---

[1]Miswritten for 'glob.'
[2]The astronomical sign for Saturn, used to designate 'Saturday.'
[3]Miswritten for 'Codor.'

his hand*es* could not be washed of by Any
means. nor from his wiues hand*es* w*ch*
handled the bluddi daggers in hiding them
By w*ch* means they became both moch ama
zed & affronted. the murder being knowen
Dunkins 2 sonns fled the on to England the
[other to] Walles to saue them selues. they beinge
fled they were supposed guilty of the mur
der of their father which was nothinge so—
Then was Mackbeth. Crowned kinge
and then he for feare of Banko his old
Companion that he should beget king*es*
but be no kinge him self. he contriued
the death of Banko and caused him
to be Murdred on the way as he Rode
The next night beinge at supper w*th*
his noble men whom he had bid to a
feaste to the w*ch* also Banco should haue
com. he began to speake of Noble Ba
nco and to wish that he wer ther. And
as he thus did standing vp to drincke a
Carouse to him. the ghoste of Banco
came and sate down in his cheier be
hind him. And he turninge About to
sit down Again sawe the goste of banco
which fronted him so. that he fell in to a
great passion of fear & fury. Vtteringe
many word*es* about his murder by w*ch*
when they hard that Banco was Murdred
they Suspected Mackbet.

Then Mack Dove fled to England to the king*es*
sonn. And soe they Raised an Army and cam
into scotland. and at dun ston Anyse over
thrue Mackbet. In the meantyme whille
Macdouee was in England Mackbet slewe
Mackdoues wife & children. and after in
the battelle mackdoue slewe mackbet.

Obserue Also howe Mackbet*es* quen did Rise in
the night in her slepe & walke and talked and
confessed all & the docter noted her wordes.

GLOSSARIAL INDEX

abjure, to deny solemnly, as upon oath, iv, 3, 123

abuse, to deceive, delude, ii, 1, 50

access, avenue of approach, i, 5, 45

accompt, account, v, 1, 43

Acheron, iii, 5, 15

actual, in the way of acts, v, 1, 13

addition, title, i, 3, 106; distinction, iii, 1, 100

address, to apply, ii, 2, 25

adhere, to be consistent, be suitable, i, 7, 52

admir'd, amazing, iii, 4, 110

advantage, a good opportunity, v, 4, 11

advise, to inform, instruct, iii, 1, 129

afeard, afraid, i, 3, 96; i, 7, 39

affection, disposition, character, iv, 3, 77

affeer, to confirm legally, iv, 3, 34

afoot, in motion, mobilized, iv, 3, 185

after these ways, ii, 2, 34

agents, iii, 2, 53

agitation, v, 1, 12

ague, malarial fever, pestilence, v, 5, 4

aid (upon his), iii, 6, 30

air-drawn, iii, 4, 62

alarm, a call to arms, a rally, an attack, onset, v, 2, 4

alarum, to summon to arms or to action, ii, 1, 53

alarum bell, the bell that calls to arms or summons all to assemble, ii, 3, 79; v, 5, 51

alarum within, trumpet call to arms or to the attack (behind the scenes), i, 2, *stage direction*

all-thing, altogether, iii, 1, 13

all to all, iii, 4, 92

always thought, iii, 1, 132

amaze, to daze, confuse utterly, ii, 3, 114; v, 1, 86

amazedly, like one in a trance, iv, 1, 126

amazement, utter confusion, ii, 4, 19

an, if, iii, 6, 19

angel, evil angel, demon, v, 8, 14

angerly, angered, angry, iii, 5, 1

annoyance, injury, v, 1, 84

anointed temple, ii, 3, 73

anon, in a moment, presently, i, 1, 9; ii, 3, 22

antic, fantastic, iv, 1, 130

apply, iii, 2, 30

appoint, to arrange, plan, ii, 3, 58

approve, to prove, i, 6, 4

argument, subject, subject matter, ii, 3, 126

arm'd, clad in armour, iii, 4, 101

armed head, iv, 1, 68

aroint thee, begone, i, 3, 6

artificial, produced by art magic, iii, 5, 27

as, as if, i, 4, 11; ii, 2, 28; ii, 4, 17; v, 5, 13; in view of the way in which, i, 7, 78; as may well be, for, iii, 1, 7

assay, attempt, effort, iv, 3, 143

at a point, iv, 3, 135

at once, iii, 4, 118

attend, to accompany, i, 5, 21; to await, v, 4, 15

audit, account, report (as on money deposited), i, 6, 27

auger hole, ii, 3, 128

augure, an augury, a sign from the flight of birds, iii, 4, 124

authóriz'd, vouched for, iii, 4, 66

avouch, to authorize, justify, iii, 1, 120; to vouch for, assert, v, 5, 47

aweary, weary, v, 5, 49

aye, ever, forever, iv, 1, 134

baby of a girl, iii, 4, 106

badg'd, marked, ii, 3, 107

baited, v, 8, 29

ball, iv, 1, 121

bane, destruction, v, 3, 59

bank, i, 7, 6

banquet, iii, 6, 35

barefac'd, open, frank and undisguised, iii, 1, 119

basis, foundation, iv, 3, 32

bath, ii, 2, 38

battle, a division of an army, battalion, troop, v, 6, 4

be, are, iv, 2, 48

be, to happen, occur, iii, 4, 110

be-all, i, 7, 5

bear, to manage, conduct, exercise, i, 7, 17; iii, 6, 3, 17

bear in hand, iii, 1, 81

bear-like, like a baited bear, v, 7, 2

beards, i, 3, 46

beguile the time, i, 5, 64

behind, i, 3, 117

being, existence, life, iii, 1, 55, 117

beldam, a hag, iii, 5, 2

bellman, watchman, town-crier, ii, 2, 3

Bellona, the goddess of war, i, 2, 54

bend up, to stretch to its utmost tension, make ready for instant action, i, 7, 79

benison, a blessing, ii, 4, 40

bent, determined, iii, 4, 134

beside us, v, 7, 29

bestow'd (are), are settled or placed, have taken refuge, iii, 1, 30

bestows himself, keeps himself, has taken refuge, iii, 6, 24

bestride, iv, 3, 4

best time (in), iii, 4, 5

243

betimes, early, soon, in good season, speedily, iii, 4, 133; iv, 3, 162

better part, v, 8, 18

better (the), iii, 1, 26

beyond my practice, v, 1, 65

bill, a writing, document, list, iii, 1, 100

bind, to oblige, i, 4, 43

Birnam Wood, iv, 1, 93

birthdom, native land, iv, 3, 4

birth-strangled, iv, 1, 30

bladed, iv, 1, 55

blanket, i, 5, 54

blaspheme his breed, iv, 3, 108

bleeding, bloody, v, 2, 4

bless you, iv, 2, 65

blindworm, the slowworm, iv, 1, 16

blood-bolter'd, having the hair matted with blood, iv, 1, 123

bloody, ii, 3, 147; iii, 1, 116

blow, i, 3, 15

bodement, a prophecy, iv, 1, 96

bolter, iv, 1, 123

bond, iii, 2, 49; iv, 1, 84

borne in hand, deluded with false hopes, iii, 1, 81

bosom interest, i, 2, 64

botch, a defect due to bungling, iii, 1, 134

bound in, shut in, confined, iii, 4, 24

brainsickly, insanely, ii, 2, 46

brave, noble, splendid, i, 2, 5, 16

bravely, finely, splendidly, v, 7, 26

breach, ii, 3, 119

break, to broach, propose, suggest, i, 7, 48

breech'd, covered (as with breeches), ii, 3, 122

breed, iv, 3, 108

brew'd, ii, 3, 130

bridegroom (Bellona's), i, 2, 54

brief, short-lived, v, 5, 23

briefly, quickly, hurriedly, ii, 3, 139

brinded, brindled, striped, iv, 1, 1

bring, to conduct, escort, guide, ii, 3, 52; iv, 1, 156

bring forth, to reveal, iii, 4, 125

broad, free, unconfined, iii, 4, 23; unrestrained, too free-spoken, iii, 6, 21

brows, face, appearance, iv, 3, 23

bruit, to report, proclaim, v, 7, 22

buckle, v, 2, 15

but, only, i, 7, 6, 8, 60

by, by means of, iii, 4, 125; to judge by, v, 8, 36

by the way, iii, 4, 130

cabin'd, shut up in a cabin, iii, 4, 24

Cæsar, Octavius Cæsar (Augustus), iii, 1, 57

calls upon us, v, 8, 72

cannot want, iii, 6, 8

captain, general, commander, i, 2, 34

card, compass, i, 3, 17

careless, uncared-for, worthless, insignificant, i, 4, 11

casing, all-embracing, iii, 4, 23

cast, ii, 3, 46

cast the water, v, 3, 50

cat, iv, 1, 1

cat i' th' adage, i, 7, 45

catalogue, a mere list, iii, 1, 92

cauldron, iv, 1, 34

cause, a consideration, iii, 4, 136; (of state), public business, iii, 1, 34

'cause, because, iii, 6, 21

censure, judgment, opinion, v, 4, 14

chafe, to be resentful or discontented, iv, 1, 91

chalice, cup, goblet, i, 7, 11

challenge, to call to account, blame, censure, iii, 4, 42

chamber, hall, i, 7, 29

chamberlain, a groom of the chamber, a personal attendant and guard in one's bedroom, i, 7, 63

champion, to meet as an opposing champion in the lists, iii, 1, 72

chance (in dice play), iii, 1, 113

chaps, jaws, i, 2, 22

charge, *n.*, ii, 2, 6; iv, 3, 20

charge, to burden, v, 1, 60; v, 8, 5

charnel house, iii, 4, 71

chastise, to rebuke and suppress, i, 5, 28

chaudron, liver and lights, iv, 1, 33

check, to rebuke, call to account, iv, 3, 33

cheer, *n.*, welcome, iii, 4, 33; comfort, iv, 3, 239

cheer, to make happy, v, 3, 21

cherubin, cherub, child-angel, i, 7, 22

child crowned, iv, 1, 86

child of integrity, iv, 3, 115

choke their art, i, 2, 9

choppy, chapped, i, 3, 44

chough, a kind of crow, iii, 4, 125

chuck, pet (a term of endearment), iii, 2, 45

cistern, tank, reservoir, iv, 3, 63

clear, with an unruffled countenance, i, 5, 72; free from blame, i, 7, 18; unstained, ii, 1, 28

clearness, freedom from suspicion, iii, 1, 133

cleave not to their mould, i, 3, 145

cleave to my consent, ii, 1, 25

cling, v, 5, 40

clipt, called, iii, 1, 94

clog, to retard, iii, 6, 43

cloister'd, as in a cloister, dark and solitary, iii, 2, 41

close, *adj.*, secret, iii, 5, 7; in concealment, v, 1, 24

close, to enclose, to put into, iii, 1, 99;

to come together again, reunite, iii, 2, 14

cloudy, frowning, gloomy-faced, iii, 6, 41

cock (second), ii, 3, 27

coign of vantage, i, 6, 7

cold, *adj.*, cool, i, 2, 50

Colmekill, ii, 4, 33

combin'd, secretly allied, i, 3, 111

combustion, tumult in the state, ii, 3, 63

come in time, ii, 3, 5

comfort, v, 8, 53

commend, to put, apply, commit, i, 7, 11; to entrust (with best wishes), iii, 1, 39

commission, i, 4, 2

compass, to surround, encircle, v, 8, 56

composition, a truce, terms of peace, i, 2, 59

compt (in), on account, on deposit, i, 6, 26

compunctious, i, 5, 46

confineless, boundless, iv, 3, 55

confirm, to prove, v, 8, 41

confound, to ruin, destroy, ii, 2, 12; iv, 1, 54

confusion, ruin, destruction, ii, 3, 71; iii, 5, 29

cónjure, to adjure, call upon solemnly, iv, 1, 50

consent, party, ii, 1, 25

consequence, the sequel, that which may follow, the future, i, 3, 126; i, 7, 3

consequences (mortal), the future in human lives, v, 3, 5

constancy, firmness, self-possession, ii, 2, 68

construction, meaning, interpretation, i, 4, 12

contend against, to vie with, offset, i, 6, 16

content, satisfaction, happiness, ii, 1, 17; iii, 2, 5

contented (well), well and good, ii, 3, 140

continent, restraining, iv, 3, 64

convert, to change, turn, iv, 3, 229

convey, to manage craftily or secretly, iv, 3, 71

convince, to overcome completely, overpower, i, 7, 64; to baffle, iv, 3, 142

cool, to feel the chill of terror, v, 5, 10

copy, tenure by copyhold, iii, 2, 38

corporal, corporeal, material, i, 3, 81; bodily, i, 7, 80

counsell'd (be), to take one's advice, accept the suggestion, ii, 1, 29

counsellors to fear, v, 3, 17

countenance, to keep in countenance, be in keeping with, ii, 3, 85

counterfeit, imitation, likeness, semblance, ii, 3, 81

courier, courser, steed, i, 7, 23

course, ii, 2, 39; v, 7, 2

course, to ride rapidly after, i, 6, 21

cousin, i, 2, 24; i, 3, 127; iii, 1, 30

coz, cousin, iv, 2, 14

crack, a charge (of powder), i, 2, 37

crack of doom, iv, 1, 117

crave, to beg, iv, 3, 20; to require, iii, 1, 35

craz'd, cracked, half-mad, iii, 1, 83

cribb'd, shut up in a crib (a hut), iii, 4, 24

crime, fault, vice, sin, iv, 3, 96

cross, to thwart, iii, 1, 81

Cumberland, Prince of, i, 4, 39

cur, a nondescript dog, iii, 1, 93

curtain'd sleep, ii, 1, 51

dainty of, particular or punctilious about, ii, 3, 150

damned, i, 2, 14

dareful, boldly, v, 5, 6

dear, heartfelt, weighty, v, 2, 3

death of thy soul, v, 3, 16

dedicate, to offer up, devote, iv, 3, 75

defect, ii, 1, 18

deftly, skilfully, iv, 1, 68

degree, rank (in society), iii, 4, 1

delinquent, an offender, iii, 6, 12

deliver, to report, relate, iii, 3, 2

demand, to ask, iv, 1, 61

demerits, iv, 3, 226

demi-wolf, a cross between a dog and a wolf, iii, 1, 94

denies his person, iii, 4, 128

deny, to refuse, v, 3, 28

desert, any desolate or solitary spot, iii, 4, 104

deserve, to win, earn, iv, 3, 15

despair thy charm, v, 8, 13

detraction, slander, iv, 3, 123

devil-porter it, ii, 3, 20

dew, to bedew, water, v, 2, 30

died every day, iv, 3, 111

digg'd, dug, iv, 1, 25

direction, instructions, iii, 3, 4; guidance, iv, 3, 122

direness, horror, v, 5, 14

discharge, to unload, reveal, v, 1, 81

discovery, the act of spying; *hence*, scouts, v, 4, 6

disjoint, to come apart, go to pieces, iii, 2, 16

dismal, threatening disaster, ill-omened, i, 2, 53; iii, 5, 21

disorder, fit of distraction, wild conduct, iii, 4, 110

dispatch, management, i, 5, 69

dispatch, to make haste, v, 3, 50

disposition, mental and moral make-up, nature, iii, 4, 113

dispute, to resist, withstand, iv, 3, 220

disseat, to unseat, dethrone, v, 3, 21

distance, alienation, enmity, iii, 1, 116

distemper'd cause, v, 2, 15

flowers (in caps), iv, 3, 172
foison, abundance, store, iv, 3, 88
follows, i, 6, 11
fools, ii, 1, 44; v, 5, 22
foot of motion, ii, 3, 131
for, in exchange for, i, 5, 49; because of,
   iii, 1, 121; as for, iv, 2, 15
for that, because, iv, 3, 185
forbid, under a ban, i, 3, 21
force, to strengthen, reinforce, v, 5, 5
forge, to devise falsely, iv, 3, 82
founded, firmly based or established, iii,
   4, 22
frailties, ii, 3, 132
frame of things, iii, 2, 16
franchis'd, free from guilt, void of reproach, ii, 1, 28
free, *adj.*, i, 3, 155; iii, 6, 36
free, *adv.*, freely, without restrictions, ii,
   1, 19
French hose, ii, 3, 12
from, at a distance from, iii, 1, 132;
   away from, contrary to, in distinction
   from, iii, 1, 100; because of, iii, 6, 21
from thence, away from there (from
   home), iii, 4, 36
front to front, iv, 3, 232
fry, spawn, iv, 2, 84
full, fully, quite, i, 4, 54
fume, i, 7, 66
function, one's powers of mind and body,
   one's senses and faculties, i, 3, 140
furious, mad, frenzied, ii, 3, 114
fury, frenzy, ii, 3, 112; v, 2, 14

gall, i, 5, 49
gallowglass, i, 2, 13
gaze, a sight, a spectacle, a show, v, 8, 24
general, universal, iii, 4, 89; unconfined,
   iii, 4, 23
Genius, guardian spirit, iii, 1, 56
gentle, i, 6, 3; iii, 4, 76
gently, without active defence, v, 7, 24
germen, a seed, iv, 1, 59
get, to beget, i, 3, 67
gibbet, gallows, iv, 1, 66
gild, to daub, smear (with blood), ii, 2, 56
gin, a snare, iv, 2, 35
gin, to begin, i, 2, 25; v, 5, 49
give out, to proclaim, publish, declare,
   iv, 3, 192; v, 8, 8
give the cheer, iii, 4, 33
Glamis, i, 3, 71
glass, mirror, iv, 1, 119
go for, to pass for, count as, iii, 1, 92
go off, to be lost, die, v, 8, 36
go to, v, 1, 51
God be with him, v, 8, 53
God be with you, iii, 1, 44
God 'ield us, i, 6, 13

God's soldier, v, 8, 47
golden, red (of blood), ii, 3, 118
Golgotha, i, 2, 40
good, from a good source, i, 3, 131
good morrow, good morning, ii, 3, 49
goodness, success, iv, 3, 136
goose, a tailor's pressing iron, ii, 3, 18
gore, clotted blood, ii, 3, 122
Gorgon, ii, 3, 77
gory, matted with blood, iii, 4, 51
gospell'd, iii, 1, 88
gout, a big drop, ii, 1, 46
grac'd, honoured, noble, iii, 4, 41
grace, favour, i, 6, 30; iii, 6, 27; honour,
   i, 3, 55; goodness, virtue, ii, 3, 99;
   iv, 3, 23, 90, 91; sanctity, holiness,
   iv, 3, 159
Grace, God, v, 8, 72
grace, to honour, iii, 4, 45
gracious, good, virtuous, iii, 1, 66; iii,
   6, 3, 10; iv, 3, 43
graft, to engraft, implant, iv, 3, 51
grandam, grandmother, iii, 4, 66
grapple, to attach closely (as with grap-
   pling irons), iii, 1, 106
grave, weighty, iii, 1, 22
graymalkin, grey cat (a familiar spirit),
   i, 1, 8
green, sallow, i, 7, 37
groom, a man servant, a groom of the
   chamber, ii, 2, 5, 50
grow, i, 4, 32
guise, manner, fashion, way, v, 1, 22
gulf, gullet, iv, 1, 23

hair, iv, 1, 113
half a soul, iii, 1, 83
hand (to), iii, 4, 139
hangman, executioner, ii, 2, 28
harbinger, i, 4, 45; v, 6, 10
hard, hardening, iii, 4, 143
hardy, stout, valiant, i, 2, 4
harm, iv, 3, 55
harness, armour, v, 5, 52
harp'd, iv, 1, 74
Harpier, iv, 1, 3
hatch'd, ii, 3, 64
have thee crown'd, i, 5, 31
having, possession, i, 3, 56
head, source, ii, 3, 103
hear ourselves, confer, iii, 4, 32
heavily, sadly, iv, 3, 182
heavy, drowsy, sleepy, ii, 1, 6; sad, iv,
   3, 202
Hecate, ii, 1, 52; iii, 2, 41; iii, 5; iv, 1
hedge-pig, hedgehog, iv, 1, 2
held you under fortune, iii, 1, 77–78
hell-kite, hellish bird of prey, iv, 3, 217
here-remain, sojourn here, iv, 3, 148
hermit, a beadsman, i, 6, 20

ravell'd, tangled, snarled, ii, 2, 37
raven up, to devour ravenously, ii, 4, 28
ravin'd, ravenous, iv, 1, 24
ravishing strides, ii, 1, 55
rawness, unprotected condition, iv, 3, 26
raze out, to erase, v, 3, 42
readiness, clothing, ii, 3, 139
rebellious, i, 2, 56
rebuk'd, abashed, cowed, iii, 1, 56
receipt, receptacle, container, i, 7, 66
receive, to accept as true, to believe, i, 7, 74
receive it other, to take it otherwise, i, 7, 77
recoil, to fall back, retire, give way, iv, 3, 19; v, 2, 23
recommend (itself), suit itself, appeal pleasantly to, i, 6, 2
reconcil'd, iv, 3, 116
recorded time, v, 5, 21
reflection, shining, i, 2, 25
refrain, hold one's self back, check one's impulse, ii, 3, 122
relation, a report, iii, 4, 124; recital, iv, 3, 173
relish, taste, smack, trace, iv, 3, 95
remember the porter, ii, 3, 23
remembrance, iii, 2, 30
remembrancer, iii, 4, 37
remorse, compassion, i, 5, 45
rend'red, surrendered, v, 7, 24
rent, to rend, iv, 3, 168
repetition, recital, ii, 3, 90
require, to request, iii, 4, 6
resolve yourselves, make up your minds, iii, 1, 138
respect, honour, regard, iii, 6, 29
rest, repose, i, 4, 44
rest, to remain, i, 6, 20
ripe for shaking, iv, 3, 238
Roman fool, v, 8, 1
ronyon, scab (as term of scorn), i, 3, 6
roof'd, under one roof, iii, 4, 40
rooky, iii, 2, 51
round, circlet, crown, i, 5, 29; iv, 1, 88; a dance in a circle, iv, 1, 130
royalty, royal line, iv, 3, 155
royalty of nature, iii, 1, 50
rub, iii, 1, 134
rugged, agitated, iii, 2, 27; rough, ferocious, iii, 4, 100
rule, self-rule, self-control, v, 2, 16
rumour (hold), iv, 2, 19
rump-fed, fat-rumped, i, 3, 6
Russian bear, iii, 4, 100

's, us, i, 3, 125; iii, 1, 37; his, ii, 2, 23; ii, 3, 124
safe, safely out of the way, iii, 4, 25, 26
safe toward, i, 4, 27

safeties, iv, 3, 30
sag, to sink, decline, give way, v, 3, 10
Saint Colme's Inch, i, 2, 61
satisfy, to inform fully, iv, 1, 104; to reinforce, v, 1, 37
saucy, importunate, iii, 4, 25
scale, ii, 3, 8
scan, to consider, iii, 4, 140
scape, to escape, iii, 4, 20; iv, 3, 234
scarf, to muffle, iii, 2, 47
school yourself, control yourself, iv, 2, 15
Scone, ii, 4, 31; v, 8, 75
score, bill, reckoning, v, 8, 52
scotch, to slash, gash, iii, 2, 13
scour, to purge, clear away, v, 3, 56
screw, v., i, 7, 60
scruple, a vague suspicion, ii, 3, 135; doubt, iv, 3, 116
season, a preservative, iii, 4, 141
seat, situation, site, i, 6, 1
seated, firm, intrepid, i, 3, 136
second cock, ii, 3, 26
second course, ii, 2, 39
security, overweening confidence, iii, 5, 32
seeds of time, i, 3, 58
seeling, iii, 2, 46
seem, i, 2, 47; i, 5, 30
self and violent hands, v, 8, 70
self-abuse, self-deception, iii, 4, 142
self-comparisons, i, 2, 55
sennet, iii, 1, 10 (*stage direction*)
sense, v, 1, 29
senses, the mind, mental faculties, v, 2, 23
sensible, perceptible, ii, 1, 36
separated fortune, ii, 3, 144
sere, dry, withered, v, 3, 23
sergeant, i, 2, 3
serious, worth while, of any value or importance, ii, 3, 98
serve, ii, 1, 22
service, viands, i, 7 (*stage direction*)
set, to stake, venture, iii, 1, 113
setting down, laying siege, v, 4, 10
settled, *p.p.*, determined, resolute, i, 7, 79
sev'night, a se'nnight, a week, i, 3, 22
sewer, a server (of dishes at a meal), i, 7 (*stage direction*)
shaft, arrow, ii, 3, 147
shag-ear'd, iv, 2, 83
shall, will surely, iii, 4, 57; *for* it shall, iv, 2, 23
shard-borne, iii, 2, 42
shift away, to steal away unperceived, ii, 3, 151
shift (make a), to contrive, manage, ii, 3, 45
shine, iii, 1, 7
shoal, i, 7, 6
shook hands, i, 2, 21
shough, a kind of shaggy dog, iii, 1, 94

should, would certainly, iii, 6, 19, 20;
v, 5, 17; could, iv, 3, 49
show, appearance, i, 7, 81; a dumb
show, iv, 1, 111
show, to appear, seem, i, 2, 15; i, 3, 54;
v, 6, 2
show'd, shown, ii, 1, 21
shut up, to conclude, ii, 1, 16
sicken, iv, 1, 60
sightless, invisible, i, 5, 50; i, 7, 23
silver, white, pallid, ii, 3, 118
Sinel, i, 3, 71
single, weak, feeble, i, 3, 140; insignificant, i, 6, 16
sirrah, iii, 1, 45; iv, 2, 30
Siward, iii, 6, 31; iv, 3, 134
skipping, i, 2, 30
skirr, to ride rapidly, scour, v, 3, 35
slab, stiff, viscous, iv, 1, 32
slave (*term of abuse*), villain, i, 2, 20;
iii, 3, 18
sleave, a skein (of silk), ii, 2, 37
sleek o'er, to smooth over, iii, 2, 27
sleep, ii, 1, 51
sleight, a device, a spell, iii, 5, 26
slope, to let fall, iv, 1, 57
slumb'ry agitation, v, 1, 12
so, provided that, on condition that, ii,
1, 26
society, company, iii, 1, 42
sole, mere, iv, 3, 12
solemn supper, iii, 1, 14
solicit, iv, 3, 149
soliciting, attempt to influence, i, 3, 130
something, *adv.*, somewhat, iii, 1, 132
sometime, sometimes, i, 6, 11; iv, 2,
76
sooth, truth, i, 2, 36; v, 5, 40
sore, dreadful, iv, 3, 3
sorry, wretched, miserable, ii, 2, 21;
iii, 2, 9
speculation, intelligent sight, iii, 4, 95
speed (had the speed of), outstripped, i,
5, 36
spent, *adj.*, exhausted, i, 2, 8
spirits, eager resolution, energy of will, i,
5, 27; iii, 1, 128
spoke, spoken, iv, 3, 11; v, 1, 53
spongy, greedily drinking, drunken, i,
7, 71
spring, source, i, 2, 27
sprite, spirit, ii, 3, 84; iii, 5, 27
sprites, one's spirits, iv, 1, 127
spy, espial, observation, information, iii,
1, 130
staff, bâton, truncheon, staff of office, v,
3, 48
stage, ii, 4, 6
stamp, iv, 3, 153
stanchless, insatiable, iv, 3, 78

stand upon, to be punctilious about, iii,
4, 119
start, a nervous movement, iii, 4, 63
start, to startle, v, 5, 15; to become distracted, v, 2, 23
state, royal position, i, 4, 25; chair of
state, iii, 4, 5
state of honour, iv, 2, 66
statute, law, iii, 4, 76
staves, spears, v, 7, 18
stay, to await, iv, 3, 142
stay upon, to await, i, 3, 148
steals itself, ii, 3, 152
step, i, 4, 48
sticking place, i, 7, 60
still, ever, always, i, 6, 12, 28; i, 7, 8;
ii, 1, 27; iii, 1, 22; v, 1, 85; v, 5, 2;
v, 7, 16; v, 8, 14
stole, stolen, ii, 3, 73
straight, straightway, immediately, iii, 1,
140; iii, 6, 11
strange, iii, 4, 112
strangely-visited, iv, 3, 150
stride, a long step, ii, 1, 55
stride, to bestride, ride upon, i, 7, 22
strike beside us, v, 7, 29
studied (had been), had learned the lesson, i, 4, 9
stuff, matter, thing, etc., iii, 4, 60; v, 3, 44
stuff'd, clogged, overburdened, v, 3, 44
subject, object, iii, 3, 8
suborn, secretly to hire or induce (to
commit a crime), ii, 4, 24
success, the future, what is to follow, the
sequel, i, 3, 132; i, 7, 4
suffer, to die, perish, iii, 2, 16
suggestion, evil thought, temptation, i,
3, 134
summer-seeming, iv, 3, 86
surcease, ceasing to exist, death, i, 7, 4
surprise, to capture, seize, iv, 1, 150; iv,
3, 204
survey, to note, i, 2, 31
sway by, v, 3, 9
sweaten, sweated, iv, 1, 65
sweeter, more sweetly, iii, 1, 43
sweetly, by its sweetness, i, 6, 2
swelling, stately, magnificent, i, 3, 128
swelt'red venom, iv, 1, 8
Sweno, king of Norway, i, 2, 59

taint, a stain, disgraceful accusation, iv,
3, 124
taint, to become tainted, v, 3, 3
take off, put out of the way, get rid of,
iii, 1, 105
taking-off, i, 7, 20
tale, *n.*, count, i, 3, 97
Tarquin, ii, 1, 55
teem, to bring forth, iv, 3, 176

PRINTED IN THE UNITED STATES OF AMERICA